SPORT AND SOCIOLOGY

- How has our understanding of sport been shaped by sociological ideas?
- How can the study of sport help sociologists to understand wider society?

The sociology of sport is a subdiscipline approaching maturity. This is the first book to stand back and reflect upon the subject's growth, to trace its developmental phases and to take stock of the current fund of knowledge. It offers a 'state-of-the-art' review of the sociology of sport and investigates those areas where sport has come to influence the sociological mainstream. The book also examines how the sociology of sport has attempted to engage with a popular readership, and what the consequences of such engagement have been.

Focusing on touchstone issues and concepts within sociological discourse, such as race, gender, celebrity, the body and social theory, the book assesses the successes and failures of the sociology of sport in influencing the parent discipline, related sub-disciplines and the wider public. It also asks to what extent the sociology of sport can be said to be autonomous, distinctive and distinguished, and challenges students of sport to extend their work out of the narrow confines of the subdiscipline and across disciplinary divides.

As the first book to provide a history of the sociology of sport and to clearly locate the contemporary discipline in the wider currents of sociological discourse, this is important reading for all students and scholars interested in the relationship between sport and society, whether they are working in sports studies or in the sociological mainstream.

Dominic Malcolm is Senior Lecturer in the Sociology of Sport at Loughborough University. His main research themes are the socio-historical study of cricket, and the sociology of sports medicine.

Frontiers of Sport

Series editor: Alan Bairner

LOUGHBOROUGH UNIVERSITY, UK

Sport is ubiquitous in the modern era. As such, it is engaged with by exponents of other academic disciplines and professional groups. This innovative series explores the close relationships that exist between sport and other disciplines and professions, and traces the theoretical and professional boundaries that they share. Each book in the series introduces the key themes, topics and debates that define a particular discipline and its engagement with sport – such as sport and sociology, or sport and politics – offering an invaluable overview for all students and scholars working in sport and each mainstream discipline.

Available in this series:

Sport and Sociology
Dominic Malcolm

SPORT AND SOCIOLOGY

Dominic Malcolm

LONDON AND NEW YORK

First published 2012
by Routledge
2 Park Square, Milton Park, Abingdon OX14 4RN

Simultaneously published in the USA and Canada
by Routledge
711 Third Avenue, New York, NY 10017

Routledge is an imprint of the Taylor & Francis Group, an informa business

British Library Cataloguing in Publication Data
A catalogue record for this book is available from the British Library

Library of Congress Cataloging in Publication Data
Malcolm, Dominic, 1969-
Sport and sociology / by Dominic Malcolm.
p. cm.
1. Sports- -Sociological aspects. I. Title.
GV706.5.M344 2012
306.483- -dc23
2011026802

ISBN: 978-0-415-57121-0 (hbk)
ISBN: 978-0-415-57123-4 (pbk)
ISBN: 978-0-203-85744-1 (ebk)

Typeset in Bembo
by Taylor & Francis Books

Printed and bound in Great Britain by
TJ International Ltd, Padstow, Cornwall

CONTENTS

TABLES

Part I
The sociology of sport

1

TOWARDS A SOCIOLOGY OF THE SOCIOLOGY OF SPORT

I was recently a guest at a wedding. During dinner I was asked what I do for a living. I said that I teach in a university.

'What do you teach?'

'Sociology of sport.'

'Oh yes, what's that?'

'It's about the role of sport in society: why athletes take drugs, how football is becoming more commercial, why certain types of people take part in sport more than others. That sort of thing.'

My new friend looked bewildered. 'Oh right, that's really interesting. I love all that sports psychology stuff.'

Why the confusion I wondered?

The confusion is clearly not over the word 'sport'. Sport could be described as a cultural universal. Across the world and throughout history, people in all human societies practise, and have practised, some kind of physical leisure pursuit we would recognize as sport. Indeed, German historian Johan Huizinga (1938/1949) argued that rather than defining the human species as *Homo sapiens* ('man' of wisdom and reason) a more valid term might be *Homo ludens* ('man' the player). The most prominent contemporary sporting spectacle takes its name from the contests of the Ancient Greeks which can be traced back to Olympia in 776 BC. People might not like sport, but they know what it is. It may also appear to be something which is very basic, something natural.

Sociology is also widely known, but perhaps not as well understood as sport. This is not because sociology is particularly new. While the first sociologists were more commonly thought of as historians or political philosophers (Burke 1980: 15), the term 'sociology' can be traced to the early nineteenth century and Auguste Comte's rejection of Belgian statistician Adolphe Quetelet's notion of 'social physics' (Goudsblom 1977). During the nineteenth century the term slowly became part of the public vernacular and sociology departments were established at several major universities around the turn of the century (Chicago, 1893; London, 1907; Sorbonne, 1913). But in contrast to historians, philosophers or psychologists whose object of study is defined in fairly simple terms – the past, ideas, individual behaviour – sociology deals with something rather more abstract and ephemeral; that is to say, 'society'. Society is complex. Society is not natural.

At the conjunction of these two phenomena are people who call themselves 'sociologists of sport'. Part of that territory is to explain, and sometimes justify, to a variety of audiences what it is we do. And just as the layperson finds this association difficult to understand so sociologists of sport have trouble justifying what they do to the two worlds to which they most closely relate. As Pierre Bourdieu (1987a) aptly observed, the sociology of sport is 'doubly dominated', marginal to the sociological 'mainstream' and resisted by sportspeople who assume that outsiders cannot fully understand their social world.

Consequently, this book examines what sociologists of sport do and considers the outcomes of their efforts. In order to do this the book traces the ways in which sociology has engaged with, and sought to better understand, the world of sport, and at how others – from the fields of 'sociology', 'sports studies' and 'sport' – have engaged with the sociology of sport. The book charts how the sociology of sport has developed and identifies the ways in which it is developing. Although much of what is said along the way illustrates what sociologists of sport have done, and introduces the reader to the key research themes and advances in knowledge, as such this book is not *about* the sociology of sport, it is *a sociology of the sociology of sport.*

The sociology of professions and the sociology of sport

One way in which we can try to understand what sociologists of sport do (and why they do it) is to compare this occupational group with those we call 'professions'. One could argue that sociologists of sport are members of the sociology profession or, more broadly, the university teaching profession. But sociologists of sport are a (relatively) clearly defined occupational (sub)group, a *subdiscipline.* Sociologists of sport claim to be able to 'profess' about sport in society. Robert Dingwall warns that 'the separation of a sociology of professions from a sociology of occupations has been a blind alley' (1983: 12). Consequently, a brief look at some of the ideas in the sociology of professions will help to develop a framework through which we can structure our observations about the people who identify themselves as sociologists of sport.

A number of the arguments in Max Weber's seminal statement, 'Politics as a Vocation', are relevant here. According to Weber, 'Politics, just as economic pursuits', and here we might substitute the sociology of sport, 'may be a man's [sic] avocation or his vocation' (1991: 83). Weber noted that most citizens take part in day-to-day aspects of politics, such as voting at elections or joining the associations which today we call pressure groups. In a similar vein much of the population, albeit a disproportionate number of men, take part in the sociology of sport as an avocation. Sport is central to the identity construction of many in contemporary societies, acting at times like a 'surrogate religion' (Dunning 1999: 6). Moreover, while sports fans are usually concerned with scores and league tables, they also discuss 'social issues' in sport such as drug scandals, the relationship between the media and sport, the commercialization of sport, etc. In this respect, when people talk about sports, much of what they say touches on the subjects which sociologists of sport call their own. For many the sociology of sport is an avocation. This is somewhat ironic given the apparent incomprehensibility of the sociology of sport to the layperson.

A smaller group of people in society, Weber argues, take part in politics (again think sociology of sport) as a vocation; that is to say, in some senses 'professionally'. As Weber notes:

> There are two ways of making politics one's vocation: Either one lives 'for' politics or one lives 'off' politics. By no means is this contrast an exclusive one. The rule is, rather, that man [sic] does both … He who lives 'for' politics makes politics his life, in an internal sense. Either he enjoys the naked possession of the power he exerts, or he nourishes his inner balance and self-feeling by the consciousness that his life has *meaning* in the service of a 'cause' … He who strives to make politics a permanent *source of income* lives 'off' politics as a vocation, whereas he who does not do this lives 'for' politics.
>
> *(1991: 84)*

Sociologists of sport, like politicians, live both 'for' and 'off' their subject. Those who teach in universities use the subject as their main source of income and, in contrast to sports history (see Chapter 8), there are few 'amateurs' in the field. However, many sociologists of sport, I would suggest, also live 'for' the subject. For instance, most people who teach the sociology of sport have a passion for sport in some form (though conversely some of society's most ardent critics of sport are also sociologists of sport). (See Chapter 10.) Whereas biochemists inevitably have to switch off when they leave the lab, sociologists of sport are constantly exposed to new data. For the sociologist of sport, sport is both work and play. Unlike politicians, sociologists of sport will rarely feel, let alone enjoy, 'the naked possession of power', but, as I go on to discuss in the book, working with and in the media may afford a minor degree of celebrity and a brief opportunity to bask in the spotlight of public recognition (see Chapter 9). Others may feel that their life has meaning in the service of a cause when social changes reflect, for instance, what sociologists have argued about racial or sexual inequality (see Chapters 4 and 5). A limited number experience honour and prestige within the subdiscipline. In examining their output and products we should consider that sociologists of sport are motivated by a combination of personal interest and altruistic service.

In addition to looking at individual motivation and practice, this book seeks to examine how sociologists of sport combine and act as a profession. Though much debated, social scientists generally identify certain traits which are characteristic of 'professions'. Keith MacDonald, for instance, defines professions as 'occupations based on advanced, or complex, or esoteric, or arcane knowledge' (1995: 1). Magali Larson, more succinctly and with a different emphasis, argues that 'professions are occupations with special power and prestige' (Larson 1977: x). Eliot Freidson (1970), in his discussion of the medical profession, outlines some of the characteristics which make a profession a 'special kind of occupation'. Professions are 'special', he says, in the sense that they are typically identified as providing the authoritative and definitive voice over a particular area or practice. Professions typically have the capacity to be autonomous and self-directing and control the recruitment of new members and hence access to this authoritative status. Professions may legitimize their lack of external accountability on the grounds that what they do is so complex that others simply do not have the ability to assess their work. Subsequently they may try to reassure others of their good intentions by publishing ethical codes which, for instance, indicate that they only act in the interests of others rather than themselves (e.g., the hippocratic oath in medicine).

To what extent does the sociology of sport community exhibit these 'professional' traits? Sociologists of sport can operate some control over recruitment through the supervision and examination of Ph.D.s, the refereeing of journal articles, etc., but as subsequent chapters show, these barriers can be easily circumvented by other academics. Similarly sociologists of sport do not have ethical codes of their own but will, typically, point to the codes published by the professional bodies of the parent discipline. Sociologists of sport can, however, seek to assert their authoritative status by contrasting the scientific rigour and depth of their own knowledge with the impressionistic and ad-hoc research of journalists, or the limited engagement with sport of 'mainstream' sociologists. But whether sociologists of sport can claim to be the definitive authority over their subject matter is a more debatable point for, as I go on to spell out in some detail, sociologists of sport have constantly had their work evaluated by academics in adjacent subdisciplines, in the sociological 'mainstream' and by 'non-academic' cultural commentators on sport. A further area examined in the book is the degree to which sociologists of sport have demonstrated or convinced others that what they do is both distinctive and distinguished.

Subsequent developments in the sociology of professions have placed more emphasis on the differences rather than the similarities between professions. Comparative analysis has shown that there is no single trajectory along which occupations move towards some kind of model professional status. In fact, identifying sets of characteristics such as these tell us rather more about what a profession claims to be and do than what it actually is or does. Freidson, for instance, argued that the professional person is 'more their present than their past … more the outcome of the pressure of the situation than of what they have earlier "internalized"' (1970: 90). Descriptions of traits are, therefore, ideal types and, perhaps more importantly, the legitimizing ideologies which professions mobilize to protect their own interests. Put another way, it would be naive to accept at face value the claims of sociologists of sport that they have undertaken a specialist programme of training which has endowed them with a unique set of complex research skills, and that their immersion in the field provides a broader and more reliable knowledge base than, for instance, sociologists per se. What, in fact, they might be trying to do is to bolster their 'special power and prestige' relative to others by providing a shorthand rationale for the a priori superiority of their viewpoint. Relative expertise is an empirical question, albeit it somewhat subjectively measured.

Professions, therefore, need to be viewed not simply as altruistic groups working for the good of society but as people who undertake similar types of work and see that they might gain certain collective benefits through cooperation. While sociologists of sport, like most professionals, have internal disputes and divisions, professional bodies attempt to project an image of unity for others to consume. In this regard Larson (1977) pointed towards the 'professional project', where a combination of individual aspirations and collective action lead to two main outcomes: market control by the group and social mobility for individuals. Similarly Andrew Abbott (1988) pointed to the *system of professions* that develops through the interrelations of competing professions or groups. Thus, as we go through this book, we will look at the degree to which sociologists of sport have benefited from collaboration through an exploration of their relations with competing and complementary groups working in adjacent and overlapping subject areas.

The sociology of sport as a 'profession'

How then do sociologists of sport conceive of their 'profession'? The goals, aims and roles of this group can be identified in the mission statements of organizations established to represent sociologists of sport.[1] There are four such bodies which an English speaker might turn to in this regard: the International Sociology of Sport Association (ISSA) which is the main global body for sociologists of sport; the continental associations of the North American Society for the Sociology of Sport (NASSS) (which competes with ISSA in terms of influence), and the European Association for Sociology of Sport (EASS); and the Sport Study Group of the British Sociological Association (BSASSG). There is no equivalent national body in Australia. The multiplicity of organizational missions complicates the picture, but also provides an insight into the diversity within, and some of the tensions which underlie, the sociology of sport.[2]

The BSASSG and NASSS provide relatively terse descriptions of themselves as organizations that 'promote research and scholarship in the sociology of sport' and 'explore sociological aspects of play, games and sports' respectively. The EASS notes that its purpose, 'is the promotion of social sciences and social research in sport at the European level'. It is, moreover, the only organization that seeks to define sport within its statutes, noting that '"sport" refers to all forms of human movement which aim to maintain or improve physical fitness or mental well-being, create or improve social and cultural relationships, or obtain results in competition at all levels'. ISSA, perhaps in an attempt to assert its status over its continental competitors, speaks not of the organization's aims, but of those of the sociology of sport per se. In this it provides perhaps the most detailed statement, applying the definition of sociology – the study of human beings and the societies they form – to the sport-specific context – 'the examination of the role, function and meaning of sport in the lives of people and the societies they form.' ISSA further provides illustrative examples of the substantive areas that stem from this aim including: explaining the emergence and diffusion of sport; the process of socialization into sport; the clash between different sports (sub-) cultures; the investigation of inequalities in sport, etc.

Two aspects of the scope of the sociology of sport emerge from these comparisons. First, how broadly or how narrowly do sociologists of sport define sport? While sociologists of sport have devoted some considerable time to defining sport (see Chapter 2), most definitions include a similar combination of features: structured, goal-oriented, competitive forms of play (McPherson *et al.* 1989). Some, like Jay Coakley (2007: 6), argue that such 'traditional' definitions should be used with caution because the focus on organizational structure may lead us to overlook the sport-like activities of relatively marginalized groups who lack the power and resources to 'institutionalize'. The professional bodies representing sociologists of sport reflect these differing views. NASSS speaks of also including play (not competitive) and games (not necessarily physical), while EASS refers to a broad spectrum of human movement which may range from competitive activities to, in fact, almost any physical activity people say they enjoy. The second point of note is how narrowly or how widely sociologists of sport define sociology. We can, for instance, contrast the flexible approach of EASS which refers to social sciences and social research with the more rigid approach of ISSA which defines the borders of sociology relatively narrowly. As a profession, therefore, sociologists of sport fail to exhibit a consensus over the meaning of the two main words which make up the title of their subdiscipline.

What is seen as the purpose of these professional bodies? NASSS is described as 'organized exclusively for *educational* purposes to promote, stimulate, and encourage … sociological study' and seeks to cooperate with bodies having 'the same purposes' (emphasis added). EASS is perhaps the polar opposite, with no reference made to education, merely the provision of 'scientific advice' and the 'promotion' of sport-related research. The EASS mission explicitly refers to the goal of serving political bodies through 'support [of] European institutions such as the EU and the Council of Europe'. ISSA specifies a more diverse range of goals in its mission statement. The aims of ISSA include contributing 'to the knowledge base of sociology' and 'the formation of policy', including that of 'governments, NGO's and sport organisations'. ISSA further argues that sociologists of sport can 'highlight aspects of the general human condition' and make the world 'less wasteful of lives and resources' through debunking popular myths about sport and critically appraising the actions of those more powerful groups involved in sport. Sociologists of sport are claimed to 'seek to generate knowledge that will contribute to "human development" as opposed to "performance efficiency"'. Finally, while the BSASSG also seeks to influence public debate, engage with 'user constituencies' and liaise with groups with complementary (NB not as NASSS states 'the *same*') scholarly interests, an interesting and subtly different claim is also made. The aims of the BSASSG include the representation of 'the professional interests of those engaged in the sociology of sport'. It is, therefore, the only body to refer specifically to the 'professional project' of sociologists of sport and their place within the system of professions.

Certain tensions and divisions in the sociology of sport are evident within these very differently constructed statements. For instance, should the sociology of sport be an inward-looking profession content to generate knowledge for itself, or, as most explicitly stated by ISSA, a constitutive part of sociology? Sociologists of sport have debated this issue for many years. For instance, Rick Gruneau (1976) critiqued Donald Ball's assertion that one could identify two approaches within the subdiscipline, a sociology *through* sport and a sociology *of* sport. The former was defined as an attempt to contribute to sociological knowledge by using sport-related data, and the latter as an attempt to provide an analysis of the social aspects of sport using sociological frameworks. Gruneau dismissed such a distinction as merely 'two sides of the same coin' for one cannot understand one without the other. More concretely, we cannot understand an aspect of social life (e.g., sport) without reference to the broader social structure, and we cannot understand society without knowledge of its diverse and interlinking subcultures. Though the logic of Gruneau's argument is convincing, it remains the case that within the sociology of sport the different levels of importance which people have attached to the subdiscipline's impact on the broader world of sociology, compared, for example, to physical education, have always been a source of tension (see Chapter 2). In this regard we need to ask how sociologists of sport have sought to influence both the broader discipline and broader world of sport, and what success they have had?

Should the sociologist of sport contribute to sports performance? While ISSA explicitly rejects this idea, EASS fully embraces it. This difference reveals the historical tension between the sociology of sport and the sports sciences. Such struggles are not unique to sociologists of sport. For many years a tension was evident between those who called themselves medical sociologists and those who called themselves sociologists of medicine. The former saw their role as contributing towards medicine through the use of sociological analysis, while the latter saw themselves as sociologically critiquing medicine as a social institution (Waddington *et al.* 2006). The nomenclature used by the subdiscipline's professional groups indicates a consensus on this matter with all referring to sociologists of sport rather than sports sociologists. Yet it remains the case, as Coakley acknowledges (2007: 18–19), that some orientate their research more to 'improve athletic performance, coaching effectiveness, and the efficiency and profitability of sport organizations' because they see themselves as part of the larger field of sports sciences rather than sociology, while others focus more on the cultural issues which are related to sport because they see themselves, first and foremost, as sociologists.

A third tension revealed in these statements centres upon how and in what ways research conducted by sociologists of sport should be applied. While all sociologists of sport would, on one level, wish their scholarship to have an impact on the broader social world (see Chapter 9), disagreement arises over how the research agenda should be drawn up. Ironically, given that NASSS is the body that most explicitly prioritizes educational purposes over policy formation or collaboration with political bodies, North Americans have been at the forefront of this debate. In 1989, Andrew Yiannakis lamented the fact that an applied sociology of sport had been hindered in the 1960s and 1970s and argued that 'if sport sociologists are truly interested in the worth of their research, logic dictates that their findings be put to the test in the world of sport' (1989: 5). Countering this, Alan Ingham and Peter Donnelly expressed concern that seeking validation within the 'marketplace' might have important ramifications for the research agenda in the sociology of sport: 'which aspects of the human condition are to be selected for special consideration and … who is establishing priorities?' (1990: 61). They further raised a 'serious ethical concern', noting that they had 'little sympathy with individuals who use the time and opportunity afforded by their privileged and frequently taxpayer-supported positions in academia to establish private business ventures and to disseminate knowledge that is not submitted to knowledgeable peer review' (1990: 62). While advocating engagement with a wider public, Ingham and Donnelly argued that sociologists of sport should do so on their own terms and on agendas which they, rather than the market, have set. This approach is more in line with that taken by ISSA, which specifically identifies the challenging of inequalities, the advocacy of athletes' rights and responsibilities and the better use of human and environmental resources amongst the 'achievements' of sociologists of sport. EASS, through explicit reference to European institutions, appears more at ease with having political influence over the research agenda.

Finally, these mission statements reveal differences over the desirable degree of collaboration between the sociology of sport and other sport-related subdisciplines. EASS effectively circumvents this issue by defining sociology of sport so broadly that all social-scientific analyses of sport are included within its remit. NASSS, while recognizing that its scholarship has become more open to a greater range of sociological perspectives in recent years, seeks to 'support and cooperate with … organizations having the same purpose' and thus looks to be interested in developing alliances only with other sociologists (of sport). The BSASSG, in speaking of 'groups with complementary scholarly interests', appears open to interdisciplinary exchange. To what extent are these respective positions an insight to the relative status security of these bodies? The fact that ISSA fails to make any mention of other sport-related subdisciplines could be an indication of relative independence. Perhaps the most recent and strident statement on this issue of interdisciplinarity has been made by Alan Klein. An anthropologist by training (and the anthropology of sport has no national or international professional body), Klein has called for a movement towards a 'transnational sports studies' arguing that 'as sports scholars we must shed national identities in conjunction with turning in our disciplinary passports' (Klein 2007: 885).[3] David Andrews (2008) has made similar claims in advocating the development of an approach called 'physical cultural studies'. We will return to this issue later in the book, and in Chapters 8 and 10 in particular. Suffice to say, sociologists of sport disagree over the extent to which their work overlaps with, or is distinctive from, the work of other academic subdisciplines focused on sport. In sum, sociologists of sport are divided over whether the profession should be:

- inward-looking, content to generate knowledge for itself or part of sociology more broadly;
- closely or loosely aligned with other sports-related subdisciplines and sports sciences;
- inclined towards knowledge generation or market application;
- and overtly (or covertly) concerned to fight for its own interests.

However, this review of mission statements has served a further purpose. In light of the above statements about the sociology of professions, we can see that sociologists of sport have their own 'professional project' which they pursue in the 'system of professions'. Each of the organizations reviewed here seeks the advancement of its membership, some through the insistence on independence, others through the active collaboration with similar or higher prestige groups (sociologists in the case of ISSA, political bodies in the case of EASS). While their policies and actions contribute towards both market control and social mobility, the respective professional bodies go about their 'projects' in their own distinctive way. The mission statement of ISSA, for instance, makes reference to the '*complex*' nature of its subject matter, the '*considerable* knowledge' and '*sophisticated* understanding' within the subdiscipline, and the ability of members to provide '*expert* advice'. In this regard it is interesting that the BSASSG, which was founded in 1995, some time after NASSS and ISSA, should be the only body that explicitly identifies the professional interests of people working in the subdiscipline. To what extent is this the act of a more mature, more self-confident profession or a manifestation of the subdiscipline's insecurity stemming from its 'double domination'?

The issues over which sociologists of sport are divided could simply be seen as emerging from personal preferences or philosophical differences. Such a view, however, would be inherently *un*sociological. If, as most sociologists believe, social behaviour is patterned, with people in similar social conditions tending to act in similar ways – or to express it in more technical language, that there is a connection between human agency and the broader social structure which humans form – then as a sociologist it would be remiss not to seek a sociological explanation of these professional differences. What follows is a sociological analysis of the sociology of sport which addresses both the commonalities that pull the subdiscipline together as well as the differences that threaten to pull it apart.

Towards a sociology of the sociology of sport

While to some extent my task has been attempted before, in other respects this book represents something of a ground-breaking exercise. Over twenty years ago Coakley argued that, 'the number of "state of the field" papers focusing on the sociology of sport is truely [sic] impressive' (1987: 63). Coakley provided a number of structural reasons why this number should be so great (see Chapter 2), but he also conceded that essentially these were 'self-descriptions' that reflected on the growth of the field and the potential challenges that lay ahead. A more recent 'stocktaking' exercise of this kind was undertaken by Eric Dunning in 2004. This review took a similar form, charting advances in knowledge (and theoretical developments in particular) and identifying the principal epistemological and ontological conflicts within the field. By way of conclusion Dunning advocated a framework to address some of his main concerns about the field, which in part related to the balance between political action and the generation of knowledge that stemmed from the critical response to John Hoberman's *Darwin's Athletes* (1997, see Chapter 4), and the development of a more philosophical approach to sociology, and the growth of postmodernism in particular (Dunning 2004).

An attempt to undertake a more wide-ranging evaluation of the field came in 1995 when John Loy and George Sage issued a call for papers for a special issue of the *Sociology of Sport Journal* (*SSJ*). The guest editors felt that 'given the maturation of sport sociology, both nationally and internationally during the past quarter of a century, a sociology of the sociology of sport now seems appropriate' (1997: 315). They were, however, disappointed by the community's response. The special issue ultimately contained just three contributions. While Sage (1997) focused on the interrelationship between the sociology of sport and physical education, and David Rowe *et al.* (1997) briefly discussed the neglect of sport in 'mainstream' sociology in Australia, much of this special issue was devoted to theoretical developments of the past and potential challenges for the future. Ingham and Donnelly (1997), for instance, charted the development of North American sociology of sport in terms of the dominant theoretical approaches at particular points in time, with the initial and largely functionalist paradigm first being replaced by a Marxist approach informed by a reading of C. Wright Mills, before itself being replaced with a variant of Gramscian cultural studies. The editors specifically noted as omissions contributions concerned with the relationship between the subdiscipline and sociology per se, an analysis of race and ethnicity, and a feminist perspective on the field (Loy and Sage 1997: 315).

This book is clearly different from these previous projects. For instance, the length of the review enables it to incorporate these three omissions (see Chapters 3, 4 and 5 in particular). But I hope that this work will also be qualitatively different. As signalled by my brief discussion of the sociology of professions, I want to focus less on internal or theoretical differences and more on the combined impact of the sociology of sport community. While I will, as others before me, look at how the sociology of sport has developed and the key debates that marked the growth of the subdiscipline, I will be more concerned with how the work stemming from such debates has affected how people from the 'outside' view the subdiscipline. While I too will discuss the relationship between the sociology of sport and sociological theory, I want to be more outward-looking than my predecessors and consider how others have reacted to the emergence of the sociology of sport, be they 'mainstream' sociologists (Chapter 3–7), academics in other disciplines (Chapter 8), or people who provide competing cultural commentaries on sport (Chapter 9).

Two final points need to be made. First, in developing the analysis in this book, it has sometimes been necessary for me to define who is (and is not) a 'sociologist of sport' and what is (and is not) 'mainstream' sociology. Such distinctions can be quite arbitrary. Some would see themselves simply as sociologists, others would not see themselves as solely or primarily studying sport (as opposed, for example, to being a sociologist of race). Some sociological subdisciplines are more 'mainstream' than others (see Chapter 3). Such a distinction can also fail to represent the *processual* nature of an academic career which may entail a number of new directions and emphases. No doubt some will contest my categorizations, but I have tried to make them on the basis of comparing people's sport-related research in relation to their broader published output, and a sense of whether writers are known to sociologists of sport through, for instance, their attendance at conferences, publications in sociology of sport journals, etc. I hope that I have avoided categorizing people simply because doing so suited my argument.

Second, if I have learnt one thing from reading previous reviews of the subject area, it is that authors are generally concerned to qualify their analyses in terms of the influence of their own biography. Rowe *et al.* (1997: 341), for instance, note that 'our article is written from the inside and from a particular position within the institution we seek to analyze and should be read as such.' Ingham and Donnelly (1997: 363) similarly 'concede that our overview is a personally positioned and male-privileged read of the field over the past 30 years'. Dunning notes that his is just *a* history of the area, not *the* history, and more particularly one which reflects the fact that he is an English white male, who is also 'a (hopefully!) maturing "figurational" or "Eliasian" sociologist who has worked on sport since 1959' (2004: 1–2). These caveats, made by established and senior academics, reflect just what a contentious undertaking this project is. Because of the potential pitfalls and biases of a sociology of the sociology of sport, it might help for me to say something about my own biography and perspective.

Like all those cited above, I consider myself a 'sociologist of sport'. I am male, middle-class and 'white'. Like Dunning, I consider myself a figurational or process sociologist. While I intend to wear my theoretical clothes lightly in the forthcoming analysis, certain principles of this perspective lead me to select specific subjects and structure my approach in a particular way. First, one of the key themes of figurational sociology is a focus on studying social dynamics, which in turn leads to an interest in historical sociology or, as Elias preferred to put it, process sociology. To this end, my approach will fundamentally be developmental. Second, Elias's figurational sociology prioritized the study of interdependence (Elias 1978). The key to understanding society, Elias argued, is an examination of the 'networks of interdependence' in which we are all enmeshed, and, to this end, this sociology of the sociology of sport will focus explicitly on relationships between sociologists of sport and various other groups and individuals. Third, Elias stressed the importance of 'blind' or unplanned social processes. In this respect, my analysis is based on a belief that the development of the sociology of sport has not been predictable and that the subdiscipline has developed in directions which no individual entirely envisaged. Fourth, the figurational approach is predicated on the belief (which, Eliasians argue, is empirically supported by historical evidence) that a growth in human knowledge is more likely to occur when relatively higher levels of detachment inform the knowledge production process. To this end, wherever possible I endeavour to separate my description and explanation of the social processes under investigation from any judgements I may pass upon them.

No doubt my commitment to this sociological perspective is in part a consequence of my own personal biography. I was educated and first employed at the 'spiritual home' of figurational sociology of sport, the University of Leicester. Like other students I was greatly influenced by my teachers and latterly colleagues there. But my position within what Dunning (2002) has termed the 'five generations' of figurational sociologists has perhaps also been influential. As Richard Kilminster (2004) has argued, the cognitive abilities which sociologists develop are shaped by the social contexts in which they initially train and subsequently work. While there is no scope to develop this point here, latter generations of figurational sociologists seem to exhibit distinctive traits (compared with prior generations) which are manifest, for example, in their relations with those who do not share the same theoretical perspective and their relative openness to 'non-figurational' ideas. Finally, I am acutely aware that my age, relative that is to those authors cited above (Dunning, Loy, Ingham and Sage, for instance, might justifiably be described as among the founding fathers of the subdiscipline), adds something different to my approach. Suffice to say, the social and political context in which I have been socialized into the subdiscipline/profession will undoubtedly influence the structure and content of my analysis. As Ann Hall (1996: 7) reflects in her 'research odyssey of a feminist', being unduly critical of the work of others can be a dangerous thing: 'In hindsight, now that I am in my 50s with a whole new generation of scholars coming up behind, my own work also lacks the sophistication I know they will bring. We are products of our time in ways that we do not realize until we look back.' Much of what I have to say will no doubt be controversial. My hope, however, is to produce something which is not just a relatively adequate portrayal of the sociology of sport but one that will be of practical use to those hoping to understand it better and thus influence its future development.

2

THE EMERGENCE OF THE SOCIOLOGY OF SPORT

The invention of tradition?

The previous chapter examined the mission statements of sociology of sport organizing bodies to identify some of the divisions that exist within the subdiscipline. This discussion touched upon a definition of the sociology of sport; e.g., 'the examination of the role, function and meaning of sport in the lives of people and the societies they form'. Yet many writers of textbooks now treat the sociology of sport as so widely understood that a definition is superfluous. Coakley (2007: 4), for example, defines sociology – 'the study of social life, including all forms of social interaction and relationships' – and thereafter simply identifies some of the questions which sociologists of sport have attempted to answer using sociological concepts.

This clarity and confidence has not always been evident (see, e.g., Kenyon and Loy 1965/1969; Erbach 1966/1969; Daniels 1966/1969; Dunning 1967; Loy and Kenyon 1969; Page 1969; Snyder and Spreitzer 1974/1980; McPherson 1975; Lüschen 1980; Sage 1980). As the dates of these texts suggest, the mid-1960s marked the beginning of a phase of rapid change as people – drawn from either sociology or physical education – began to call for, define and establish the institutional manifestations of the sociology of sport. Two interdependent processes were central to these developments: the delineation of a distinct field of study and the legitimation of the area as a respectable and potentially fruitful field of academic enquiry. This chapter examines how the subdiscipline's pioneers sought to establish the field and to identify and define themselves and each other as sociologists of sport. These questions relate to the professional project of the sociology of sport and a system of academic professions.

There have been many previous attempts to map the development of the sociology of sport. These 'stocktaking' accounts are a useful resource. Many of the key phases have been documented, often by people who were centrally involved. For those not even born when the subdiscipline began to form, these accounts are an invaluable source of information. But the proliferation of such accounts makes them *sociologically* interesting also. There are three main reasons for this. First, many of the early accounts are not culturally neutral, 'factual' recordings of history, but are also 'political' texts. In the sense that these pieces were often conscious attempts to shape the emerging field, they were prescriptive as well as descriptive. What interests and motives do they reveal? Second, a comparison of these accounts reveals a number of inconsistencies. In part these may be attributable to fallible memories but they also reveal how history is an interpretive process and how, in Winston Churchill's words, it is written by the victors. Third, the majority of accounts have been written by North American sociologists of sport. Of British sociologists of sport, only Leo Hendry (1973) and Dunning (2004) have attempted a similar exercise. This suggests that the developmental processes through which the sociology of sport has passed are culturally and geographically specific. Cross-cultural comparison reveals the social construction of the sociology of sport. In examining the emergence of the sub-discipline, three apparently simple questions – when? why? and how? – reveal the ways in which individuals were enabled and constrained by the broader social context in which they were acting, and of which they were a part.

When did the sociology of sport emerge?

'State of the field' papers largely agree that the subdiscipline emerged in the mid-1960s. However, the fact that these papers invariably use a combination of evidence, and cite different foundation landmarks, highlights the subjective nature of this task. Though post-dating some significant sociology of sport meetings, Kenyon and Loy (1965/1969), for instance, define the emergence of the field by citing texts which they feel constitute an emerging sociology of sport literature. Subsequent reviews combine the identification of key texts with a discussion of organizational manifestations of the subdiscipline such as conferences and professional bodies, especially the ISSA's forerunner, the International Committee for the Sociology of Sport (ICSS).[1] Where reviews cite key texts, there is some variation in terms of which of these 'count'. A good illustration of the difficulty of precisely locating the emergence of the field is given by Loy and Sage who state that, 'Depending on one's viewpoint, one may argue that the sociology of sport in North America has had a long, a medium, or a short history' (1997: 315). They subsequently provide three possible foundational dates: 1899 and Thorstein Veblen's *Theory of the Leisure Class*; 1965 and Kenyon and Loy's programmatic paper cited above, 'Toward a Sociology of Sport'; and 1978 and the establishment of NASSS. It is probably most accurate to describe these events as processes of subdisciplinary institutionalization (see, e.g., McPherson 1975; Lüschen 1980; Coakley and Dunning 2000a), for these texts, conferences and professional bodies are merely the visible manifestations of a more significant but less tangible process: the development of a particular 'we-group' identity. These texts and meetings were the consequence of scholars becoming increasingly aware of others with whom they shared relatively distinct but nonetheless common interests. Subsequently individuals began to think that the formal recognition of these interests would be mutually and personally beneficial.

Literary emergence

As Johan Goudsblom (1977: 18) points out, while 'it is customary to write the history of sociology in terms of individual contributors', this approach is ultimately flawed, for 'no matter which name is chosen there is something arbitrary and misleading about the choice'. The difference between the texts which are included and those which are excluded, is often just 'a matter of degree' (Goudsblom 1977: 21). Many of those who have reviewed the development of the sociology of sport recognize this. For example, Sage notes that 'it is always difficult, as well as risky' to identify a specific incident or text (1980: 11). But as difficult and risky a task as this may be, it is also a common practice. Moreover, reviews of literature exhibit a distinct pattern. Three types of text are invariably identified:

1 'classical' sociological texts which address sport as part of a broader analysis;
2 texts which either address sport 'un-sociologically', or address sport-related as opposed to sport activities per se;
3 texts which while both sport-focused and sociologically orientated were deemed to be 'one-offs' and thus had marginal impact on the field.

Given that any choice of texts will be relatively subjective, it is most interesting to ask what these choices reveal about the emergence of the sociology of sport and the orientations of those involved?

Loy and Kenyon (1969) were amongst the first to identify 'mainstream' sociologists who had addressed sport. They note that psychologists from 'Freud to Dewey … have had something to say about play' (Loy and Kenyon 1969: 2) and describe in some detail the work of Mead (1934). By way of contrast, however, they also identify sociologists such as Georg Simmel (1917), Max Weber (1904/1930), Erving Goffman (1961), Thorsten Veblen (1899) and William Graham Sumner (1906) who had shown some interest in examining the 'function' of games in society. Günther Lüschen (1980: 315) similarly cites Mead, Weber and Simmel plus the work of Spencer (1861). Gruneau (1976: 12) cites Veblen, Mead and Weber, while Coakley and Dunning (2000a) cite Veblen, Weber and Sumner.

Despite their different emphases, sociologists of sport are consistent in their categorization of these 'mainstream' sociological texts as located *outside* the subdiscipline. Lüschen describes them as 'acknowledgements' (as opposed to analyses?), limited by their inability to go beyond 'the commonsense meaning of sport' (1980: 316). Coakley and Dunning describe them as 'proto-sociological' studies of sport, implying that the sport-related ideas were not sufficiently developed to constitute bona-fide sociology of sport analyses (2000a: xxii). The citation of these texts was perhaps more an attempt to establish sport 'as a legitimate object of sociological study' (Lüschen 1980: 315) and to demonstrate individuals' own sociological credentials than it was to concretely locate the origins of the sociological study of sport.

The next category of texts is divided between (1) those focused on sport-related activities (as opposed to sport) and (2) those focused on sport, but whose authors' sociological credentials are questioned. Typically identified in the first part of this category are works that focused on play. These include cultural historian Johan Huizinga's *Homo Ludens* (1938/1949), work on play and games-playing by anthropologist John Roberts and psychologist Robert Sutton-Smith (Roberts *et al.* 1959; Roberts and Sutton-Smith 1962; Sutton-Smith *et al.* 1963) and French philosopher/sociologist Roger Caillois's *Man, Play and Games* (1961). Joffre Dumazedier's (1966) work on the sociology of leisure is also sometimes cited (Kenyon and Loy 1965/1969; Loy and Kenyon 1969). In the second part of this category are studies such as Cozens and Stumpf's *Sports in American Life* (1953), McIntosh's *Sport in Society* (1960), Natan's *Sport and Society* (1958) and Morton's *Soviet Sport* (1963). Coakley and Dunning go back further, citing Beckford's *Thoughts on Hare and Foxhunting* (1796), Egan's *Boxiana* (1812) and Shearman's (1887, 1889) studies of the development of football, rugby and athletics. Once again, however, these texts are deemed to be liminal to, if not lying outside, the sociology of sport. Sage (1980: 12), for instance, describes McIntosh and Natan's work as 'basically descriptive accounts of the social dimensions of sport', and Lüschen suggests that these texts have 'hardly begun to address' a range of sociologically important issues (1980: 316).

Non-English language works are also cited in this regard. Prominent amongst these are Steinitzer's *Sport und Kultur* (1910), Risse's *Soziologie des Sports* (1921) and Magnane's *Sociologie du Sport* (1964). Though more or less explicitly both sociological and sport-related, these analyses are again classified as lying outside the subdiscipline. Andrezj Wohl, for instance, argues that Steinitzer and Risse's texts were 'the outcome of generally accepted opinion and prejudices about sports' (1966: 5), while Sage argues that they, 'lacked systematic and empirical research data' (1980: 11). The 'inaccessibility' of these texts to English scholars may have limited their impact on the emerging subdiscipline, but their treatment illustrates a desire by the subdiscipline's pioneers not solely to develop a sociology of sport but also to draw upon a particular, preconceived (English language/Anglo-American) definition of 'sociology'. For instance, we might ask whether all sociological work must contain systematic, empirical research data? Or whether sociology does not entail description? The founders of the subdiscipline had a clear and distinct understanding of how the sociological analysis of sport was to be conducted.

This latter point is particularly evident in the treatment of works by writers from the physical education community. That physical education texts are not cited amongst those which provide a lineage to the sociology of sport is indicative of the orientation of the leaders of this emerging subdiscipline. The treatment of Ernst Jokl who wrote *Medical Sociology and Cultural Anthropology of Sports and Physical Education* (1964), and who, with Ernst Simon, co-edited *International Research in Sport and Physical Education* (Jokl and Simon 1964) is a case in point. The former was the first English-language text to combine the words 'sociology' and 'sport' in its title. The latter included two chapters titled 'sociological' analyses of sport (by Leemans [1964] and Vlot [1964]) plus chapters from the aforementioned Dumazedier (1964) and renowned social theorist Max Horkheimer (1964). With hindsight, it is difficult to see how these texts were less significant to the emergence of the subdiscipline than those of Weber, Simmel, Mead and Sumner. Another notable omission was C. L. R. James's *Beyond a Boundary* (1963), a text which many now see as seminal but which was almost entirely ignored by those charting the literary emergence of the sociology of sport (see also Chapter 4). The citation of these texts would not have generated the kind of prestige through association sought by those who saw themselves as leading this subdisciplinary development and thus legitimization of the emerging field. Their omission reveals how a white, Anglo-American conception of sociology structured the formation of the sociology of sport.

Many of those who have charted the development of sociology of sport literature (e.g., Sage 1980; Loy and Sage 1997) also cite a third category: isolated or miscellaneous texts. Texts which fall into this category include Riesman and Denney's study of the cultural diffusion of football (1951), Weinberg and Arond's analysis of the boxing culture (1952), Stone's 'American Sports: Play and Dis-play' (1955), Helanko's study of sport and socialization (1957) and Grusky's work on managerial succession and organizational effectiveness in baseball (1963). All of these had an explicit sport focus yet only Stone's work is generally accepted as signalling the beginning of the sociology of sport. The rest were dismissed, not as 'unsociological' – publication in 'mainstream' sociology journals precluded this – but because they did not form part of a sustained analysis. Despite acknowledging the quantity and diversity of relevant literature, Kenyon and Loy tellingly noted that, 'few have committed their career' to the study of sport and society (1969: 5). To be defined as a sociologist of sport, one had to do more than just study sport sociologically.

In citing these various texts, authors reveal not only the wish to establish a legitimate footing for the subject but also to clearly define its boundaries in terms of empirical focus, mode of analysis and, most arbitrarily of all, the sustained nature of an individual's commitment. Thus, the subdiscipline could only 'emerge' once individuals defined themselves as sociologists of sport. This identity was in part contingent upon the organizational development of the subdiscipline.

Organizational emergence

Charting the organizational manifestations of the emergence of the subdiscipline would, on the face of it, appear to be the one of the more objective ways of illustrating the development of the sociology of sport. Though not initially recognized as such by Kenyon and Loy (1965/1969), writers now agree that the formation of the ICSS was a significant landmark in the institutionalization of the sociology of sport. A comparison of different accounts, however, illustrates discrepancies about what happened when, and which events were significant. Disagreements focus on four key issues:

1 the dating of the formation of this committee;
2 the organizations from which it emerged;
3 its programme of events;
4 its key personnel.

In attempting to chart these differences the aim is not to establish a definitive history but to highlight the socially constructed nature of the subdiscipline and some of the tensions that underlay its emergence.

Loy and Kenyon (1969: 7) date the committee from 1964, as does the committee's first chairman, Andrzej Wohl (1969: 191). Günther Lüschen, who became the organization's first general secretary, argues that the ICSS was formed over two meetings in Geneva in 1964 and in Warsaw 1965 (1980: 316), but subsequently gives primacy to the latter meeting (Lüschen and Sage 1981). The current ISSA website and Coakley and Dunning (2000a: xxiii) cite 1965. These differences suggest that the perception of which meeting was decisive has shifted over time.

The establishment of the ICSS, Wohl argues (1969), began as an initiative of the International Council of Sport and Physical Education (ICSPE) and resolved to gain International Sociological Association (ISA) accreditation for its meetings in both 1965 and 1967. In 1980 Lüschen described the ICSS as a response to initiatives 'within the International Sociological Association and the UNESCO-affiliated International Council of Sport' (1980: 316). Sage (1980: 12), however, claims that the ICSS was founded 'as an affiliate of *two* UNESCO organizations' (emphasis added): ICSPE and ISA. Loy and Kenyon (1969: 6) concur with Wohl in arguing that the ICSS was 'formed as an outgrowth' of ICSPE which *subsequently* became an affiliate of ISA but, like Sage, cite both parent bodies as UNESCO-affiliated. Over time, therefore, it appears as though there has been a shift in the perception of the respective roles of physical education (ICSPE) and sociology (ISA) in the formation of the sociology of sport.[2]

There is agreement over the venue for the first international symposium, with Sage (1980: 12), Loy and Kenyon (1969), Lüschen (1980) and Coakley and Dunning (2000a) all citing Cologne, 1966. Organized by Lüschen, the seminar was hosted and supported by the Institute of Sociology at Cologne, the director of which, René König, was also the chair of the ISA (which in turn may provide the context for Lüschen's portrayal of the ISA's role in the establishment of the ICSS). There is, however, disagreement over what resulted from this conference. Wohl (1969) indicates that the committee subsequently initiated meetings at Illinois (1967), Vienna (1968) and Leicester (1968) and planned a meeting for Switzerland in 1969 (which did take place) and Russia in 1970 (which did not happen). Loy and Kenyon, however, cite Cologne as the venue for the ICSS's first 'biennial Congress' (1969: 7) and, in line with this, Sage argues that 'the second conference sponsored by this committee was held in 1968 in Vienna' (1980: 12). McPherson (1975: 57) also depicts symposia as biennial, but implies that they occurred on odd-numbered years, citing the third, fourth and fifth events as having taken place in Canada (1971), Romania (1973) and Finland (1975) and suggesting by implication, therefore, that the first and second took place in Illinois and Switzerland (the Finland conference appears to have been moved to Heidelberg, Germany at late notice [Anon. 1976]). In contrast, Coakley and Dunning (2000a: xxiii) state that ICSS symposia were annual, listing subsequent meetings in Champaign-Urbana, Illinois (1967), Leicester (1968) and Magglingen/Macolin (Switzerland) (1969). Loy and Kenyon (1969: 6) and

Coakley (1987) refer to an 'international workshop' hosted by the University of Illinois in 1967, but do not accredit the ICSS as the organizing body, despite the central involvement of two prominent ICSS members, Lüschen and Gregory Stone. These different interpretations suggest that for the first ten years of its existence (at least) ICSS organization was somewhat ad hoc, with affiliated individuals working on a number of different fronts and having differences of opinion over what was being organized under the committee's auspices, and in what capacity individuals were involved.

There is further disagreement over the identity of the key personnel involved in this movement. Wohl (1969) argues that he, Joffre Dumazedier, Lüschen and Günter Erbach prepared 'three programmatic documents' to initiate discussions about the formation and remit of the committee. The initial committee consisted of these four, plus Kalevi Heinila, Peter McIntosh, Alexander Novikov and Stone. In 1965, Kyuzo Takenoshita, Rolf Albonico and Ruiz Randol were co-opted. Coakley and Dunning (2000a: xxiii), however, recognize the role not only of Lüschen, Wohl, McIntosh, Stone, Albonico and Heinila, but also of Michel Bouet, Norbert Elias, Eric Dunning, Barbara Knapp (the only female), Gerald Kenyon, John Loy, John Phillips, Walter Schafer, Robert Sutton-Smith and Takaaki Niwa as 'participants in these early meetings'. Ingham and Donnelly (1997: 366) argue that, 'judged by their words and organizational deeds', the key players in this movement were Wohl, Lüschen, Erbach, Heinila and Stone (all committee members), Dunning, Kenyon, Loy and Sutton-Smith (who were not but whom Coakley and Dunning also mention) plus Fred Gras. Thus of the ten members of the committee during autumn 1968 identified by Loy and Kenyon (1969), four (Wohl, Lüschen, Heinila and Stone) are cited by both Coakley and Dunning and Ingham and Donnelly, two (Albonico and McIntosh) are cited by Coakley and Dunning but not by Ingham and Donnelly, one (Erbach) is cited by Ingham and Donnelly but not by Coakley and Dunning, and three (Dumazedier, Novikov and Takenoshita) are omitted from later accounts. Ruiz Randol, a Cuban member of the IRSS editorial board until it was restructured in 1972, is not mentioned by anyone. One must assume therefore that these accounts are influenced by interpretations of the significance of individual contributions. Such perceptions are relatively subjective and are likely to be influenced by an individual's theoretical and disciplinary orientation and geographical location.

These different interpretations illustrate that it is sometimes only in the context of later developments that particular events and individuals come to be deemed as having been significant. By way of illustration one can point to the parallel organizational developments in North America at this time:

- the sociology of sport session at the 1966 American Alliance for Health, Physical Education and Recreation (AAHPER) conference;
- the formation of 'a committee on sport sociology' sponsored by physical education departments in the American Midwest by 1967 (Loy and Kenyon 1969);
- the sessions at the 1968 American Sociological Association (ASA) and American Association for the Advancement of Science (AAAS) conferences;

- or the 'first major sociology of sport conference in the United States' at the University of Wisconsin in 1968 under the sponsorship of the Committee for Institutional Cooperation (CIC) (Lüschen 1969; Coakley 1987).

These conferences are probably regarded as less significant events because of the length of time it took until the establishment of NASSS at the second CIC conference in 1978 (Coakley 1987). This is, nevertheless, essentially a post-hoc rationalization. That Warsaw (1965) and Cologne (1966) are deemed more significant points of origin is perhaps also related to Wohl and Lüschen's personal involvement and subsequent roles in the ICSS. In the chronicling of the development of the subdiscipline, therefore, we see evidence of the maxim that history is written by the victors.

Why did the sociology of sport emerge?

There are two main ways in which people have attempted to explain why the sociology of sport emerged: as a 'logical' corrective to the traditional neglect of sport in sociology and/or as a consequence of the enhanced social significance of sport. This section reviews these parallel claims and examines the consequences of these respective positions for the external legitimacy of the subdiscipline. As we will see, these arguments do not fully capture the complexity of the subdiscipline's social construction for, like the above discussion, they underplay the significance of individual agents who had their own professional projects.

Among those who have discussed why the sociology of sport did not emerge earlier are Sage (1980: 9–10) and Snyder and Spreitzer (1974/1980). Sage identifies five reasons why sport featured so rarely in the 'mainstream' of the social sciences. The first two – that sport has been perceived as a 'lower form of culture' and thus not worthy of serious study; and that sport has been seen as 'frivolous and ephemeral' and thus not easily addressed by social-scientific theories – essentially highlight the same cause. Sage's other three reasons are that:

1. as a field of enquiry, sport had offered few opportunities for academic prestige;
2. there had been limited publishing outlets for sport-related research;
3. the poor quality of existing literature had retarded study.

These, however, verge on the teleological in that they could equally be said to be *consequences* of the neglect of sport within the social sciences.

Snyder and Spreitzer (1974/1980) provide a more adequate explanation. By pointing to an element of 'snobbery' within sociology and a belief that sports are not part of the 'real' world, Snyder and Spreitzer embrace the best aspects of Sage's argument. Citing Dunning (1967), however, they go on to suggest that these views may stem from the North American commitment to the Protestant work ethic. Pre-empting the emergence of the sociology of the body (see Chapter 6), they further note that as a consequence of sociology's traditional orientation towards the social rather than the physical, sport has not been a natural field of enquiry.

Both approaches implicitly seek to legitimize the sociology of sport by questioning the adequacy of existing sociological approaches. The analyses therefore indicate that the orientations of the founders of the subdiscipline lent more towards sociology and away from physical education. To cite the failings of physical education as retarding the development of the sociology of sport would, of course, implicitly suggest that physical education, rather than sociology, was the subdiscipline's 'spiritual home'.

Snyder and Spreitzer also provide the beginnings of an explanation of *why* the sociology of sport emerged when it did. Post-war affluence, they argue, increased the salience of leisure and recreation and thus sport's social significance (1974/1980). Coakley (1987) also points to the growing social prominence of sport at this time but argues that, as part of the broader trend towards journalistic investigations of social institutions (c.f. Watergate), media scrutiny of sport also increased. He notes that over two dozen book-length exposés about sport were published between 1969 and 1978. Sport, moreover, overlapped with key social and political issues:

- race-related civil rights (see Chapter 4);
- gender equity (see Chapter 5);
- pacifism and post-Vietnam concerns about violence;
- the relative merits of competition and cooperation, the distribution of social power and authority and the role of higher education in society.

Coakley thus argues that the sociology of sport emerged, 'at least partially as a response to the awareness of problems generated by muckrakers, and to the call for changes by reformers' (1987: 67).

Other North American accounts put a greater emphasis on physical education as the seedbed of the sociology of sport. Sociology had been fundamental to the 'new physical education' which developed in the USA from around 1910 (Sage 1997: 321), but pressure 'to demonstrate a basic academic body of knowledge' (Sage 1997: 324) transformed physical education 'from a profession, to a loose coalition of subdisciplines' (Gruneau 1976: 27). Led by Franklin Henry's seminal paper 'Physical Education: An Academic Discipline' (1964), the sociology of sport emerged alongside biomechanics, exercise physiology and sports psychology as a discipline-defined approach to sport. The proliferation of subdisciplines was a 'symptom of sport's rationalization' (Gruneau 1976: 28). The 'publish or perish' ethos that ensued (Ingham and Donnelly 1997: 363) meant that the revamped physical education field provided much of the emerging sociology of sport literature. For Sage, these developments combined with the increasing prominence of sport in North American culture and some 'serious scholarly studies about sport' such as sociologist James Coleman's *The Adolescent Society* (1961) and (returning to a central theme of Coakley's account) journalist Robert Boyle's *Sport: Mirror of American Life* (1963). The 'roots' of the sociology of sport are, however, 'firmly embedded in departments of physical education' (Sage 1997: 333), and Sage is correct to claim that 'the development of the sociology of sport has been a joint venture for physical educators and sociologists' (1997: 325). Joint, however, does not necessarily mean equal.

Dunning's 'European' perspective embraces five 'interrelated and interacting' (2004: 2) developments which occurred in conjunction with the institutionalization of the sociology of sport in the mid-1960s. These were:

1 the recognition by physical educators that sports are culturally and historically relative social practices;
2 the recognition by some sociologists (Adorno, Elias, Page and Stone) that sports were important social practices, the investigation of which would enhance sociology per se;
3 the expansion of universities and the increased competition within and between disciplines;
4 the 'permissive revolution', grounded in the relative empowerment of subordinate groups (females, minority ethnic groups, the working classes and youth), and fuelling left-oriented and radical ways of thinking which in turn boosted the popularity of sociology;
5 the Cold War and the increasing use of sport for political ends.

To this end we might add that sociology was undergoing a parallel process to the fracturing of physical education at this time, with the development of many new fields and subdisciplines during the 1990s (Haney 2008).

Comparison of the different emphases of European and North American accounts illustrates differences in the balance between physical education and sociology in the two contexts. Though in North America physical educators and sociologists may have been relatively equal partners, it is telling that a European (Dunning) rather than an American gives prominence to the role played by two 'mainstream' American sociologists (Page and Stone). This differential power balance between 'mainstream' sociologists and physical educators in these two contexts can be understood structurally. As Loy and Kenyon noted in 1969, of over thirty US 'sport in society' courses, 'nearly all' were in physical education departments, while sociology departments seemed more predisposed to studies of leisure. In Europe, 'no simple pattern exist[ed]', with sociology of sport courses evenly divided between these two types of department (1969: 7–8). Thus, in North America the strongest networks for sociologists of sport existed in physical education departments.

The comparison also illustrates the relative introspection of North American sociologists of sport. Coakley, Sage, and Snyder and Spreitzer all focus on factors 'internal' to the USA, whereas Dunning cites the international political context of the Cold War. Not one American identifies the organizational development of the subdiscipline in Europe as a significant precursor to the development of the field in North America. Indeed, Kenyon and Loy's programmatic statement of 1965, published at a time when the ICSS was in formation, discusses 'European Interest' in just a brief paragraph.

How did the sociology of sport emerge?

Thus, the establishment of an international body for sociologists of sport may have arisen out of a broad amalgamation of social changes, including changing (academic and social) perceptions of the cultural centrality of sport, but these were the *necessary*, as opposed to the *sufficient*, conditions for the emergence of the subdiscipline. In order to survive in an increasingly competitive higher-education environment, the pioneers of the sociology of sport had to establish a critical mass and an internal coherence, while at the same time seeking legitimacy through external validation. These were interacting and sometimes contradictory processes. The balance between critical mass and internal coherence was delicate; larger groups tend to be less unified. Moreover, in attempting to demonstrate credibility to a broader constituency, it was expedient to shape the subdiscipline in a style that played to the strengths of some, but inevitably not all. In analysing how the sociology of sport emerged, therefore, we can identify three key tensions:

1 over the scope of analysis (physical culture vs. sport);
2 over the method of analysis (subjective promotion vs. social scientific objectivity);
3 over disciplinary breadth (multidisciplinarity vs. sociology).

Though I would not wish to suggest that the 'battle lines' were explicitly, coherently or strictly drawn, in each case physical educators would have come from an environment where the former position had been the norm. In each case, however, the latter position won the day.

Despite their geographical differences, locating the emergence of the sociology of sport in terms of macro-sociological factors provides considerable explanatory purchase. These accounts, moreover, add legitimacy to the subdiscipline by depicting its emergence as inevitable – academics merely responding to social 'needs' or changing social context – and logical – addressing the shortcomings of existing sociology. The latter also locates the emerging subdiscipline as more legitimately rooted in 'mainstream' sociology than in 'sport' or physical education. Yet in proposing these explanations there is a tendency to deny the impact of human agency. McPherson (1975) alerts us to this in his discussion of occupational socialization, noting that the first generation of sociologists of sport developed their interest in the area some point after their formal education ended. Members of this group were trained in sociology and interested in sport, or trained as physical educators and interested in social phenomena. These were, therefore, 'marginal men, neither sociologists nor physical educators', whose early careers were 'characterized by role conflict as they sought to legitimate both the introduction of new courses and the type of research they were undertaking' (McPherson 1975: 57). These individuals were therefore not neutral or ambivalent to, but active agents in, these processes.

Scope of analysis

One of the key means by which sociologists assert their expertise is through the use of 'scientific terminology, a taxonomy which enables us to classify social phenomena in a clear and coherent conceptual framework' (Goudsblom 1977: 25). This 'taxonomizing propensity' is particularly 'characteristic of fields in formation' (Ingham and Donnelly

1997: 367). Sociologists of sport therefore followed a conventional path, developing the subdiscipline alongside attempts to clarify their object of study.

In their overviews of the field Snyder and Sprietzer (1974/1980), Lüschen and Sage (1981) and Ingham and Donnelly (1997) all cite something akin to 'definitional attempts' as among the main strands of literature in the emergent field. Loy (1968), Lüschen (1970), Edwards (1973) and Ingham and Loy (1973) are identified as amongst the key works. Defining sport may have enabled communication between those in the subdiscipline but, just as importantly, it was an attempt to establish a position of authority in the field. Through definitional discussions, sociology of sport pioneers sought to separate their work from common-sense understandings. Snyder and Spreitzer argued that sport as a concept is 'self-evident until one is asked to define it' (1974/1980: 17). Gruneau similarly argued that this definitional work is important as 'most *conventional* definitions of sport are misleading', often overlooking its multidimensional character (1976: 12; emphasis added). Though never explicitly stated, we can presume that journalistic investigations of sport were regarded as replete with these common-sense understandings and hence this literature served to distinguish the academic subdiscipline from rival forms of cultural analysis.

The outcome is as revealing as the process, for these definitional attempts ultimately led to a relatively narrow field of analysis. This is not to deny that a broader definition did have its advocates. Erbach (1966/1969), for example, continually referred to 'the field of physical culture and sport', and Dumazedier (1966; 1974), a prominent figure in the initial organizational manoeuvres in the subdiscipline, published on the sociology of leisure. But ultimately a relatively narrow conception of sport as overtly competitive came to dominate the subdiscipline. This led the analytical focus away from physical activity and thus distanced the sociology of sport from both physical education and the sociology of leisure. The definition which became ascendant fitted the interests of those who wanted to establish a relatively independent *sociological* field.

Method of analysis

In order to justify their attempts to establish a new subdiscipline, sociology of sport pioneers needed to be able to demonstrate that their research represented something of a departure from what had gone before. One means was to address the tendency among physical educators, 'to evangelize about the "social development" objective of games and sports' (Sage 1997: 322). Erbach, for instance, in arguing that 'our present-day system of physical culture must be substantially perfected' (1966/1969: 24), sought to define the emerging subdiscipline via the traditional legitimating ideology of physical education as serving some broader social benefit (e.g., health, character building, social integration). In contrast to this, Daniels (1966/1969), Kenyon and Loy (1965/1969), and others professed the value-neutrality of the subdiscipline; 'the sport sociologist is neither a spreader of gospel nor an evangelist for exercise' (Kenyon and Loy 1965/1969: 38).

The debate about analytical method invoked a related question: did the existing approach to the study of sport have unique characteristics? Though recognizing that it had connections with 'kindred or principal branches of science', Erbach argued that 'the science of sport' could, and indeed should, continue to develop 'into an independent discipline' (1966/1969: 30). Lüschen (1980) argued the opposite. There was no general theory of sport, and, as the sociology of sport could not lay claim to any special theory or method, a sociology *through* sport, rather than an isolated sociology *of* sport, was to be preferred (see Chapter 1). By the conclusion of this debate, the subdiscipline would become closely aligned to, and dominated by, 'the standard canon of social science research methods' (Lüschen 1980: 324). Sage emphasizes Kenyon's role in this: 'Kenyon emphatically situated the sociology of sport firmly within the positivistic perspective of science ... it is clear that Kenyon was asserting that the scientific legitimacy of sport sociology was tied to ... the positivist, empirical-analytical paradigm of the established sciences' (Sage 1997: 326).

It was not simply that this methodological approach was forwarded, rather that the 'value-free social science' of the emerging subdiscipline was explicitly *contrasted with* the 'physical activity is good' assumptions traditionally held by physical educators (Kenyon and Loy 1965/1969: 38). The sociology of sport needed to offer the promise of something new, and the novelty of the subdiscipline was enabled by distancing it from its physical education roots. As part of this process the term 'sociology of sport' became preferred to 'sport sociology' (see Chapter 1). By giving primacy to the word 'sociology' rather than 'sport' the nascent subdiscipline was more likely to be recognized by the sociological 'mainstream'. Ingham and Donnelly's (1997: 373) argument that 'sport sociologists in departments of physical education were constrained by the instrumental positivism that was associated by the natural scientific pretensions of the new subdisciplinary orientation' does not sufficiently account for the 'pull' of 'mainstream' sociology and the *enabling* consequences of developing a positivist orientation to the field. The internal divisions that this battle for methodological uniformity exacerbated were offset by the potential for status enhancement for the subdiscipline.

Disciplinary breadth

The tension between 'critical mass' and 'internal cohesion' was evident in early discussions and practices regarding the balance between who to include within, and exclude from, the field. Wohl notes that the ICSS had an initial target of 'no more than 70 corresponding members' (1969: 191), but this target was reached by the end of 1966, with membership exceeding 100 in 1969. By 1980, Lüschen would claim that the ICSS had 250 'full and corresponding members' (1980: 319) but argues that by 1978 there were eighty-two 'sociologists of sport on the international scene'. The citation of corresponding members in these early membership figures implies interest rather than output and was thus probably an attempt to legitimate the field by maximizing perceptions of its size. Lüschen's eighty-two research active scholars held positions in sports science (thirty-eight), sociology (twenty-nine), anthropology (three), education (three), philosophy (three), psychology (two), English (one) and planning (one) (plus three unknown), again indicating an inclusive ethos.[3] The limits initially placed on the number of corresponding members perhaps reflect the limited resources of the committee or a desire to assert 'quality control' measures for the profession. The latter is underscored by the ICSS's early policy of vetting potential members, 'according to involvement in research and academic teaching' (Lüschen 1980: 319). The desire to not only cast the net as wide as possible but also to exert a degree of control over those who wished to define themselves as sociologists of sport parallels the treatment of texts discussed earlier. Both should be seen as a manifestation of status insecurity and an attempt to establish legitimacy for the emerging subdiscipline.

In addition to physical educators and sociologists, a third and now sometimes overlooked group were (social) psychologists. In their early definitions of the field, Erbach describes the questions posed by sociologists and social psychologists of sport as 'closely interrelated' (1966/1969: 31), while Kenyon and Loy note that the two 'have much in common' (1965/1969: 37). Kenyon and Loy further suggest that students of the sociology of sport should have a broad knowledge base within the social sciences, and Daniels goes even further, advocating that sports sociology should be 'the accepted identifying label' for a 'field of study [which] must logically be the social sciences' (1966/1969: 15). Consequently, in the subdiscipline's early years, any study involving a group was defined as the sociology of sport, regardless of whether the theoretical focus was psychological, social psychological or sociological (McPherson 1975). All the early conferences were multidisciplinary (Lüschen 1969; Sage 1997). The presence of Sutton-Smith at the formation of the ICSS meant that social psychologists were represented from the outset (Loy and Kenyon 1969; McPherson 1975). Moreover, when Snyder and Spreitzer presented an outline of research in the field in 1974, two of the five areas they highlighted ('small groups' and 'social-psychological aspects') would, with the passing of time, become more firmly situated within psychology. Lüschen and Sage's (1981) overview, and Ingham and Donnelly's (1997) more recent account, demonstrate a similar division, with one ('sport as a subsystem') of three themes, and two (socialization and group dynamics) of seven themes respectively, becoming subjects which would ultimately be partly or wholly positioned outside the subdiscipline. The multidisciplinarity which was a cornerstone of the earliest incarnations of the sociology of sport reflected the traditions of physical education rather than sociology.

As the field developed, however, the focus on sociology became more uniform. Ingham and Donnelly attribute the split between social psychology and sociology of sport to various factors. In part, the division had 'methodological origins', there being a chasm between the 'field study, field experiment, laboratory experiment' of sports psychology and the ethnographic study of sociologists (Ingham and Donnelly 1997: 370). In addition to this, sociologists of sport's engagement with the work of Marx and C. Wright Mills, and the private trouble/public issue duality in particular, 'facilitated the break with the psychology of sport' (Ingham and Donnelly 1997: 375). But, with the establishment of the International Society of Sports Psychology in 1965 (Sage 1980: 13), we can see how, in Ingham and Donnelly's words, 'in the early days, it was issues that brought scholars together before subdisciplinary specializations set them apart' (1997: 371). The continued citation of psychological research in early 'state of the field' papers does, however, suggest a thwarted desire for inclusion rather than their active attempt to exclude psychology.

Conclusion: the search for legitimacy

In contrast to the pioneers of the subdiscipline whose work I have examined here, those who come across the sociology of sport in the twenty-first century are liable to take its existence for granted. The sociology of sport may have corrected a previous omission within sociology, and it may have been spurred by wider social processes that bolstered the cultural centrality of sport, but it is essentially manufactured, and its specific manifestation is a consequence of the actions of individuals within, and who constituted, this broader social context. There is, I would argue, no logical inevitability to there being a distinct and identifiable subdiscipline called the sociology of sport, for, given different advocates, it could alternatively have been consumed, for example, within the sociology of leisure/leisure studies, a sociology of physical culture or a more broadly social science, 'sports studies'. We will return to this point in Chapter 10. Given that the emergence of the subdiscipline was a contested process, we need, moreover, to be aware that there were both winners and losers. The contentious nature of Erbach's role in the emergence of the sociology of sport probably owes something to his regular appearance on the 'wrong' end of the early debates that shaped the field. Through a comparison of the differing accounts of when, why and how the sociology of sport emerged, we can see how this tradition, as others, was 'invented' (Hobsbawm 1983).

Underlying the subdiscipline's institutionalization was the search for recognition and respect, the drive to be seen as a distinctive area of study, yet one that is sociologically distinguished. To some extent this clamour for outside validation led to a 'strong affinity among social scientists in this speciality' (Snyder and Spreitzer 1974/1980: 30), but there were also casualties. Internal cohesion was developed through the exclusion of certain (types of) scholars: Jokl, sociologists of leisure such as Dumazedier, 'non-conforming' physical educators and perhaps also social psychologists such as Sutton-Smith. Debates over the appropriate boundaries for the subdiscipline would continue to shape its constitution.

The reason why so many 'state of the field' papers were written by North Americans was that the links with physical education were strongest there, and thus professional insecurity most pronounced. That it was a 'mainstream' sociologist, Page, rather than one of the emergent American sociologists of sport who could say, 'sports writers are among my favorite list of sociologists' (cited in Sage 1980: 196) is indicative of the relative levels of status security. The desire for 'mainstream' recognition, moreover, shaped the research agenda. According to Ingham and Donnelly (1997: 373), the subdiscipline's North American pioneers' 'quest for legitimacy through emulation of the parent discipline could not have dissuaded them from adopting both structural functionalism and instrumental positivism as "models" of scholarly activity'. In Europe, left-orientated theories were significant in stimulating interest in the sociology of sport (Dunning 2004). We turn to these issues in the next chapter.

Part II

The *sociological* impact of the sociology of sport

3

SOCIOLOGY OF SPORT AND SOCIAL THEORY

As we saw in the previous chapter, theoretical considerations shaped the emergence of the sociology of sport. This was evident in the propensity of the subdiscipline's pioneers to identify citation of sport in the works of 'classical' sociologists as a stimulus to the field. Perhaps most significant, however, was the dominance ultimately achieved by those who sought to align the subdiscipline with the value-neutral positivism that formed the 'standard canon of social science', rather than establish a (semi-)autonomous 'science of sport' (Lüschen 1980: 324; Erbach 1966/1969: 30).

These actions stemmed from a desire to establish legitimacy for the new field through gaining the respect of those who might be considered the sociological 'mainstream'. Defining the sociological 'mainstream' is, however, as potentially problematic and subjective as the process by which the sociology of sport was defined. In some respects we could define the 'mainstream' in terms of those areas that are regularly represented within university departments of sociology and sociological textbooks. According to this criterion we could locate the sociology of medicine and sociology of race within the 'mainstream'. However, both areas could also reasonably be described as sociological subdisciplines, just like the sociology of sport. More compellingly, one could argue that only sociological theory (and perhaps sociological research methods) truly constitutes the 'mainstream' of the discipline, because theory is the only ever-present component of sociological study. As the relationship between the sociology of sport and other sociological subdisciplines will dominate later sections of this book, the aim of this chapter is to use the subdiscipline's engagement with sociological theory as a gauge of the changing relationship between the sociology of sport and the 'mainstream' of the discipline.

As we saw in Chapter 2, however, there were important differences between the development of the sociology of sport in North America and Europe. The relatively limited number of textbooks that explicitly attempt to combine sport and social theory reminds us of these differences. There are, to date, five English-language books that fall into this category: Rees and Miracle's *Sport and Social Theory* (1986), Jarvie and Maguire's *Sport and Leisure in Social Thought* (1994), Maguire and Young's *Theory, Sport and Society* (2002), Giulianotti's *Sport and Modern Social Theorists* (2004a) and Smith's *Sociology of Sport and Social Theory* (2010). If we divide these texts between North American (Rees and Miracle, Smith and Young) and British (Giulianotti, Jarvie and Maguire) editors or authors, we can again see North American–European divisions. Given that there are considerably fewer sociologists of sport in the UK, these texts illustrate a relative reluctance amongst North Americans to explicitly deal with sociological theory.

Tellingly, both Rees and Miracle (1986: vii) and Smith (2010: xi) indicate that their aim is to demonstrate how social theory *might be* applied in the sociology of sport. In so doing, the majority of chapters in both texts are devoted to empirical expositions of theory. Both texts also lament the relatively poor theorization of sports research. Kenyon (1986: 8–9), opening the Rees and Miracle volume, presents a quantitative analysis of literature that suggests that 'theoretical' works account for less than 5 per cent of sociology of sport publications. Nearly twenty-five years later it was Smith's belief that sociology of sport research was so poorly theorized that it is 'often derided for its atheoretical underpinnings' (2010: xii). In contrast, the texts produced by British authors focus primarily on individual social theorists and the way in which their work *has been* applied to sport. Indeed, far from bemoaning the absence of theory, they reflect upon the way in which 'rancorous exchanges' have led to sectional divisions within the field (Giulianotti 2004b: 1). These tensions have obscured the 'common ground which does in fact exist between the different traditions of social thought' (Jarvie and Maguire 1994: 3).

It would be an error to portray this pattern as uncomplicated, for North American universities – and Canadian universities in particular – provide almost half of the seventeen authors in Giulianotti's text and the overwhelming majority in Maguire and Young's collection. But if, as Kenyon (1986: 17) suggests, 'the true test of intellectual independence comes when the sport sociologist takes on social theory per se', such independence is unevenly distributed. These cross-cultural differences are probably more a consequence of the relationship between the subdiscipline and physical education than of the characteristics of sociology in these respective regions. For instance, in the International Sociological Association's survey of the most influential books of the twentieth century, five of the top-ten texts were written by American authors (see Table 3.1). Given what Dunning (1986a: 37) has described as an 'American hegemony over the sociological world', the relative absence of theory in North American sociology of sport appears to be a peculiarity of the subdiscipline.

The next section examines the role of social theory within the sociology of sport. What are the main theoretical influences in the subdiscipline and how have they changed over time? To what degree has work in the subdiscipline been theoretically orientated? Following this, social theorists' engagement with sport is discussed, focusing in particular on the work of Bourdieu and Elias. In this regard, it is worth reminding ourselves of the distinction drawn between the sociology *of* sport and a sociology *through* sport (see Chapter 1). To what extent has an engagement with sport

TABLE 3.1 International Sociological Association's 'most influential books of the twentieth century'.

Author(s)	*Title*
Max Weber	*Economy and Society*
Charles Wright Mills	*The Sociological Imagination*
Robert K. Merton	*Social Theory and Social Structure*
Max Weber	*The Protestant Ethic and the Spirit of Capitalism*
P. L. Berger and T. Luckmann	*The Social Construction of Reality*
Pierre Bourdieu	*Distinction: A Social Critique of the Judgement of Taste*
Norbert Elias	*The Civilizing Process*
Jürgen Habermas	*The Theory of Communicative Action*
Talcott Parsons	*The Structure of Social Action*
Erving Goffman	*The Presentation of Self in Everyday Life*

Source: International Sociological Association (1998).

led to the generation of social theory and thus a more sophisticated sociological understanding of the social world? To what extent does this engagement reflect the differences between North American and European sociologists of sport?

Theory in the sociology of sport

Sociology of sport textbooks generally identify a wide range of theories that have been influential in the subdiscipline. Coakley, for instance, cites functionalism, conflict theory, critical theory, feminism and interactionism (2007), while Coakley and Dunning (2000a) identify functionalism, Marxism, cultural studies, feminism, figurational sociology and post-structuralism. Donnelly (2003) takes a different tack, suggesting that there have been three relatively distinct phases in the use of theory in the sociology of sport. These phases relate to the emphasis on the role of sport relative to broader society. During the first phase, sport was depicted as a *reflection* of society; in the second as serving to *reproduce* society; and in the third as a forum for *resistance* to broader social trends and dominant forces. Coakley and Dunning (2000a: xxx) suggest that it is possible to relate the various theories to particular ontological issues such as materialism versus idealism, agency versus structure and synchronic versus diachronic studies. As with any system of classification, decisions about what is included/excluded are partly a consequence of the purpose for which the system was designed. In the case of textbooks, the purpose is breadth of coverage allied to simplification for clarity.

In contrast, this review will be developmental and focus on the individual theories that were dominant at particular times. It builds on and develops Ingham and Donnelly's (1997) analysis of the development of North American sociology of sport. Again, this approach, as Ingham and Donnelly acknowledge, simplifies for clarity's sake and runs the risk of obscuring the conflicts that have always existed in the field between different theoretical approaches. That said, Ingham and Donnelly's overview of the subdiscipline can act as a useful starting point. They suggest that the sociology of sport was initially dominated by structural functionalism and that this was subsequently superseded by more critical approaches informed by a Marxist understanding of political economy, before Gramsci-informed cultural studies became ascendant in the late 1990s. Three additions to this model are necessary. First, some of the most theoretically explicit developments in the subdiscipline have drawn on feminism. Second, to incorporate developments outside North America, mention also needs to be made of figurational sociology. Finally, since Ingham and Donnelly wrote, the commitment to post-structuralism has grown in the sociology of sport, and, in recent years, this has come to challenge the cultural studies hegemony. I will review each of these phases, and key sociology of sport texts, in turn.

Structural functionalism draws an analogy between biological organisms and social systems. It suggests that, like the human body, all societies require certain 'functions' to be performed if they are to continue to exist (e.g., the socialization of young people into acceptable social roles, the reward of 'functional' behaviour). Moreover, each social institution (e.g., sport) contributes a 'function' to the whole (society). Early sociologists of sport argued that sport performed socio-emotional, socialization, integration and social mobility functions (Stevenson and Nixon 1972). As Dunning has noted, there was a structural-functionalist bias in sociology as a whole in the 1960s and early 1970s (1986a: 37) so it is not wholly surprising that the subdiscipline should follow this lead. While Loy and Booth (2000) have argued that structural functionalism was never the dominant paradigm in the sociology of sport, pioneers such as Bouet, Heinila, Kenyon, Lüschen and, indeed, Loy himself, predominantly engaged with this theoretical perspective and thus made it particularly prominent in the subdiscipline. In that structural functionalism also had parallels with some of the more advocacy-driven traditions of the physical education community (suggesting that sport built character, resolved social problems, etc.), the theory gained a significant degree of influence.

Despite this, most of the key theoretically driven statements about sport were inspired by Marxism, figurational sociology and feminism, with the former two primarily being European interventions. Marxism suggests that human societies can be distinguished according to their different 'modes of production' and that economic structure provides the key to a deeper understanding of any society. All past modes of production have been inherently exploitative, and the current system – capitalism – is the most exploitative of all. Bero Rigauer's *Sport and Work* (1969) provided the first sustained Marxist analysis of sport, identifying the reproduction of the central characteristics of the capitalist mode of production (e.g., specialization, commodification and alienation) in sport.[1] Where Rigauer presented a kind of 'correspondence theory' that depicted sport as a simple reflection of economic production, French sociologist Jean-Marie Brohm (1978) produced a form of 'reproduction theory' in which sport's relative autonomy from the economy enabled it to provide certain ideological functions supporting economic production. *Sport: A Prison of Measured Time* contains a selection of Brohm's writings which argue, for instance, that sport legitimates nationalism and de-politicizes the masses and thus diverts people's attention away from their economic exploitation. As Bairner argues, however, Marx holds an ambiguous position in the sociology of sport, 'less likely to be mentioned in sociological writings about sport and society than any number of considerably less innovative and influential thinkers' (2007: 21).[2]

Figurational sociology stems from the work of Norbert Elias (mentioned in the previous chapter). This perspective stresses the examination of long-term social processes and seeks to explain changes to individuals' behaviour and emotional norms with reference to the structure of society. Key in this regard is what Elias called the 'civilizing process' in which, he suggested, there had been observable changes in the way people feel about witnessing and taking part in physical violence over time (Murphy *et al.* 2000). The first book-length study to employ this approach in relation to sport was Dunning and Sheard's *Barbarians, Gentlemen and Players* (1979/2005). *Barbarians, Gentlemen and Players* provided a theoretical framework for interpreting the characteristics specific to modern sport forms through an examination of five overlapping stages in the development of rugby football. *Barbarians, Gentlemen and Players* expands upon Elias's theory of the civilizing process by illustrating how Britain's pioneering role in the development of modern sport was linked to the country's broader social and class structure.

Feminism is somewhat different from the approaches discussed so far in that it is more adequately understood as a 'dynamic and continually evolving complex of theories or theoretical traditions' (Birrell 2000: 61). That said, there are generally argued to have been two schools of feminist thinking which were initially prominent: liberal feminism and radical feminism. A central premise of liberal feminism is the belief that the principles of equality, liberty, etc., upon which Western democracies are based are not rigorously applied to gender relations. Liberal sports feminists seek to identify and remove the barriers that prevent women from competing on equal terms with men. Conversely, radical feminism proposes systemic change organized around an opposition to patriarchy (the system of relations by which men dominate women). Patriarchy is seen as the most fundamental form of human oppression because it is rooted in inherent physical and psychological differences between the sexes. Whereas liberal feminists seek to change sport 'from within', radical feminists advocate the overhaul of sport as a social institution, or the establishment of distinct and separate female cultures which are not inherently masculinist and competitive or which place less value on 'male attributes' such as strength and aggression. The first books to apply these approaches to the study of sport were Ann Hall's *Sport and Gender: A Feminist Perspective on the Sociology of Sport* (1978), and Mary Boutilier and Lucinda San Giovanni's *The Sporting Woman* (1980). The relationship between feminism and sport is discussed at greater length in Chapter 5.

Of these three perspectives, figurational sociology has changed the least over time. The tradition initiated by *Barbarians, Gentlemen and Players* continued, perhaps most significantly, through the publication of Elias and Dunning's *Quest for Excitement* (Elias and Dunning 1986a). (See the next section of this chapter.) Dunning *et al.*'s *The Roots of Football Hooliganism* (1988) was also seen to be closely associated with this theoretical perspective although references to Elias are sparse. Edited texts which drew upon and developed this perspective included Dunning and Rojek's *Sport and Leisure in the Civilizing Process* (1992) and, to a lesser extent, Dunning *et al.*'s *The Sports Process* (1993). Dunning's *Sport Matters* (1999) included a figurational analysis of a range of sporting issues such as gender, race and violence, while Maguire's *Global Sport* (1999) forwarded a figurational approach to the study of globalization (see also Maguire 2005). Dunning *et al.* (2004a) also published an edited collection of figurationally informed essays on the developmental trajectories of a variety of sports in *Sport Histories* (see Chapter 8).

In contrast, Marxist and feminist studies of sport have undergone significant development. Key to both has been a movement towards cultural studies. Cultural studies has its roots in Marxism, and Gramscian Marxism in particular. It stresses the ideological rather than material forces that subordinate particular groups and the continuing struggle of those groups against their domination. Cultural studies research therefore scrutinizes the way cultural forms (e.g., sport) consolidate, contest and reproduce power structures. While the distinction between the analysis of sport from Marxist and cultural studies perspectives is not always clear-cut, the distinction between feminist cultural studies and earlier forms of feminism is more readily apparent.

During the 1980s, Marxism, 'neo-Marxism' or cultural studies informed an increasing number of sociology of sport texts. Cantelon and Gruneau's *Sport, Culture and the Modern State* (1982) combined a range of authors using variants of Marxism in their study of sport. Gruneau's *Class, Sports and Social Development* (1983/1999) is often depicted as a Marxism-inspired historical analysis of sport in Canada, though Gruneau rejects this theoretical positioning in his foreword to the 1999 edition. John Hargreaves's *Sport, Power and Culture* (1986) is a Marxist exposition of the development of sport in Britain and has been described as 'one of the most cited sociological works employing Gramsci' (Rowe 2004: 106). Bairner, however, points out that direct reference to Gramsci in either of these texts is generally exaggerated (2007: 29).

A more explicit commitment to, and therefore movement towards, cultural studies became evident in Jennifer Hargreaves's *Sport, Culture and Ideology* (1982) and Ingham and Loy's *Sport in Social Development* (1993). In 1989, the *SSJ* published a series of articles about how emerging feminist cultural studies scholarship could and should be used to inform and advance the sociology of sport (Deem 1989; Sparkes 1988; Whitson 1989), and, as discussed in Chapter 5, work on gender and sport moved towards something of a feminist cultural studies consensus around this time (see Birrell 2000). Indicative of the influence cultural studies exerted over the subdiscipline, Talbot (1988) and Young (1991) published articles calling for the greater use of cultural studies in the sociology of sport (in relation to gender and victimology respectively), and the *SSJ* (Donnelly 1992) published a special issue that debated the potential of British cultural studies to contribute to the sociology of sport in 1992. Cultural studies continue to be applied to sport, notably in Sugden and Tomlinson's edited work, *Power Games* (2002), Hughson *et al.*'s *The Uses of Sport* (2005) and most explicitly in Carrington and McDonald's *Marxism, Cultural Studies and Sport* (2009). Andrews (2002) and King (2006) have also made recent statements about the relevance and use of cultural studies in the sociology of sport. As evident from the dates cited in this paragraph, the commitment to cultural studies has been one of the more enduring theoretical trends in the sociology of sport.

A theorist whose work has been significant in the sociology of sport, but who does not fit neatly into this (or, it seems, any) typology of theories is Pierre Bourdieu.

Consequently, many textbooks do not cite Bourdieu in the theoretical overviews they offer (e.g., Cashmore 2005b; Coakley 2007; Coakley and Dunning 2000b; Jarvie 2006; Scambler 2005). Bourdieu's work (key aspects of which are detailed in the next section) has similarities with Marxist 'reproduction theory' in that sport (and other cultural forms) provides ideological functions that maintain the class structure of a society. Bairner (2007), for instance, discusses Bourdieu's debt to Marx and suggests that 'the other forms of capital that Bourdieu highlighted [social capital, cultural capital, physical capital] are in fact secondary to and determined in the final analysis by economic capital' (2007: 28), but advocates deny that Bourdieu's ideas embrace the kind of economic determinism with which Marxism is often associated. In that Bourdieu examines how cultural forms consolidate and contest power structures, his work shares some of the premises of cultural studies. Andrews (2000), conversely, expresses an inclination to include Bourdieu in an overview of post-structuralist sociology of sport research but rejects this on the basis that Bourdieu (1987b) describes himself as a constructivist structuralist or structuralist constructivist. Temporally Bourdieu's influence on the subdiscipline has been concurrent with that of post-structuralism (see also Chapter 6) as a number of readings attest (Clement 1995; Defrance 1995). My own inclination is to recognize Bourdieu's debt to Marx, while seeing his emphasis on embodiment/habitus as a significant original development, akin to Gramsci's extension of Marx through his stress on the ideological dimensions of class domination.

In the past decade, research in the sociology of sport has increasingly been influenced by the post-structuralist turn in social science. Post-structuralism arose as a critique of modernist theoretical perspectives that seek to provide a comprehensive and causal explanation of social life. Post-structuralism emphasizes the difference and diversity in the subjective experiences of individuals and argues that the truth-claims of so-called experts are merely competing narratives. Prominent in this regard is David Andrews who was particularly significant in introducing the work of Foucault to sociologists of sport (Andrews 1993; Rail and Harvey 1995). Starting with Rail's *Sport and Postmodern Times* (1998), other books informed by this perspective include Crabbe and Blackshaw's *New Perspectives on Sport and Deviance* (2004), Caudwell's edited collection *Sport, Sexualities and Queer/Theory* (2006) and Markula and Pringle's *Foucault, Sport and Exercise* (2006). In 2007, the *SSJ* published a special issue on post-structuralism and the sociology of sport (see, e.g., King and MacNeil 2007), and a year later King published the first 'review essay' assessing the impact of this perspective on the field. King claimed that the number of post-structuralist sociology of sport essays and books had reached approximately 120 (2008: 420). Post-structuralism was therefore well-established in the field at this time.

It is impossible in this context to give anything more than an indicative description of theoretical trends in the sociology of sport. But it is clear from this review that social theory has been, and continues to be, strongly debated within the subdiscipline. It is thus more accurate to depict the sociology of sport as a vibrant and critical community of scholars than something akin to a theoretical desert. Moreover, especially given the sizes of the respective sociology of sport communities, the relative prominence of European scholars (notable in relation to figurational sociology, cultural studies and the use of Bourdieu) again shows the degree to which the subdiscipline in North America is more closely aligned to its physical education roots than to sociology. Indeed, where North American sociologists of sport do explicitly engage with social theory, the orientation is largely towards European theorists. Overall, however, sociologists of sport can legitimately claim to have aspired to the goals of the subdiscipline's pioneers, embracing social theory and conforming to the 'best practice' of the sociological 'mainstream'. An additional question, however, is to ask to what degree *trends* in the subdiscipline match those in sociology more generally? To what extent does theorization in the sociology of sport have a relatively autonomous relationship with 'mainstream' social theory as Giulianotti suggests (2004b)?

The theoretical orientations of the subdiscipline can be gauged through an analysis of the content of its leading journals. Table 3.2 shows the findings of an electronic search of the three major journals in the field (NASSS's *Sociology of Sport Journal* [*SSJ*], ISSA's *International Review for the Sociology of Sport* [*IRSS*], and the *Journal of Sport and Social Issues* [*JSSI*, published by Northeastern University, Massachusetts]) and two 'mainstream' sociology journals (the *American Journal of Sociology* [*AJS*] and the International Sociological Association's *Current Sociology* [*CS*]). The content of each of these journals was searched for the names of theoretical perspectives and/or key theoreticians.

The table shows significant differences between sociology of sport journals. In part, this must reflect differences in their respective cataloguing practices. It is also apparent that different theorists feature more prominently in different journals. Though again absolute numbers may reflect recording differences, if we assume internal consistency for each journal we can see that the *JSSI* shows a marked preference towards feminist sociology and postmodernism while Bourdieu and Elias figure highly elsewhere. The minimal reference to Marx/Marxism across the journals underscores Bairner's (2007) point that this perspective has been increasingly (and unfairly) discredited within the subdiscipline. Perhaps the most striking finding, however, is the degree to which cultural studies dwarfs all other theoretical perspectives in both the *IRSS* and *JSSI*, while being joint top with Elias in the *SSJ*. We can therefore conclude that this has historically been the dominant perspective in the field, although Ingham and Donnelly would subsequently pose the question, 'Does the concept of hegemony still have hegemony?' (1997: 365).

From this survey it would be rather harsh to conclude that the subdiscipline should be derided for its atheoretical character. Kenyon's 5 per cent assessment in 1986 now seems way off the mark. Differences between the journals do, however, support the contention that a relatively small proportion of American sociologists of sport are inclined to engage with social theory (which in turn may reflect their closer and continued links with physical education). Even allowing for cataloguing differences, however, the relative scarcity of explicit reference to social theorists in the *SSJ* is striking. Finally, comparison with the contents of the *AJS* and *CS* suggests that, *pace* Giulianotti, with some notable variations the subdiscipline has broadly followed the theoretical trends evident in the sociological 'mainstream'. What, however, has been the impact of sport on the generation of social theory?

TABLE 3.2 The prominence of social theory and theorists in the sociology of sport.

	Baudrillard	*Bourdieu*	*Cultural Studies*	*Elias*	*Feminism*	*Foucault*	*Marx*	*Postmodernism*	*Post-structuralism*	*Total*
SSJ	2	14	20	20	9	17	8	1	2	93
	(2.2)	(15.1)	(21.5)	(21.5)	(9.7)	(18.3)	(8.6)	(1.1)	(2.2)	
IRSS	22	125	775	142	99	80	74	79	7	1,403
(1.6)	(8.9)	(55.2)	(10.1)	(7.1)	(5.7)	(5.3)	(5.6)	(0.5)		
JSSI	9	39	397	28	104	63	32	41	7	720
	(1.3)	(5.4)	(55.1)	(3.9)	(14.4)	(8.8)	(4.4)	(5.7)	(1.0)	
AJS	178	823	1998	415	611	664	632	562	110	5,993
	(3.0)	(13.7)	(33.3)	(6.9)	(10.2)	(11.1)	(10.5)	(9.4)	(1.8)	
CS	24	132	706	71	95	101	236	52	5	1,422
	(1.7)	(9.3)	(49.6)	(5.0)	(6.7)	(7.1)	(16.6)	(3.7)	(0.4)	

Notes: On 6 April 2011 the contents of each of these journals were searched for the name of the theorist/perspective appearing in the top row. Figures in brackets refer to the percentage of that journal's total number of articles identified in the search.

Sport in sociological theory

While historically various theories can be seen to have influenced sociologists of sport, often the relationship has not been entirely reciprocated. In Bairner's review of the place of Marxism in the sociology of sport he notes that few Marxist theorists have made any 'direct contribution to the development of the sociology of sport' (2007: 31). Feminist theoreticians also rarely engage with sport (see Chapter 5 for a discussion). Perhaps most conspicuous, however, has been the neglect of sport within cultural studies. As Silk and Andrews (2010) suggest, cultural studies has generally failed to 'engage the complex and diverse practices and representation of active embodiment'. This is particularly surprising given the prominence of cultural studies in the sociology of sport and the obvious synergies between this empirical focus and the conceptual approach. Where the sociology of sport partly emerged out of physical education, cultural studies is explicitly multidisciplinary. Where significant elements of the sociology of sport advocated the social benefits of sports participation, cultural studies incorporates an explicitly political agenda for social change. Where the sociology of sport has fought against an element of 'snobbery' within 'mainstream' sociology that leads sport to be depicted as not part of the 'real' world, cultural studies rejects elitist conceptions of culture and commits to examine the lived experiences of dominated groups. Yet if one considers cultural studies readers and leading cultural studies journals in both the UK and America, 'sport is one prominent absence from the roster of activities normally considered by cultural studies work' (Blake 1996: 13).

Indeed, amongst leading sociological theorists there have perhaps been only three who have explicitly discussed sport to any significant degree: Jean Baudrillard, Pierre Bourdieu and Norbert Elias. Baudrillard, for instance, has examined relations between sports spectators and authorities, changing attitudes towards physical exercise and the body, the role of 'symbolic exchange' in modern sport which enables it to be enjoyed simply because it is seen as wasted time (and therefore may transgress productive relations), and how the notion of 'hyperreality' explains the mediation of contemporary sports events and our inability to distinguish between the real and simulation. While Giulianotti (2004c: 226) argues that Baudrillard's 'regular *aperçus*' on sport and leisure 'help to elucidate the key elements of his imaginary', for two reasons my primary focus here will be on the latter two theorists. First, Bourdieu and Elias are perhaps the most widely acclaimed of the three social theorists. For instance, Bourdieu's *Distinction* and Elias's *The Civilizing Process* are ranked sixth and seventh respectively in ISA's books of the twentieth century (see Table 3.1). Second, of the three, these are the theorists whose work has been employed most widely in the sociology of sport (see Table 3.2) and whom sociologists of sport have identified as contributing most significantly to the field.

Bourdieu and the sociology of sport

Bourdieu's interest in sport is evident in his most important and well-known text, *Distinction* (1984; originally published in 1979). Reference to sport appears frequently throughout the text, and a sustained analysis appears in the second half of the third chapter ('The Habitus and the Space of Life-styles'). Either side of its publication, Bourdieu presented two conference papers on sport. The first, a keynote address to the International Congress of the History of Sport and Physical Education Association in Paris in 1978, was later published as 'Sport and Social Class' in the journal *Social Science Information* (Bourdieu 1978) and subsequently in revised form, 'How Can One Be a Sportsman?', in a collection of his works, *Sociology in Question* (1983). The second, 'Program(me) for a Sociology of Sport' was originally presented at the 8th ICSS Symposium in Paris in 1983, published in *In Other Words* (Bourdieu 1987a), and reprinted in the *SSJ* in 1988. In addition to this Bourdieu published a rarely cited appendix on the Olympics in *On Television* (1998a) and a journal article on the state, economy and sport in *Sociétés et Représentations* (1998b) which has not (to my knowledge) been translated into English.

As Jarvie and Maguire (1994: 184) note, Bourdieu's 'essential proposition appears to be that the appeal of sport and leisure practices to social groups lies in distinctive uses of the body. These practices act as taste signifiers in a constant struggle to gain or maintain distinction.' In other words, Bourdieu argues that an individual's leisure pursuits are lifestyle choices made not solely on the basis of the economic resources and time one can devote to that activity but also on the basis of an assessment of the relative costs (economic, physical, cultural) and benefits (e.g., enhanced social status or physique) which might accrue to the individual. Moreover, different social classes assess these costs and benefits differently and are therefore predisposed, have a preference or taste for, particular leisure/sport activities. A key division between the working and middle classes, as Bourdieu sees it, is the former's utilitarian conception of the body as a tool to be used for particular means and the latter's conception of the body as a project, or an end in itself. Thus, sporting preferences, as indeed all lifestyle choices, are both structured by and structuring of broader social hierarchies. As Laberge and Kay (2002: 253) note, Bourdieu's analysis of sport and physical activity 'is in line with his broader effort to reveal the extent to which cultural practices embody power relations'.

This analysis of sport is evident in, and consistent with, the broader themes of *Distinction*. Bourdieu restates and refines this position in his other sport-related works, while making a number of additional explicit claims about sport which are less commonly included in reviews of his sport-related work. For instance, Bourdieu argues that the Olympics are 'doubly hidden' in that 'no one sees all of it [the Games] and no one sees that they don't see it. Every television viewer can have the illusion of seeing *the* (real) Olympics' (1998a: 79). To properly understand the Games, he further suggests, sociological investigators need 'to assess all the objective relations between the agents and institutions competing to produce and sell the images of, and commentary about, the Olympics' (1998a: 80); namely, the International Olympic Committee, TV networks, multinational sponsors, journalists, and the policy-makers and professionals who 'industrialize' the production of sports. He also expresses concern about the 'field of professional production of sports goods and services' (Bourdieu 1987a: 165), developments in which have altered sports such that those with no previous practical experience increasingly consume sports but do so very differently, and therefore in conflict with, those consumers *with* previous practical sporting experience. In 'How Can One Be a Sportsman?' Bourdieu suggests that increases in doping and player and spectator violence may be the consequence of the changing media portrayal of sport (1983), and he argues that sport 'represents one of the few paths of upward mobility open to the children of the dominated classes' (1983: 127). The arguments about media representation are perhaps widely ignored by sociologists of sport as they are not distinctively Bourdieuian, whereas those about deviance and social mobility have probably been ignored because they are seen as somewhat simplistic interpretations of sporting phenonema.

Although Bourdieu's use of sport in *Distinction* primarily appears to be descriptive, he was also to make more expansive claims for the explanatory purchase of sport and its potential for the generation of theory. For instance, Bourdieu (with Wacquant) uses sport to illustrate the concept of field in *An Invitation to Reflexive Sociology* (Bourdieu and Wacquant 1992: 98). In his 'Program(me) for a Sociology of Sport' he further argues that as the relationship between sport and social position is not direct or fixed, 'the priority of priorities is the construction of the structure of the space of sporting practices whose effects will be recorded by monographs devoted to particular sports' (Bourdieu 1987a: 158). Sport, moreover, he describes as 'one of the terrains in which is posed with the maximum acuteness the problem of the relations between theory and practice, and also between language and the body' (Bourdieu 1987a: 166). An understanding of the teaching of bodily practices involves theoretical questions 'of the greatest importance' (Bourdieu 1987a: 166).

These incursions into the field of sport are widely acclaimed as unusual amongst social theorists, not least by Bourdieu himself. Bourdieu and Wacquant somewhat immodestly claim that 'Bourdieu is virtually alone among major sociologists – Elias being the other one – to have written seriously on sports' (1992: 93). Tomlinson repeats this claim, adding that in *Distinction*, 'sport is acknowledged as a *major* focus of sociological analysis' (2004: 161, emphasis added). Perhaps most extreme is MacAloon's claim that sport has provided 'a *capital* project in the development of Professor Bourdieu's general theory' (1998: 150, emphasis added). Neither of these latter two claims really stand scrutiny; sport forms the focus of about twenty of the 600 pages in *Distinction*. In more measured terms, Jarvie and Maguire (1994: 193) argue that 'Bourdieu is unusual as a major social theorist in that he himself has applied the main corpus of his work in the study of sport and leisure practices'. Laberge and Kay (2002: 243) similarly note that while Bourdieu gives 'major attention' to sport and physical activities, he 'has not devoted a complete project' to the area.

How then might we assess Bourdieu's work on sport? Is Bourdieu's a sociology *of* sport or a sociology *through* sport? How seriously does Bourdieu view the sociology of sport? Does Bourdieu's empirical engagement with sport enable him to develop theoretical ideas which he would not otherwise be able? It may well be that Bourdieu's interest in sport enabled him to develop his core theoretical concepts. While that in itself is unusual amongst major social theorists, and not to be disregarded, it is probably true to say that the substance of *Distinction* would not be significantly altered by the omission of sport from the text. The fact that the inclusion of sport in *Distinction* is quite significant says more about the general neglect of sport in social theory than it does about Bourdieu's commitment to sport.

While Bourdieu did subsequently appear to become more convinced of the theory-generative potential of sport, to see the importance of a sociology *through* sport, particularly when emphasizing and developing the embodied aspects of his sociology, against this we might note that his sport-related publications stemmed from invitations to present papers at sports history and sociology of sport conferences. As Laberge and Kay (2002) note, Bourdieu did not act upon his own advice and develop the sport-related empirical studies he identified as particularly important. Indeed, the degree to which Bourdieu engaged with ideas and literature within the sociology of sport suggest that he did not have a particularly high opinion of this area. In my reading of Bourdieu I have only come across mention of three/four pieces of sociology of sport literature: the work of Jean-Paul Clement in 'Program(me)' (no reference given); that of Jacques Defrance (1976) in *Distinction* and 'Sport and Social Class'; and Elias's 'Essay on Sport and Violence' (1986b); and, if you include it in this category (as Wacquant himself has disputed this), Wacquant's work on boxing (1989) in *Invitation*. Indeed, perhaps not inaccurately, Bourdieu described sport as 'a minor sociological topic by any measure of the hierarchy of scientific objects' and explained his own interest in it as a 'strategic' and 'opportunistic' research site 'for uncovering the logic of "practical sense"' (Bourdieu and Wacquant 1992: 93).

As a final gauge of the role of sport in Bourdieu's work we might consider the degree to which those who have written about Bourdieu's theory view the significance of his analysis of sport. Despite describing his contribution as 'otherwise excellent, wide ranging and searching', Jarvie and Maguire (1994: 207) accuse Richard Jenkins (1992) of deliberately and unapologetically excluding discussion of Bourdieu's analysis of sport. Jenkins, however, is not unusual in this. Few books introducing or examining Bourdieu's theoretical ideas (e.g., Harker 1990; Fowler 2000; Kauppi 2000; Lane 2000; Robbins 2000a, 2000b; Shusterman 1999; Swartz 1997) include any mention of sport in the index, or citation of Bourdieu's writing on sport.[3] Interestingly, even those texts that do cite sport (e.g., Webb *et al.* 2001) refer not to the work to which sociologists of sport draw attention but to Bourdieu's other discussions of sport, namely *Practical Reason: On the Theory of Action* (1998c) and the aforementioned appendix to *On Television*. Seen in this light, the degree to which Bourdieu undertook either a sociology *of* sport or a sociology *through* sport is perhaps overstated by those within the subdiscipline.

Elias and the sociology of sport

Like Bourdieu, Elias mentions sport in his most important and well known text, *The Civilizing Process* (originally published 1939). For Elias, however, the mention is only in passing, arguing in the space of a paragraph that in 'modern', relatively 'civilized', societies sporting contests constitute a social context in which relatively high degrees of 'belligerence and aggression' are largely tolerated (2000: 170). Following this, and widely attributed to Eric Dunning's influence (Mennell 1992; Waddington and Malcolm 2008), Elias went on to co-author and author a number of theoretical-empirical studies. Initially published as journal articles or book chapters, these were subsequently combined to produce *Quest for Excitement* (Elias and Dunning 1986a), a text that constitutes Elias's 'major statement on sport and leisure' (Giulianotti 2004d: 146). The text contains Elias's explanation, through an analysis of fox-hunting, of modern sport's initial development in eighteenth-century England, his comparison of the character and status of sport in Ancient Greece and two works which Elias saw as significant contributions towards his sociology of the emotions: the thesis of the 'quest for excitement in unexciting societies' (see below) and the analysis of sport as part of a broader 'spare-time spectrum' that attempted to debunk the conventional dichotomy of work and leisure.[4]

Again, like Bourdieu, it is clear that in some ways Elias sees sport as a convenient vehicle through which to demonstrate certain concepts that inform his sociological approach more broadly. His first excursus into sport, 'Dynamics of Sports Groups with Special Reference to Football' (Elias and Dunning 1966), published in the *British Journal of Sociology*, essentially critiqued symbolic interactionism (Elias and Dunning refer to 'small group theory') and instead promoted Elias's concept of figuration. (This paper may also have been stimulated by the influence of psychology within the sociology of sport at this time.) Elias (1978) similarly used sport to illustrate his 'game models' theory in *What Is Sociology?* These writings parallel Bourdieu's use of sport to illustrate his concept of field.

Yet, compared with Bourdieu, Elias was to subject sport to rather more direct scrutiny and empirical investigation. As Jarvie and Maguire (1994: 145) note, core questions for Elias include: What are the characteristics of people's leisure needs in more complex societies such as our own? And what are the characteristics of the leisure events that satisfy these needs? While these questions directly stem from Elias's 'central theory' of civilizing processes, working in conjunction with Dunning, he expands upon and extends his previous work. In the chapter, 'Quest for Excitement in Leisure', Elias and Dunning (1986b) suggest that the social significance of sport in contemporary societies is directly related to, and fundamentally interdependent with, broader social changes affecting the control of violence, bodily habits and emotional expression. Elias (1986a: 19) argues that he (and Dunning) were keenly aware that 'knowledge about sport was knowledge about society', and in seeking to understand the social context from which sport emerged in its modern form, Elias makes some of his most explicit observations on the development of English society. While the main focus of the second part of *The Civilizing Process* is the socio-genesis of state formation in France, 'Elias' work on sport … constituted his main attempt to contribute to the understanding of English social development' (Dunning 1992: 98). Thus, in 'An Essay on Sport and Violence', Elias's (1986b) notion of sportization (the process by which folk games are transformed into rule-bound, codified, standardized and formalized modern sports forms) emerges in conjunction with the concept of the 'parliamentarization of political conflict' (the rule-bound and relatively peaceful transference of political power). In 'The Genesis of Sport as a Sociological Problem',

Elias contrasts contemporary sport with that practised in Ancient Greece in seeking to understand how the structural characteristics of sport have changed over time, and therefore how particular English pastimes 'set the pattern for a world-wide leisure movement' (1986c: 128). He argues that sport could only have developed in its contemporary form in a country which was characterized by a specific balance of power between elite groups that permitted freedom of association and relative independence from the monarch (in contrast, for instance, to the absolute rule in France). Elias not only saw sport as a kind of '"natural laboratory" for shedding light on key aspects of human existence … [but also] as constituting a problem area which merits investigation in its own right' (Dunning 2002: 215). Elias's was, thus, both a sociology *through* sport and a sociology *of* sport.

Like Bourdieu, Elias is recognized as 'highly unusual among leading sociologists' in seeing sport and leisure as important social phenomena (Giulianotti 2004d: 145). Jarvie and Maguire similarly note that within his 'overall project, Elias took the study of sport and leisure as a serious area of investigation' (1994: 130). For instance, in 'Genesis', Elias stated that the adoption of sports such as boxing and horse racing in a range of European countries, and the timing of the diffusion of ball games such as tennis and football in the second half of the nineteenth century are 'as significant to our understanding of the development of European societies as it is for that of sport itself' (1986c: 127). Dunning states the case rather more strongly, arguing that Elias 'is the only sociologist with a claim to major status who has contributed significantly to the field' (1986a: 37), and describing him as 'one of the pioneers of the sociology of sport' (2002: 213). Like Bourdieu, Elias was conscious that his interest in sport marked him out as unusual amongst social theorists. In his 'Introduction' to *Quest for Excitement,* he reflects on his collaboration with Dunning, saying, 'we helped a little' to make sport a respectable subject for academic study (Elias 1986a: 19).

How then might we assess Elias's work on sport? While the claim that Elias was a pioneer of the field is somewhat disputed (see Chapter 2), claims that he has significantly contributed to it largely depend on perceptions of significance. For figurational sociologists (such as Dunning and myself), these works are clearly important, but for others their significance has faded over time. However, given that the bulk of Elias's work on sport was written in the late 1960s and early 1970s when the field was in its infancy, it would at least be true to say that, in contrast to Bourdieu, at *one* point in time Elias had contributed a relatively significant number of theoretically guided empirical examinations of sport.[5] Sport, moreover, allowed Elias to develop his theoretical ideas in distinct ways, most notably in terms of a 'quest for excitement' in contemporary societies, but also in his understanding of the way English state-formation processes contrasted with those of France and Germany. Like Bourdieu, Elias could hardly be said to have been immersed in the subdiscipline for, when writing alone (as opposed to with Dunning), he makes few references to sociology of sport texts. Unlike Bourdieu, however, Elias's primary research leads him to consult historical texts on football, boxing, fox-hunting and sport in Ancient Greece. One could reasonably suggest, therefore, that Elias's engagement with sport is qualitatively different from that of Bourdieu and in many ways more significant to his broader project.

Judging the impact of Elias's sociology of sport on the broader sociological and social theory communities is perhaps more difficult than doing so for Bourdieu. Giulianotti's claim that 'Elias makes few impressions in textbooks and compendia for modern social theory courses' (2004d: 154) is not without substance, especially when contrasted with the impact of Bourdieu. Yet Elias's appearance in the ISA list of key texts, and indeed the visibility of his theories in 'mainstream' sociology journals (see Table 3.2), suggests that Giulianotti underestimates Elias's broader significance. Tellingly, however, those who write more generally about Elias's social theory attach considerably more value to his work on sport than do those who write about Bourdieu. In contrast to the almost complete absence of reference to sport in texts on Bourdieu's social theory, books exploring Elias's theoretical ideas (e.g., Dunning and Mennell 2003; Fletcher 1997; Goudsblom and Mennell 1998; Loyal and Quilley 2004; Mennell 1992; Mennell and Goudsblom 1998; Smith 2000; van Krieken 1998) invariably devote entire chapters or sections to Elias's work on sport and its impact on his broader theoretical development.

What accounts for Bourdieu's and Elias's interest in sport? Laberge and Kay (2002) claim that Bourdieu's interest is probably attributable to his participation in rugby as a young man and his interest in developing a theory of embodiment. Dunning (1992) similarly attributes Elias's interest to his sporting background (boxing in his youth, skiing until his mid-sixties and swimming daily until over eighty years old) plus Elias's early medical training which inspired an interest in embodiment and the need for a 'sociology of the body'. Dunning (2002) has also claimed that Elias's broader rejection of dualistic thinking, such as that between mind and body and between work and leisure, was significant in alerting him to the interest in and potential of sport. Moreover, Elias was critical of the fracturing of sociology into discrete subdisciplines (1986a: 20). To this we might add Dunning's own role in stimulating Elias's interest in sport. It has been argued that Dunning is overly modest in giving Elias credit for their joint work, thereby understating his own contribution to the field (Waddington and Malcolm 2008). In Loïc Wacquant Bourdieu perhaps had his own potential collaborator akin to Dunning's relationship with Elias, though Wacquant's own career developed along a significantly different trajectory from that of Dunning, who has been rather more intrinsic to the development of the field (see Chapter 6 for a further discussion of Wacquant's interest in and attitude towards the sociology of sport).

Conclusion

The relationship between the sociology of sport and social theory is therefore rather mixed. It is clear that amongst those who might first and foremost be considered social theorists sport is rarely the subject of analytic focus. In contrast to the work of Bourdieu and Elias, social theorists more commonly fail to engage with sport, and sociologists of sport regularly bemoan their failure to do so. The subdiscipline remains a theoretical backwater, and the rather exaggerated claims for Bourdieu's sport-related project illustrate the degree to which sociologists of sport would dearly like this not to be the case.

However, I have also argued that within certain sections of the sociology of sport there has been a prolonged and critical engagement with social theory. This belies the rather pessimistic analyses of some sociologists of sport. Moreover, in contrast to Kenyon's assessment that the subdiscipline's 'frontiersmen' were the most theoretically committed (1986: 11), there are signs, borne out in subsequent chapters in this book, that the sociology of sport has become thoroughly engaged with theory. It is certainly the case that this review of sport and social theory is markedly at odds with the earlier texts that identified sparse references to sport made by social theorists such as Weber and Simmel as significant (see Chapter 2).

As Kenyon rightly notes, a 'distinction should be made between theory use and theory development' (1986: 17), and amongst sociologists of sport it is difficult to identify work that has *developed* theory in significant ways. Indeed Carrington (2010: 11) contends that 'much of the work within the sociology of sport rarely uses sport as *generative* of social theory and at best shows how concepts and ideas developed in other contexts can be *applied* to sport'. These claims form the backdrop to the next four chapters which begin to assess more empirically driven research in both the sociology of sport and the sociological 'mainstream'. Part of that assessment relates to the way theory is used and informed by such studies. But it also enables us to gain an appreciation of the broader impact of the subdiscipline within sociology.

4

SPORT, 'RACE' AND ETHNICITY[1]

In 1990, Norman Tebbit, a senior politician in Margaret Thatcher's Conservative government, made a statement in an interview with the *Los Angeles Times* that was to bring sport to the heart of race and ethnicity politics in Britain. Introducing his so-called 'cricket test', Tebbit argued that if a British immigrant, or one of his or her descendants, chose to support a team such as India or the West Indies when that team was playing cricket against England, this could, and indeed should, be used as a gauge of his or her patriotism and thus acceptability as a British citizen. Whilst Tebbit argued that the comments were designed to promote national integration, they effectively forwarded the argument that assimilation (i.e. that immigrants should forsake their ethnic roots and be subsumed into the culture of the host nation), as opposed to multiculturalism (i.e. the celebration and promotion of ethnic diversity within a nation), should form the basis of British race-relations policy. Tellingly he felt that sport, and cricket in particular, offered the most vivid illustration (and provocative example) of his argument.

Unlike a number of other areas discussed later in this book, the sociological study of race and sport is by no means a recent development. Indeed, C. L. R. James's *Beyond a Boundary*, a text which many now regard as a seminal account of race and sport, and indeed colonial and post-colonial relations more generally, was first published in 1963, before the emergence of the sociology of sport. While this reminds us of the questions previously raised about the emergence of the subdiscipline (see Chapter 2), a different problematic underpins this chapter. The opening sentence of the first book to bear the title *Race and Sport* notes that, 'The role of sport in race relations has not been given the attention it deserves' (Thompson 1964: 1). Similarly, the introductory chapter of the most recent analysis of this area, *Race, Sport and Politics*, states that 'the sociology of sport has been negligent in failing to take the racial signification of sport seriously … To think race *and* sport sociologically has, until relatively recently, meant to occupy an intellectual niche of such supposed specificity as to invoke outright incredulity' (Carrington 2010: 13).

This chapter considers whether the state of scholarship has changed so little in the half-century between the publication of these two texts. To this end, a developmental analysis of sociological studies of sport and race illustrates how the field has grown and how it has changed empirical and theoretical focus. The chapter further looks at the degree to which sociologists of race have studied and embraced scholarship on sport.

The emergence of the sociology of sport and race

American sociologists provided the first examinations of race. Their dominant theoretical assumption was that social and economic inequalities would be ameliorated through the assimilation of minority populations. By the 1950s, British race studies emerged, characterized by two main themes: issues related to immigrants defined as 'coloured' and the reaction of 'whites' to this new phenomenon; and the role played by colonial history and imperialism (Jarvie 2000). This section highlights how these themes – American dominance, assimilation theories and colonialism – were evident in a 1960s trilogy of books that might be defined as the first sociologies of sport and race.

Issues of race and colonial history were the first to emerge, as exemplified in James's *Beyond a Boundary* (1963). A Marxist philosopher and political activist, claiming James as a sociologist might not be strictly accurate. However, his part-autobiographical text, *Beyond a Boundary*, describes how cricket had been just as significant in shaping Caribbean society as had political movements, economic forces and educational systems. By revealing how cricket clubs remained strictly demarcated according to colour, class, status and religion, James showed that the game replicated and reproduced the pattern of social relations that had evolved under slavery. James's discussion of the stratification of cricket clubs according to both colour and class illustrated that everyone 'knew his place' and revealed how deeply internalized and how universally accepted social inequalities were. The 'black masses' did not reject this game, created and imposed by the 'white masters', in the post-colonial era, but thoroughly embraced it. Cricket thus contributed to a 'remarkable Caribbean conservatism' (Stoddart 1995: 384). James's achievement was to illustrate how an understanding of the social impact and importance of a sport is necessarily predicated on an understanding of the broader social context in which the sport is played. *Beyond a Boundary* has subsequently exerted a significant influence over both sociological and historical writing on sport (see Stoddart and Beckles 1995), Struna describing it as a 'classic essay' (2000: 194) which has stimulated research on the sporting experiences of people of African descent.

Richard Thompson's *Race and Sport* (1964) continued the colonialism theme. Thompson, a sociologist at the University of Canterbury, Christchurch, New Zealand, forwarded an argument consistent with much American sociology of race scholarship at this time, namely that 'modern sport undermines any system of social stratification based on colour' (1964: 11).[2] The book examined various issues relating to the role of sport in South Africa, including the organization of Apartheid and the consequences of sporting boycotts of South Africa, and explained the examples of relations between New Zealand and South Africa in both rugby union and cricket.

James's now classic question, which prefaces *Beyond a Boundary* – 'What do they know of cricket who only cricket know?' – replicates the subdisciplinary mission to understand sport in its social context. Yet neither James's nor Thompson's work was initially 'claimed' as part of the sociology of sport (see Chapter 2). Why? First, both texts were explicitly political and thus in marked contrast with the value-neutral orthodoxy of the subdiscipline's founders. Second, it was probable that James's work was not seen as *sufficiently* sociological, illustrating the relatively narrow disciplinary lines along which the sociology of sport was initially drawn. And while Thompson's work was explicitly sociological, citing American sociologists of race relations such as Robert Park and J. S. Coleman, his incorporation within the subdiscipline was probably limited due to his specific focus on race (and sport), as opposed to a more general interest in sport. The sociology of sport does not appear to have been ready for, or could not recognize, a sociology of sport and race.

This began to change with the publication of the third book in this trilogy: Harry Edwards's *The Revolt of the Black Athlete* (1969/1970). *The Revolt of the Black Athlete,* like *Beyond a Boundary*, is semi-autobiographical and marks the beginning of a period of American hegemony in studies of sport and race. Edwards though was a sociologist, an athlete and chair of the Olympic Project for Human Rights, which sought to alert the world to the injustices faced by black athletes. The project culminated in the famous Black Power salute by two American sprinters, John Carlos and Tommie Smith, as the American national anthem was played during the men's 200-metres medal ceremony at the 1968 Mexico Olympic Games. Edwards describes the build-up to this protest, including threats to disrupt college football and the boycott of the New York Athletics Club meeting in 1968. Edwards further highlights racist policies in colleges, Apartheid sport in South Africa, allegations about the lack of employment rights for (black) college athletes who 'are treated like slaves' (1969/1970: xx), the lack of black coaching appointments, the restrictive rules of the National Collegiate Athletic Association (NCAA) and the organization's resistance to change. Chapters on the history of black participation in sport and media representations perpetuating stereotypes of black people as incapable of leadership (and thus needing 'white' direction), provide the backdrop to his argument that black participation in American sport has done little to alter broader patterns of racial discrimination. Edwards effectively charts the process of the creation of a new consciousness; the black athlete had 'left the façade of locker room equality and justice' (1969/1970: xxviii).

The consolidation of the sociology of sport and race

The American hegemony signalled by Edward's *Revolt* became shaped by two important sport-specific contingencies. First, race and sport literature continually engaged with popular ideas linking performance with an innate biological advantage of black people. Second, sociologists of sport and race felt compelled to critique the apparent dominance (as opposed to discrimination) of black athletes in American sport.

Popular biological explanations of sports performance were exemplified by Martin Kane's (1971) 'An Assessment of Black Is Best'. Kane argued that the dominance of black athletes in sport could be attributed to three factors: race-linked physiological traits, race-linked psychological traits and the historic specificities that had developed these traits in particular ways (i.e. slavery exacerbated evolutionary selection such that only the very strongest survived). The place of publication (appearing in *Sports Illustrated*), and Kane's 'validation' through testimony from black and white athletes and coaches rather than academics (see Chapter 9), cemented the popular legitimacy of this argument.

Sociologists of sport have continually responded to Kane and others who have made similar arguments. For example, Harry Edwards (1973) argued that Kane's sample group was far from random and that making conclusions about entire 'races' on the basis of a physically atypical select few was highly problematic. Edwards further noted that Kane overlooked the heterogeneity of black athletes' physical types and that he underplayed the influence of cultural factors in shaping physicality. In countering arguments about psychological differences, Edwards implicitly raised what many later identified as the problem of the pathologization the black athlete (i.e. the tendency to only see black sporting performance as 'the' problem or anomaly). Edwards argued that the most likely causal link between psychology and race lay not in biological difference but in white responses to beliefs about black biological superiority. Finally, Edwards asked why, if slavery had 'naturally' selected a black biological elite, was it not also the case that the most intelligent survived? Why were black people not also more academically talented than white people?

In addition to challenging prevalent and populist beliefs linking race and sporting achievement, sociologists of sport interrogated the apparent equality of opportunity in American sport. Forged in a context in which the segregation of races (both in sports leagues and, e.g., on buses) was part of a recent past, sociologists of sport drew attention to the phenomenon in American team sports whereby the overall presence of significant numbers of black athletes masked internal, or *positional,* segregation. Initiated by Loy and Elvogue (1970), a series of studies illustrated how members of minority ethnic groups experienced 'stacking'; that is to say, how they tended to be disproportionately over-represented in certain roles while remaining largely excluded from others.[3] Empirically, the pattern was relatively simple to illustrate. Raw data were readily available and seasonally refreshed. The methodological approach conformed to the positivist leanings of those dominant in the nascent subdiscipline. Loy and Elvogue argued that 'racial segregation in professional team sports is positively related to centrality' (1970: 7), centrality being defined both in terms of spatial location in team formations and the frequency and diversity of contact with other team members. The quarterback in American football was the archetypal 'central' position. Central positions, it was thought, required decision-making abilities and thus conflicted with stereotypical notions of black intellect.

Sociologists of sport focused on illustrating the broad applicability of this trend, but the approach could only generate speculative explanations. Edwards (1973), for instance, argued that positional location was not structured according to centrality but according to 'outcome control' (which, Edwards argued, explained why black athletes 'underperform' in individual sports and are excluded from management). Yetman and Eitzen (1984) argued that black athletes were disproportionately 'star' athletes, who needed to outperform their white counterparts in order to be employed, and that this influenced positional occupancy. Alternative explanations included the 'uncertainty hypothesis' (Lavoie and Leonard 1994), which suggested that discrimination was greater for positions in which a player's performance could not be objectively assessed and Medoff's (1986) 'economic explanation', which controversially suggested that playing position was linked to athletes' rational choices of probable economic gain (controversial because it again pathologized the black athlete). Empirical variations on this theme were to look at longitudinal (Yetman and Berghorn 1993) and gendered (Berghorn *et al.* 1988) patterns of stacking. Theories were tested beyond the USA, through studies of French-Canadian involvement in ice hockey (Lavoie 1989), Aboriginals in Australian rugby league (Hallinan 1991) and black footballers and black and Asian cricketers in England (Maguire 1988; Malcolm 1997).

Richard Lapchick's work has largely been located within this quantitative framework, but with a more overtly political stance. The son of a famous basketball player and coach, Lapchick has been a prominent activist campaigning against Apartheid in South Africa, highlighting aspects of racial inequality in American college and professional sports and promoting conflict resolution through sport in the USA and beyond. Lapchick founded the Centre for the Study of Sport and Society at Northeastern University, Boston, in 1984, which publishes an annual 'Racial and Gender Report Card' highlighting the inequitable employment practices of leading sports organizations in the USA. The Centre also publicizes NCAA graduation rates as a way of signalling the failure of colleges to ensure that athletic scholarships, of which black athletes are significant beneficiaries, entail a meaningful educational experience.

Among Lapchick's publications are *Broken Promises: Racism in American Sports* (1984) and *Five Minutes to Midnight: Race and Sport in the 1990s* (1991). While both are targeted at a mass rather than academic market, with neither particularly drawing on the sociology of sport literature, they are powerfully written. *Five Minutes to Midnight* opens with a rather harrowing account of an attack on Lapchick by masked men who warned him to stop campaigning against Apartheid in South Africa before beating him and carving 'Nigger' into his stomach with a knife. More substantively, the book charts 'limited progress' towards racial equality:

> Black athletes still graduate at a significantly lower rate than whites, are over-represented in basketball and football, are academically and sometimes physically separated from black students, have few black mentors on campus, have absolutely unrealistic expectations of making the pros, and still have a long fall back to the streets if they neither make the pros nor get a degree. In pro sports, the front offices … are still predominantly white outposts.
>
> *(1991: 320)*

Few sociologists of sport have suffered so personally as Lapchick, but his concern with South African sport (1975) was widely shared. Analyses were written by political activists (Ramsamy 1982), political historians (Archer and Bouillon 1982) and latterly cultural historians (Nauright 1997; Booth 1998). Sociologically, the most significant text was Grant Jarvie's *Class, Race and Sport in South Africa's Political Economy* (1985). Jarvie distinguished his own approach from those of others by drawing on the theories of Gramsci and by emphasizing the 'complex interaction between racial and class dynamics' (1985: 1). He argued that South African sport must be understood in the context of a mixture of social relations: colonization, capitalist development and Western imperialism. He further argues that the desire for capital accumulation had led to an increased white dependence on the black masses, increased black resistance and, thus, to what Gramsci termed 'organic crisis'. Through his account of the history of white responses to non-racial sporting organizations, Jarvie argues that South African sporting policy is 'no more than a facelift, part of the ideology of reform constructed by the dominant culture in response to a growing crisis' (1985: 5).

Political change in South Africa signalled a shift in focus in the sociology of sport, but equally significant was Susan Birrell's (1989) seminal critique of race-related research in the subdiscipline. Birrell had previously written little about race, but drawing on the theoretical insights of feminist cultural studies of sport (see Chapters 3 and 5), her comments anticipated how the area would develop. Addressing the dominance of quantitative research, she argued that:

> We continue to produce studies on centrality and stacking, not because of their theoretical significance but simply because the data are there. Twenty years ago such studies provided major insight into stratification by race, and it is startling to know that such patterns persist today, but there is no theoretical news in this tradition.
>
> *(Birrell 1989: 214)*

Birrell further suggested that the sociology of sport and race could learn much from adopting the theoretical insights of cultural studies, Marxism and feminist theories which viewed sport as a complex site of dominance–subordinance relations. Noting that while most sociologists of sport rejected popular beliefs about meritocratic underpinnings of sport (contrast this with Bourdieu's rather simplistic comments about sport and social mobility; see Chapter 3), she argued that, 'we have yet to launch any sort of sophisticated analysis of racial relations' (Birrell 1989: 213). Rather, she noted, there was a mistaken tendency to:

- equate race with black and thus 'idiosyncratically' assess racial equality only in cases where that minority group had been 'allowed' to play;
- 'obliterate gender' by equating black experience with black male experience;
- underplay the relationship between sport and sexuality/masculinity;
- obscure class relations.

The result was the examination of race as homogeneous and undifferentiated in the context of sport. Birrell attributed this shortcoming to an ignorance of the broader study of race and ethnic relations. Birrell's critique signalled the beginning of the end of the tradition of stacking research in the sociology of sport (stacking appeared in all of the early editions of Coakley's *Sport in Society* but was dropped from the 2001 seventh edition), but created the broad theoretical framework for studies of sport and race from the 1990s to the present day:

> our approach has been to assert that race exists and to ask what effect membership in a particular race or ethnic group has on sport involvement. A more profound approach is to conceive of race as a culturally produced marker of a particular relationship of power, to see racial identity as contested, and to ask how racial relations are produced and reproduced through sport.
>
> *(Birrell 1989: 214)*

Sport and race in the 1990s

Underscoring earlier arguments about cross-cultural differences in the subdiscipline (see Chapter 3), as the influence of British sociologists of sport researching race has grown so the area has become increasingly theoretically oriented. The 1990s opened with Grant Jarvie's edited collection, *Sport, Racism and Ethnicity* (1991a). Citing Birrell's critique, Jarvie called for literature on sport and race to look at 'the role of sport in either consolidation or challenging the racist values of various dominant groups' (1991a: 4–5). The contents of the collection showed a sensitivity towards both gender and the sporting experiences beyond simply those of black athletes. The book included analyses of stacking in British team sports and the role of sport in the popular struggle against Apartheid in South Africa, discussion of the relationship between Caribbean cricket and carnival and the first ethnographies of both male and female British South Asian sporting experiences. It also showed the underdevelopment of race and sport research in Britain, drawing on two North American authors (Othello Harris and Vicky Paraschak) for contributions on the experiences of college athletes and Native Canadians respectively. The latter demonstrated that ethnicity was now being studied alongside race.

Scott Fleming's *Home and Away: Sport and South Asian Male Youth* (1994) was perhaps the first sociology of sport monograph devoted to the study of race in the UK.[4] The book attempted to address the general lack of understanding of South Asian experiences of sports participation, and physical education experiences in particular. Betraying a cultural studies orientation through the citation of C. Wright Mills and Stuart Hall, Fleming suggested that it was important to focus on cultural change and continuity, on both personal problems and public issues. The study concludes by citing four findings:

1 the prominence of cultural continuity, with leisure choices shaped by British South Asians' religious commitments and cultural patterns;
2 that sports participation that cross-cuts ethnic group membership illustrates the fallaciousness of stereotypes of ethnic/racial group difference;

3 the heterogeneity of South Asian male youth experience highlights the risk of 'false universalism';
4 a strong interdependence of class and race.

Despite these developments, knowledge advances through UK scholarship on race and sport were slow and limited in breadth. A decade after Jarvie's *Sport, Racism and Ethnicity* (1991a), Ben Carrington and Ian McDonald edited *'Race', Sport and British Society* (2001a). Offering an explicit attempt to 'raise the quality' of analysis of race issues in the 'sometimes insular' world of the sociology of sport, the editors argued that sport provides one of the clearest and most public ways of demonstrating British multiculturalism. Invoking Paul Gilroy's (1987) *There Ain't No Black in the Union Jack*, they suggest that the sight of Black British athletes celebrating Olympic victory draped in the national flag poses distinct and highly visible challenges to British nationalist and racist ideologies. They express caution, however, noting that the relationship between sport and race is complex. While challenging some forms of racism, sport is also complicit in reproducing others.

Carrington and McDonald (2001a: 8) suggest that their review of British literature on sport and race clearly demonstrates that 'racial equality is still not considered an area worthy of investigation by many in sports sociology'. They are critical of Dunning (1999) for choosing to use American material to illustrate his figurational analysis of race and sport – 'are there no sociologically relevant issues relating to sport and "race" in Britain?' (Carrington and McDonald 2001a: 8) – and Lincoln Allison (1998) for his 'tabloid style commentary' and empirically unsubstantiated claim that 'racial discrimination exists largely in the minds of black people' and that 'if blacks had a different self image … the structural inequalities they faced would largely disappear' (2001a: 10–11). They note that Jarvie's (1991a) text, while successfully centring power in analyses of sport and race, paid too little attention to the British context, and they are critical of the tendency in North American scholarship towards narrow empiricism and the advocacy of sport and integration models.

Structured in three parts, *'Race', Sport and British Society* documents the extent of racism in various British sports and contexts: cricket (Carrington and McDonald 2001b), football (Back *et al.* 2001a), rugby league (Spracklen 2001) and Scottish football (Dimeo and Finn 2001), and draws on public controversies over race to argue that the law can only play a limited role in combating racism (relative to education and social policy [Gardiner and Welch 2001]) and critique the analysis of race in sports science (Fleming 2001). The third section, 'Challenging Discourse/Contesting Identities', explores 'new agendas', including discussion of South Asian footballing experiences (Johal 2001), calls for a more gender-sensitive approach to the study of race (Scraton 2001) and two personal, critically reflexive accounts by a black female sports journalist (Lindsey 2001) and the educationalist, cricket writer and race campaigner Chris Searle (2001). Though the book represented a significant development at the time, the inclusion of journalists and popular writers such as Mike Marqusee (2001) illustrated the continued absence of a critical mass of British sociologists of sport producing race-related research.

Contemporary trends in the sociology of sport and race

There have been considerable advances in both the quantity and theoretical sophistication of sociological studies of sport and race in recent years. In the last decade or so a number of key works on race and sport in both Britain and North America have appeared which, following Birrell, examine how a variety of racial identities are constructed and contested and how racial relations are produced and reproduced through sport. Many of these texts include extensive theorization and are deeply informed by a reading of the broader sociology of race literature. The degree of theorization is, however, more consistent in the works of British authors.

Offside Racism: Playing with the White Man is written by Colin King (2004). A sociologist, political activist and professional football coach, King is critical of previous studies which have been fixated with explaining the 'peculiarity' of the black athlete, for such studies neglect the way white men perpetuate racism. King attempts to show the black experience as heterogeneous and thus to illustrate that black athletes should not be depicted as singular characters. He also describes the pressures on black and Asian players to 'act white' in order to be accepted. King contrasts 'onside' racism (visible and conscious) with 'offside' racism, or the often unthinking ways in which 'white men create forms of familiarity which ensure that they are never made accountable for the ways they exclude predominantly black men' (2004: 3). Whiteness is thus a 'performance' that affects both sides of 'the colour line', and King suggests that racist physical threats, beliefs about the black body as animalistic and the pathologization of a black mentality permeate football cultures. He concludes that the lived reality of black players involves the routine acceptance of racial abuse from white fans and relationships with white coaches and managers that force tolerance of these acts 'as part of the performance of being in the English game' (2004: 20). Black players, King argues, are expected to 'toe the line', 'be reasonable' and not to have a 'chip on their shoulder'. Racialized discourse may be delivered in a joking style, followed by an apology or justified as 'part of the game', but these 'strategies' simply make racist actions less visible and therefore less able to be confronted, challenged and changed.

Similar ideas inform Dan Burdsey's *British Asians and Football* (2007a). Burdsey aims to 'illustrat[e] the heterogeneity of British Asian communities and cultures, and the myriad ways that they approach and interact with professional football'. Like King, Burdsey attempts to challenge the perception that:

- cultural practices (e.g., religion) are self-excluding;
- minorities are both 'the problem' and masters of their own destiny.

Rather, Burdsey highlights the social significance of football as a venue in which 'young British Asians are asserting their right to celebrate both their "sameness" and their "difference" to the game's dominant (sub)cultures and identities' (2007a: 153). British Asians must actively modify their identities to gain inclusion; they 'consciously deprioritize their ethnic identities and seek to share the dominant habituses of their white and African-Caribbean team-mates' (2007a: 14). In examining the complex

diasporic lifestyles of racial, generational and spatial subjectivities, Burdsey emphasizes the dynamic and unfinished character of culture, stresses the hybridity, fusions or creolizations of British-Asian identities, and illustrates football's role in this. He further examines institutional approaches to anti-racism and concludes that while football 'construct[s] and maintain[s] racial inequality and disadvantage' (2007a: 4), the 'dominant claims that football is "colour-blind" or meritocratic are actually a means of sustaining white hegemony in the structures and subcultures of the professional game' (2007a: 9).

In what is perhaps the theoretically most explicit work, *'Race' and Sport: Critical Race Theory* (2009), Kevin Hylton argues that the problem with traditional approaches that focus on charting racial inequalities is that the 'naturalness of "races" is not questioned or disturbed' (2009: 4). Race ideology permeates public perception, and thus, while researchers may express a desire to challenge racial inequalities, in accepting the basic existence of the category 'race', they effectively legitimize and reproduce the notion that physical differences underpin differential (sporting) experiences. Rather, Hylton undertakes an examination of the meaning of 'whiteness', the relationship between the media, sport and racism, sport-related anti-racism movements and the premises and conclusions of genetics and scientific racism. Hylton's aim is to consider how racism operates, the divisions created by it and the intersection of race with other axes of power and difference.

Carrington's *Race, Sport and Politics* is an examination of sport's role in shaping racial discourse and 'an account of the political meanings and global impact of the "black athlete"' (2010: 2). Carrington argues that black athletes are never 'ordinary' or neutral but always 'remarkable', or 'othered'. Furthermore, their 'othering' is not solely, or primarily, about their blackness, but is structured by white colonial self-definition. *Race, Sport and Politics* contains two underlying arguments:

1 that belief in the apolitical nature of sport (ironically) makes it a highly effective social sphere for the (political) act of constructing race identities;
2 that sport acts as 'a homosocial space for the projection of white masculinist fantasies of domination, control and desire for the racialized Other' (Carrington 2010: 4).

Carrington's synthesis of cultural studies, postcolonial studies, the concept of diaspora and elements of psychoanalysis builds on Gramsci and draws on Aimé Cesaire, Frantz Fanon and Gilroy. Carrington argues that the concept of 'diaspora helps to challenge static and at times Eurocentric models of history and place' (2010: 52), and he defines the 'sporting black Atlantic' as 'a complex, transnational cultural and political space, that exceeds the boundaries of nation states, whereby the migrations and achievements of black athletes have come to assume a heightened *political significance* for the dispersed peoples of the black diaspora' (2010: 55). Carrington provides a history of the white colonial discourses that defined the black athlete as a 'fantasmatic figure' (2010: 96) and compares the media portrayals of British boxer Frank Bruno and American boxer Mike Tyson to illustrate how 'various tropes of madness and savagery have infused the media representations of … high profile black men' (2010: 105). The final empirical chapter focuses on multiculturalism and the role of sport (and race) in shaping contemporary notions of British and English national identities. Carrington concludes that 'sport remains a critical site for the reproduction (and rearticulation) of forms of racial knowledge and commonsense and an important location in the contested and ongoing struggles over ideology, politics and identity' (2010: 175).

While the focus in the section so far has been on the development of research on race by British sociologists of sport, there have also been significant developments in the North American literature. For instance, Gary Sailes's *African-Americans in Sport: Contemporary Themes* (1998) is an edited collection mainly consisting of previously published material (the majority initially published in 'sociology of race' journals). Sailes attempts to illustrate the 'complex and diverse social worlds' in which African Americans give meaning to sport and construct their social identities. Unapologetically focused on males, the book covers the role of sport in African-American culture, focusing on masculinity, community significance and participation rates, and media portrayals of athletes such as O. J. Simpson, Mike Tyson and Tiger Woods. The book examines biological beliefs about sport and racial difference and explores the extent of racist exploitation in college and professional sports.

Theoretically more sophisticated is C. Richard King and Charles Springwood's (2001) *Beyond the Cheers: Race as Spectacle in College Sport,* which focuses on college 'revenue' sports (basketball and football) in an attempt to move beyond narrow statistical representations of racism and to look at how racism is practised and imagined. Following Birrell's call for multi-ethnic analyses, King and Springwood note the specific developmental trajectories of African-American and Native-American participation in sport that highlight 'the construction and contestation of redness, blackness, and whiteness' (King and Springwood 2001: 14). Starting from the premise that through sports Euro-Americans celebrate their own race and mimic others, chapters examine the 'contradictory stagings' of race and sport. Initially black athletes were legally segregated and Indians were incorporated and stereotyped for physicality and savagery. Subsequently the position inverted, with the rise of black athletes parallel to the marginalization of Native Americans. Ironically, however, the practice of 'playing Indian at half time' through the use of Native American mascots, emerged as being central to the identity of sports teams (King and Springwood 2001: 4–5). King and Springwood examine how contemporary media remake blackness through (white) ideas of criminality, etc., but also construct and defend 'whiteness'. Theoretically inspired by Guy Debord, Michel Foucault, Jean Baudrillard and Antonio Gramsci, King and Springwood argue that through the discourses and spectacle of sport that locate, structure and perform race and racial identity, 'Americans have come to know and think of themselves as a freer, more racially harmonious society' (2001: 6). Yet sport is infused with racial inequalities, and King and Springwood conclude that we can see that notions of race are not simply constructed as binaries but within a more complex network of relations.

But perhaps the most significant sociology of sport and race publication, and certainly the most controversial in recent years, is John Hoberman's *Darwin's Athletes: How Sport Has Damaged Black America and Preserved the Myth of Race* (1997).[5] A 'racial history of modern sport', *Darwin's Athletes* examines the prominence of black athletes in

American sports, arguing that their media-generated images 'probably do more than anything else in public life to encourage the idea that blacks and whites are biologically different in a meaningful way' (1997: xxiii). Hoberman argues that the cult of black athleticism continues the tradition of emphasizing the physical superiority of blacks which started with the retreat of European empires and the parallel decline of white athletes. Concomitant with ideas of black physical superiority, were and are beliefs that white dominance stemmed from mental superiority relative to blacks. Considerable scientific effort was devoted to 'proving' these ideas in the nineteenth century (hence the book's titular reference to Charles Darwin and evolutionary theory).

Hoberman argues that African Americans have bought into the collective fantasy of physical difference, basking in the symbolism of black athletes' victories over whites. While many whites may retreat from sport, perceiving their disadvantage to be innate, those who remain are compensated with coaching and administrative roles of responsibility and power. Athletic success leads to peer-group pressures that ridicule black academic achievement and fosters a culture of anti-intellectualism. Moreover, the media's conflation of 'the athlete, gangster rapper and the criminal into a single black male persona' (1997: xxvii) and the prominence of such images have led to the invisibility of the African-American middle class and professionals. The black middle classes and black intelligentsia remain 'infatuated with sports' and thus 'cannot campaign effectively against racial stereotyping that preserves the black man's physicality as a sign of his inherent limitations' (1997: xxxiv).

Though not central to this discussion, it should be noted that *Darwin's Athletes* launched a nationwide public debate in the US media, prompted a walkout demonstration at the 1997 NASSS conference, where Hoberman had been invited to give a keynote speech, and led to fierce debate in the academic community (see the IRSS special issue, e.g., Bale 1998). Critics argued that Hoberman was out of touch with the lived reality of African-American youths and pathologized black communities through his portrayal of anti-intellectualism. Hoberman responded by asking whether at the heart of these debates was the question of whether a white middle-class male could accurately analyse (and legitimately speak about) the experience of black working-class youth. Beyond dispute is the fact that *Darwin's Athletes* clearly illustrated that the sociology of sport and race was more vibrant and intellectually critical than in earlier times. It is interesting that this was largely a methodological and empirical dispute rather than a theoretical one.

Sport and the sociology of race

While studies of race in the sociology of sport have thus significantly developed in recent years, what is the status of sport within the sociology of race? In *Race, Sport and Politics,* Carrington refers to his 'multiple disappointments of engaging with radical intellectual works that … constantly and consistently fail to address the centrality of sport in the making of race and of race in the structuring of sport' (2010: 16). He is critical of analyses of black popular culture that overlook '*the* most significant and public of popular cultural forms, namely sport' (Carrington 2010: 16, emphasis in original), the failure of post/colonial theorists to consider or theorize sport at all (2010: 46) and of 'the repetitive and perfunctory "Jamesian" nod' via which mention of *Beyond a Boundary* is deemed sufficient recognition of sport (2010: 48). To what extent do these comments accurately reflect the way in which sport has been explored by sociologists of race?

There is clear evidence to support Carrington's assessment. As he goes on to note, despite its integral role within empires and colonialism, 'sport hardly surfaces' in Edward Said's (1994) *Culture and Imperialism* and is similarly absent in the work of Gayatri Spivak and Homi Bhabha. He further cites six 'key texts' within diaspora studies that focus on writers and intellectuals, film, dance and literature, but rarely athletes or sport (Carrington 2010: 52–3). One could also highlight the range of readers, edited collections and reference works that eschew any mention of sport. Typical is Alison Donnell's *Companion to Contemporary Black British Culture,* described as 'a gesture towards recording the immense and yet often unrecognised talent and significance of black British culture' (2001: xv). Donnell emphasizes the collection's diversity and hence the inclusion of, for example, an entry on hairdressing, yet (unconvincingly) identifies space limitations as the reason for the omission of any mention of sport or Black British athletes. The absence of sport from Ellis Cashmore and James Jennings's *Racism: Essential Readings* (2001) might, given Cashmore's own work (see below), be one of the more peculiar omissions. Kwesi Owusu's (2000) inclusion of a chapter by Carrington (2000) on the 'double consciousness' of Black British athletes representing both the 'nation' and their 'race' is very much the exception.

But in other respects the analysis of sport amongst scholars of race is less moribund than Carrington portrays. Of course, much depends on the rather subjective process of deciding what does and does not count and how much is 'enough', but Carrington himself cites a significant number of race scholars who consider sport. For instance, he quotes Frantz Fanon's distinction between sports in capitalist and underdeveloped nations, warning that for the latter commercialism may undermine the national consciousness generated through the practice of sport (Carrington 2010: 169). Reminiscent of the introduction to his previous collection (Carrington and McDonald 2001a), Carrington cites Stuart Hall's (1998) discussion of the role of black athletes in the (re)imagination of the national community. He further mentions bell hooks's (2004) analysis of the relationship between sport (and Mike Tyson in particular) and the generation of ideas of black masculinity, and of the commodification of contemporary black athletes that strips them of their radical potential (in contrast to predecessors such as Jack Johnson and Joe Louis) (hooks 1994). Though Carrington is critical of hooks's failure to see how contemporary black athletes can both confirm and challenge hegemonic readings of black masculinity, this does not equate to neglect.

There are other works that we might cite in this regard: Ossie Stuart's (1996) study of the dynamics of a Caribbean cricket club in Oxford; Sallie Westwood's (1990, 1991) study of the relationship between football and black masculinity; Pnina Werbner's (1996) 'Our Blood Is Green', examining the social significance of cricket amongst British Muslims; Bob Holland's evaluation of anti-racist campaigns in football (1995) and racial harassment of footballers (1997); and Searle's various accounts of race and cricket (1990, 1993, 1995, 1996). Carrington recognizes Gilroy's (1993) analysis of Frank Bruno (and similarly draws on Kobena Mercer 1994) but omits to mention Gilroy's (2000) discussion of sport's role in reifying black physicality and racialized bodies, as well as the masking of white supremacy via the economic success of black athletes. Gilroy (2001) has also discussed the conflation of sport, post-colonial nationalism, whiteness and exclusion in the preface to Carrington and McDonald's *'Race', Sport and British Society*, as well as the social significance of England women's football coach, Hope Powell (Gilroy 2008). While we might be critical of some of Gilroy's analysis, for instance his hasty prediction of the 'terminal decline' of English cricket (2001: xv), his work acknowledges the cultural centrality of sport if not constituting a more sustained empirical focus.

Moreover, it would be reasonable to claim that there are a number of sport-related research monographs, authored by scholars whose primary interest is or was race, which focus on sport. Two of these, James's *Beyond a Boundary* and Thompson's *Race and Sport,* were discussed at the outset of this chapter. The third is Cashmore's *Black Sportsmen* (1982). Based on interviews with professional black sportsmen, Cashmore concluded that the experience of being black was not used as a basis for defeatism but as a resource, citing boxer Maurice Hope's belief that being black and experiencing racism made him work 'twice as hard'. Cashmore discusses the history of black sports participation, contests biological explanations linking race and sports performance (c.f. Kane 1971) and discusses how family and school experiences, perceptions of blackness as disadvantageous and individuals' responses to perceived obstacles explain how and why sport becomes a central life interest for black children. For young black males, Cashmore argues, sports participation 'generates a fresh, exhilarating and positive image of himself, in short, a new identity' (1982: 10). Because of his subsequent work, Cashmore is often viewed as 'belonging' to the sociology of sport (and his work is roundly critiqued as such; see Hylton 2009; Carrington 2010), but prior to the *Black Sportsmen* project Cashmore had written more on race, and on Rastafarianism and black youth in particular, than on sport.

The status and quality of *The Changing Face of Football: Racism, Identity and Multiculture in the English Game* (Back *et al.* 2001b) is perhaps less contentious, with authors Les Back and John Solomos being two of the UK's most prominent sociologists of race. The book is premised on 'the need to go beyond the convenient and simplistic stereotypes that shape much popular discussion about racism in football or other spheres of life … [and expose the] contradictions and ambivalence within the culture of racism in football' (Back *et al.* 2001b: 2). Back *et al.* note that while football authorities either deny the existence of a problem or caricature clubs/hooligans as racist, the reality is much subtler. The book begins by examining 'Fan Cultures and Local Cultures of Racism', exposing the varieties of racism within the rituals of football and arguing that the conceptualization of racism needs to be widened. It then looks at racism experienced by players and the way it has been responded to by clubs and in campaigns, before examining experiences of travelling with England fans and watching football with members of the British Jamaican community during the 1998 Football World Cup. Back *et al.* seek to highlight two main forms of racism:

1 'the racialized body' and the way sport exemplifies notions of racial physical difference;
2 'ossified notions of culture' which are defined through inter-group relations and different groups' relations with sport.

They introduce the concept of a '"cultural passport" that equips and facilitates belonging and identity' (Back *et al.* 2001b: 279) to describe how black and minority ethnic groups gain acceptance into football culture, but do so on terms defined within 'exclusive white preserves'. By looking at the banal and prosaic as well as the loud and explicit, they examine 'the normalizing whiteness that is at the centre of football culture' and argue that the dominance of the 'racist-hooligan couplet' leads to 'implicit forms of exclusion … disguised or rendered invisible in "white eyes" by their very normalcy' (Back *et al.* 2001b: 285).

Finally, mention should be made of three American texts on race and sport. Earl Smith's *Race, Sport and the American Dream* (2007) examines the impact of black athletes on African-American civil society. Smith addresses biological beliefs about sporting performance and the exploitative and colonizing relations in college and professional sport (particularly NASCAR [National Association for Stock Car Auto Racing] and NBA [National Basketball Association]). He explores the restriction of African Americans from leadership roles and the distinct portrayal of 'deviant' black athletes and thus portrays sport in America as contributing to racial oppression. Like Wacquant's work on race and boxing (see Chapter 6), *Black Men Can't Shoot* (Brooks 2009) stems from the urban sociology subdiscipline. An ethnography of the everyday lives of children and their support networks, Scott Brooks explores the skills and status development of basketball players and the complexities of the process of getting 'known' and publicly recognized for one's basketball-playing ability. Finally, Douglas Hartmann's *Race, Culture and the Revolt of the Black Athlete* (2003) focuses on the previously discussed events of 1968 (Edwards 1969/1970). Hartmann, however, examines both the story of the revolt – where it came from, why it was so controversial and how memories of it have changed – and its impact on and outcomes for sport and American culture. He locates the protest within 'a decade of disruption' and in relation to subsequent race-based activism in sport and establishment responses that renegotiated race–sport relations culminating in the reincorporation of Carlos and Smith at the 1984 Los Angeles Olympics. Hartmann argues that three features of sport – its myth-making qualities, the element of 'deep play' whereby sport can be simultaneously serious and trivial and the link between sport and ideas of America as a melting-pot meritocracy – make it an ideal site to examine how 'racial formations are constantly – and very publicly – struggled over' (2003: xiii). Yet he also says that it is too limited to portray these events as simply sports protests. Rather, they illustrate how 'sport is implicated in the history and structure of race and racism' (Hartmann 2003: xix). To this end, he repeats the critiques of colour-blind ideologies as masking the effects of the social construction of whiteness and the inadequacies of research that pathologize the black athletes and their communities.

Conclusion

Where early writers such as Thompson, Edwards, Loy and Elvogue sought to highlight the way in which racial inequalities persisted in sporting practice, more recent analyses have questioned whether the very concept of race is any more than a social construction that needs to be deconstructed before change can be evoked. Within the literature latterly reviewed in this chapter there is considerable consensus over the interdependence of sport and race. Sport is a racially structured institution via which members of ethnic minorities are 'othered', in terms of biological or psychological difference (for black athletes in particular), or in terms of cultural distinctiveness (particularly British Asians and Native Americans). Research draws attention to the heterogeneous and dynamic nature of ethnic minorities' experience of sport, of the complexity of ways in which entry into the 'white domain' of sport is negotiated and the context-specific ways in which white hegemony can be both consolidated and contested in sport. Sport plays a central role in publicly reaffirming ideas of innate biological difference. Moreover, writers largely agree that through sport white people seek to define themselves in terms of their own 'achievements', that relations are subtly and covertly structured in such a way that white hegemony is not only sustained but, via the ideology of sport as colour-blind and meritocratic, is also insulated from more radical critique (see, for instance, the *SSJ* special issue on Whiteness in Sport, McDonald 2005). All recognize the intersection of race with other axes of power and difference.

Twenty years on, we can see how much of Birrell's critique of studies of race in the sociology of sport has been addressed. Racial identity is viewed as contested. Racial relations are viewed as produced and reproduced through sport. There is a recognition of the need to go beyond bipolar, black–white studies of race relations and to incorporate aspects of class and masculinity in our analyses. With notable exceptions (e.g., van Sterkenburg and Knoppers 2004; Scraton *et al.* 2005), however, there is a marked bias towards the study of male athletes, and understanding of the racialized experiences of female athletes remains a lacuna. Birrell's assessment that the previous (lamentable) state of affairs stemmed from an ignorance of the broader, or 'mainstream', study of the sociology of race can also be seen to have been addressed. Indeed, a comparison of the texts published by people who might largely be seen to be sociologists of sport and those who have embraced sport as one aspect of a more sustained analysis of race relations indicates a considerable overlap in terms of assumptions, approaches and theories. There are, of course, differences, but there is little in Burdsey's work that Back *et al.* would disagree with and vice versa and little over which one would think Carrington and Gilroy would disagree.

Two interconnected issues require final comment here. First, to what extent has sport been incorporated into the work of sociologists of race? On the basis of this review, it seems that there are distinct pockets of sport-sensitive research within the broader area of race and ethnic studies. The degree to which these are sustained analyses varies, and may not satisfy some, but there are elements of both breadth and depth which sociologists of sport should find encouraging. Looking at leading 'race studies' journals, such as the *Journal of Ethnic and Migration Studies*, *Race and Class* and

Race and Ethnic Studies illustrates an acceptance of sport as a relevant site for research and theoretical advancement.

Second, to what extent is it still the case, as Thompson (1964) stated in the 1960s and Carrington (2010) recently endorsed, that sport in race relations has not been given the attention it 'deserves'? The discussion in this chapter reveals – with the exception of the racialization of female sport – an impressively broad coverage of analysis. This includes research on multiple ethnicities, the international/global spread of sport, the sporting experiences from grass roots to the professional game and the racialized nature of media portrayal. The degree to which race is incorporated into the literature on sport celebrities is testament to the influence/diversity of this body of work (see Chapter 7). In contrast to its early decades, this field has undergone significant development, both in terms of quantity (the number of different analyses) and quality (the degree to which they are theoretically informed).

There would, however, appear to be two main considerations for the future vitality of this area. The first stems from politicization, for a characteristic of this field since its outset has been a fusion of scholarly activity and political campaigning. Just as this was evident in the James–Thompson–Edwards trilogy discussed in the opening section, so it is evident in the work of Burdsey, King, Back *et al.* and, of course, Lapchick. Each of these authors mentions their anti-racist activities in the introductory sections of their respective books. It is surely no coincidence that it should be a book on race and sport (*Darwin's Athletes*) which has been the focus of the most acrimonious relations in the subdiscipline for many years, if not its entire existence. Hoberman does not have a background as an activist.

The second issue relates to intellectual rigour. There exists, for instance, an element of circularity in this field. Sociologists of sport continually seem to respond to popular ideas linking sport, race and biology. This relates to the 'de-bunking motif' of sociology (Berger 1966), the need to illustrate the distinctiveness of a sociological approach (compared to the analysis of sport by media commentators) and to show the continuing relevance of sociology to a broader, non-academic constituency (see Chapter 1). Yet the regularity with which such arguments are rehearsed, and the frequency with which ideas such as Kane's continue to resurface, suggests an inability of sociologists of sport to define the research agenda and thus to advance the field. Brett St Louis, identified by Carrington as an 'important exception' (2010: 49) to those more generally interested in post/colonialism for his interest in and embrace of sport, is as culpable as anybody. His 2003 *Body and Society* article (St Louis 2003), save for a few comments addressing recent advances in genetics research, says little that Edwards had not said thirty years ago.

Indeed, rather than being theoretically moribund or empirically under-researched, my reading of this field suggests that coverage is relatively comprehensive, but that core theoretical debates, if they exist, are rarely explicitly aired. As illustrated in the introductory comments to this conclusion, a relatively high degree of consensus characterizes research within the field. Perhaps the biggest challenge relates to engaging with the public and challenging popularly held ideas about race and sport. We examine these questions in Chapter 9.

5

SPORT AND GENDER

In 2010 Caster Semenya was included amongst the *New Statesman*'s *50 People Who Matter*.[1] Semenya was the only sportsperson amongst politicians, business leaders and a handful of entertainment celebrities, 'with global influence and the power to change the world'. Such rankings are notoriously subjective but the reason for Semenya's inclusion is both interesting and relevant here. After winning the women's 800 metres at the 2009 World Athletics Championships in Berlin aged eighteen, Semenya was suspended by the IAAF amid media speculation about whether she was male or female. No details of what tests found (or did not find) were ever released, and Semenya, who denies having undergone hormone therapy, resumed competing in women's athletics eleven months later. The *New Statesman* thus included Semenya in recognition of her importance to gender politics. Indeed, it would be unthinkable (impossible?) that anyone from any other walk of life could pose this kind of challenge to such a fundamental premise of contemporary society: the division of the human population into two discrete categories, male and female. This chapter looks at the relationship between sport and gender and between the sociology of sport and the sociology of gender and asks what these relationships reveal about the significance of the subdiscipline in the broader sociological landscape.

The emergence of gender studies has been one of the more contested developments within sociology (of sport). One reason for this is the link between empirical subject matter (gender) and theoretical approach (feminism). While '[f]eminist theory is not to be confused with a focus on "women in sport"' (Birrell 2000: 61), the central focus of *all* works informed by feminist theories is gender relations. Moreover, atheoretical analyses of gender and sport have all but disappeared. By 1993 Ann Hall could write, 'gone are the simplistic chapters on women in sport' (1993: 51). Thus, like no other area, the empirical focus (gender) entails a particular theoretical commitment with advocates of one theory confined to a focus which is largely overlooked by advocates of others. This empirical-theoretical link was the focus of divisions within the subdiscipline. Messner and Sabo (1990: 3) argue that institutional sexism has contributed to a situation 'within sports studies, [where] feminist scholars have often found themselves marginalized and ghettoized'. Moreover, theoretical divisions are largely also sexual divisions. In Hall's view (1993: 51), 'there is little critical scholarship by men that is informed by feminist writing, and even less in the sociology of sport'. Hargreaves (1990: 288) considered herself to be adopting 'a controversial position' when she argued that both males and females could be 'sports feminists'. This gender dynamic is significant to an understanding of the impact of this field of research.

A second matter of controversy relates to the principle that feminist research should have a fundamentally political application. This poses a challenge to the premises of the sociology of sport which, as noted in Chapter 2, emerged alongside a debate about the methodological orientation of the subdiscipline. Feminist sociologists of sport largely eschew the social-scientific objectivity that enabled the sociology of sport to become distanced from its physical education roots in favour of making 'political intervention[s] into the world of sports scholarship' (Hargreaves 1994: 1). Some explicitly blame social-scientific objectivity for contributing to the ghettoization of women in sport and seek to 'challenge traditional research orthodoxies which … have rendered women's presence both marginal and in many cases invisible' (Clarke and Humberstone 1997: xiv; Hargreaves 1992).[2] Feminist sociologists argued that only women could truly understand the social experiences of women. Consequently, some critiqued feminist theory's value-laden approach as 'pseudo-science' (Phillips 1993, cited in Birrell 2000). The centrality of both political advocacy and feminist epistemology is important to an understanding of the relationship between gender and sport.

The first section of this chapter examines the historical development of work on gender in the sociology of sport, mapping the emergence of theoretically informed research, the establishment of a feminist cultural studies consensus and more recent trends towards post-structuralism. The second section looks at how sociologists of gender have viewed sport and incorporated it into their analyses.

Gender and the sociology of sport

At its inception, the sociology of sport, like sociology more generally, was dominated by men who wrote about men. This much is evident from the names of the individuals who featured in the subdiscipline's institutional establishment and who produced its early literature (see Chapter 2). Hall (1996: 6) states that a review of sociology of sport texts and anthologies published prior to 1976 indicated that less than 10 per cent were (co-)authored by females and less than 3 per cent of content focused on females. Conversely, Jay Coakley would later claim that gender was the most popular topic in the field in the 1990s (cited in Theberge 2000a). By the end of the decade, encyclopaedias devoted to 'women in sport' emerged (Christensen *et al.* 2000; Greenberg *et al.* 1998; Oglesby 1998). How did gender become 'one of the most dynamic and important areas within the sociology of sport' (Theberge 2000a: 331)? To what extent does it remain so?

Ironically, given the relationship between the study of gender and feminist sociological theory, one of the earliest works on gender in the sociology of sport was produced by two male figurational sociologists: Ken Sheard and Eric Dunning. 'The Rugby Football Club as a Type of "Male Preserve"' describes the development of rugby club subcultural norms (e.g., violence, obscenity, drunkenness) as concomitant with the emergence of first-wave feminism and the suffragette movement (Sheard and Dunning 1973). Sheard and Dunning argue that it was within the middle and upper classes, from which most rugby players and suffragettes were drawn, that women posed the most acute challenge to male dominance. Males responded by establishing all-male groups hostile to women. Songs and rituals mocked, objectified and vilified women and the sexual act and, in being overtly heterosexual, countered charges of homosexuality fuelled by the men's homosocial preference. Sport provided men with a source of identity reaffirmation and thus Sheard and Dunning argue that it may have developed as a response to threatened masculinity.

It was probably because this research focused on men that it was not seen as particularly relevant by, or to, the pioneers of the study of gender in the sociology of sport. After all, their primary concern was to correct the bias evident in the 'malestream' of the subdiscipline. Instead, edited collections such as Ellen Gerber's *The American Woman in Sport* (1974) and Carole Oglesby's *Women in Sport: From Myth to Reality* (1978) began to chart women's shared experiences of oppression and inequality in sport. For instance, the latter contained Betty Spears's (1978) review of historical material describing sport in Ancient Greece, medieval Europe and the twentieth-century USA which illustrated that through time and across cultures the majority of women have either been discouraged or completely excluded from sport. Susan Greendorfer (1978) identified gendered socialization processes that led females to see sport as a relatively unwelcoming social sphere. Dominant at this time were 'psychological rather than sociological analyses of women's place in sport' (Hall 1996: 5), which again mirrored the relative prominence of psychology in the subdiscipline at this time. These works would later be described as characterized by a 'categoric' approach (Hall 1993: 49; Birrell 2000), because they identified males and females as separate experiential groups and sought to explain the differences between them with reference to biology, personality and/or socialization.

Studies of gender and sport advanced during the late 1970s and early 1980s through the more consistent and rigorous use of feminist theory. This development was stimulated by a variety of broader social processes including the academicization of physical education (Hall 1996: 4; see also Chapter 2) and legislative changes such as Title IX in 1972 in the USA and the 1975 Sex Discrimination Act in Britain. In 1973, Billy Jean King defeated Bobby Riggs in a tennis match designed to 'test' whether the sexes could compete on equal terms. Personal experiences of disadvantage were also important. Ann Hall's (1996) career was stimulated by the discrimination she experienced as a physical education teacher, while Mary Boutilier and Lucinda San Giovanni (1980) talk about their realization that the feminist dictum 'the personal is political' was deeply relevant to their own sporting experiences – from the resistance they encountered in developing female sporting opportunities to their role in monitoring compliance with Title IX in their university. The development of second-wave feminism was also clearly significant, but feminism has never been a unified approach.[3] There are generally argued to have been two schools of feminist thinking which were prominent at this time – liberal feminism and radical feminism – with some work also influenced by Marxism and socialism (see Chapter 3).

While Ann Hall's *Sport and Gender: A Feminist Perspective on the Sociology of Sport* (1978), and Mary Boutilier and Lucinda San Giovanni's *The Sporting Woman* (1980) signalled the growth of a more theoretically nuanced analysis within the sociology of sport, in reality it is difficult to identify studies which are exclusively influenced by any single perspective. Tellingly, there are few if any sociologists of sport who would identify themselves and their research as liberal feminist. Reviews of the area reflect this ambiguity. Hargreaves (1990) cites just the work of Australian geneticist K. F. Dyer (1982) and a range of (UK) Sports Council reports as examples of liberal feminist approaches to sport, and while Birrell (2000) argues that liberal feminism 'underlies the bulk of research' charting gender inequalities, she provides a token citation to Acosta and Carpenter (1994). Scraton and Flintoff (2002) cite the aforementioned Greendorfer and Oglesby. Sometimes the works of popular or non-sociologist writers are defined as liberal feminist. In practice, liberal feminism is often used to describe the boundary between atheoretical and theoretical, populist and bona-fide sociological studies of gender and sport. Such boundary-marking practices are typical of professional groups seeking to establish an identity and legitimacy for their work, a process which was a particular struggle for pioneers in this field (Birrell 1988).

In the mid-1980s, sociologists of sport started more explicitly to distance their work from liberal feminist research. Theberge's 'Toward a Feminist Alternative to Sport as a Male Preserve' (1985) was critical of much of existing sport and gender research which was largely informed by liberal feminism and, further, (a) implied that the 'problem' of role conflict between sports participation and femininity lay with women (akin to the pathologizing of black athletes) and (b) falsely abstracted 'sport' socialization from other areas of social practice. Drawing on the emerging feminist literature which highlighted the centrality of sexuality and physicality to male domination, Theberge argued that sport significantly impacts on gender relations in all spheres of social life. While largely oppressing women, however, sport was seen to also have considerable potential for liberation. Helen Lenskyj's *Out of Bounds: Women, Sport and Sexuality* (1986) identified the ideological and cultural dimensions of women's domination in sport. In the nineteenth and early twentieth centuries, male 'experts' in medical science and religion propagated beliefs that defined female sexuality and physicality in ways which were largely restrictive for women. In relation to sport, the notion of compulsory heterosexuality was linked to a belief that either sports participation made women masculine or that only masculine women enjoyed sports participation. Such ideologies legitimated the constraints placed on women in relation to sports participation, and sport became a forum in which male physical dominance was acted out and affirmed. Birrell and Richter's (1987) ethnographic analysis of women's softball provided one of the first empirical examinations of female resistance to sport as a male preserve. Purposively sampling self-proclaimed feminists, Birrell and Richter found that participants were often critical of 'male sport' and developed practices that critiqued its competitive, hierarchical, exclusive and elitist traditions. Thus, feminist softball players constructed an activity that rejected the ethos of physical endangerment and the disparagement of opponents and thus the alienation of players from each other. 'Under their direction, sport is transformed from a mechanism for the preservation and reproduction of male values to a celebration of feminist alternatives' (Birrell and Richter 1987: 408). While Birrell and Richter described their thesis as 'radical', they identified interactionism and cultural studies as their theoretical influences.

Although Theberge (1984) and Hall (1985) theorized the relationship between Marxism and feminism, most empirical studies employing Marxist feminism (and socialist feminism) were UK-based and focused on women's leisure activities more broadly (e.g., Deem 1986; Green *et al.* 1987; Wimbush and Talbot 1988). These studies showed the relationship of paid and domestic labour with sports participation. Working-class women in particular lacked the economic independence to take part in sport. Domestic duties further curtailed temporal freedom. Studies that focused on the inequality of resources or opportunities were described as part of a 'distributive approach' to gender. While post-structural studies would more explicitly problematize the notion of sport as a theoretical effect rather than an object of study (Birrell and Cole 1994: vii), it was Marxist feminist studies that initially signalled how problematic a narrow definition of sport could be in delineating the scope of the subdiscipline. How could there be a sociology *through* sport if sport systematically excluded so many people?

The feminist cultural studies consensus in the sociology of sport

If the mid-1980s saw sociologists of sport produce their first theoretically sophisticated analyses of gender, by the early 1990s there were indications that the area was now firmly established. First, a number of review articles attempted to map the scope of the 'gender and sport' area and/or examined the application of feminist approaches to sport (e.g., Birrell 1988; Hall 1988, 1993; Hargreaves 1990; Cole 1993). Second, a number of 'gender and sport' readers and anthologies were published as teaching aids. Some, like Greta Cohen's *Women in Sport: Issues and Controversies* (1993) and Margaret Costa and Sharon Guthrie's *Women and Sport: Interdisciplinary Perspectives* (1994) were explicitly interdisciplinary. Pamela Creedon's *Women, Media and Sport* (1994) combined feminist approaches with media studies of sport while Birrell and Cole's *Women, Sport and Culture* (1994) was the most distinctly sociological in focus, examining ideologies of women and sport, the gendered organization of sport, the media's portrayal of female athletes, women's experiences of challenging the male preserve of sport and the politics of sexuality in sport. In 1994, Jennifer Hargreaves published *Sporting Females*, perhaps the most comprehensive monograph devoted to 'the lived experiences of women in sports *and* the structural forces influencing participation' (1994: 2; see Chapter 8 for a more detailed discussion). Gender now had a significant presence in the sociology of sport.

This development was concomitant with a significant theoretical retrenchment, with 'a noticeable shift from the categoric research of biology and psychology, and the atheoretical distributive research of sociology, to more theoretically informed relational analyses within feminist cultural studies' (Hall 1993: 62). Feminist cultural studies, like cultural studies more generally, emerged from a tension within Marxism (and by extension also Marxist feminism) over the degree of determinacy attributed to economic relations and social class. It was also informed by critiques that women of colour had been largely excluded from existing analyses of gender and sport (Birrell 1990; Smith 1992). A commitment to analyse gender within a 'matrix of power relations' emerged, though a paradox of this position is that if gender is decentred and becomes just one factor in a broader matrix of power relations, to what extent are these studies still 'feminist'? The approach was further underpinned by the belief that power is usually maintained through ideology as much as material conditions. It would later occur to gender and sport researchers that the social psychological work on sex roles informed by liberal and radical feminist perspectives perpetuated and replicated the very categories of existence which feminists sought to challenge (Hall 1996).

Because of its flexibility – both empirically and analytically – something of a consensus emerged around feminist cultural studies of sport. As with previous theoretical typologies, however, mutual exclusivities are hard to establish. For Cole (1993), feminist cultural studies combined cultural studies, socialist feminism and insights from Foucault, while for Birrell and Cole (1994: vii) it drew on 'insights from poststructuralism and postmodernism'. Hall similarly suggests that the work of post-structuralists and postmodernists (citing Foucault and Jacques Derrida) had informed feminist cultural studies, while Birrell would later suggest that feminist cultural studies 'served as *a bridge* to more interdisciplinary, postmodern sensibilities' (2000: 69; emphasis added). Scraton and Flintoff (2002) concur with Birrell's depiction of a more distinct break, categorizing some of the literature which others define as feminist cultural studies as post-structural feminism. A gradual movement towards the increased use of post-structuralism informed particularly by Foucault (1992) and Butler (1990) is clear. However, while there is little conceptual precision to the term 'feminist cultural studies', it is agreed that it defines most of the sociology of sport literature on gender from the 1990s onwards.

Two different but overlapping typologies of feminist cultural studies of sport provide indicative overviews of the area. Birrell (1988) identified four main themes of the feminist cultural studies project and in 2000 argued that these themes still received significant attention (Birrell 2000). These themes were:

1 the production of an ideology of masculinity and male power through sport;
2 the media practices through which dominant notions of women are reproduced (namely the under-representation of women, the trivialization and marginalization of female sporting achievements, the heterosexualization of females in sport characterized by homophobia and a focus on feminine appearance);
3 physicality, sexuality and the body as sites for defining gender relations;
4 the resistance of women to dominant sport practices.

Hall's review of literature (1993) emphasized:

1 the importance of historically grounded studies (see Chapter 8 for a discussion of these and their reception within sports history);
2 a sensitivity to difference;
3 a focus on the body;
4 the study of men, sport and masculinity.

It is these latter two categories, identified by both Birrell and Hall, that merit the most extensive discussion.

Men, sport and masculinity

Birrell describes the production of masculinity and male power through sport as 'the primary assumption of the field' (2000: 67). Major statements on this topic have come from Michael Messner and Don Sabo, and, while Sabo's contributions began at the beginning of the decade (e.g., Sabo and Runfola 1980), it was the mid-1980s development of 'men's studies' (discussed below) that acted as a significant stimulus. Key themes in Messner and Sabo's *Sport, Men and the Gender Order* (1990) included sport's role in the historical construction, contemporary validation and potential challenge to masculinity. Their collaboration with Jim McKay a decade later on *Masculinities, Gender Relations, and Sport* (McKay *et al.* 2000) not only focused again on the everyday constructions of and challenges to hegemonic masculinity but also on the role of violence in the construction of gender identities.

Research on the historical construction of masculinity is largely based on the belief that the development of modern sport is linked to a perceived 'crisis in masculinity' (c.f. Sheard and Dunning 1973; see also Dunning 1986b). In late-nineteenth-century America that crisis occurred in conjunction with the processes of urbanization, modernization and the growth of an active women's movement. Urban industrialism both bolstered and undermined men's power over women. By taking men's production away from the domestic sphere, men came to be more economically dominant, but women's increasingly dominant role in the socialization of young males led to fears that the next generation of men would be relatively effeminate. The establishment of social practices such as sport which fostered masculinity are interpreted as one response. Male dominance was supported by the association of males and maleness with aggression, force and violence (Messner 1990, 1992).

In line with the feminist cultural studies' commitment to examine a matrix of power relations, much of the sociology of sport literature on men and masculinities utilizes Connell's (1987) concept of 'hegemonic masculinity' to identify males as a disunited group. Typically, while Messner notes that sport is a gendered institution, he also argues that it has been continually contested, especially in relation to class and race. The sports which had been defined by the dominant male classes imposed a particular kind of masculinity upon the working classes and men of colour. Thus, while sport disseminates and reinforces values such as male superiority, competition, work and success, there are several strains in the sport–masculinity relationship. In particular, three factors undermine the construction of a single dominant conception of masculinity:

1 the 'costs' of athletic masculinity to men (in terms of health, but also in terms of failing to generate the kinds of relationships men want);
2 athletic experiences, variously shaped by class, race and sexual orientation, which lead men to come to understand themselves as distinct from, and competitive with, each other;
3 the new experiences and alternative sports models posed by the rise in women's sport and mixed sex participation.

Important in relation to the first of these points is research that problematizes the violence inherent in many male sports (Young 1993) and the subsequent impact on male participants in the form of injuries (Young and White 2000). This body of work is also best understood in relation to sociological studies of the body and sport (see Chapter 6). Klein's work has been significant in highlighting the paradoxical features of male bodybuilding as a cultural practice. In focusing on 'hustling' – the practice of selling sex to gay men in order to raise money, e.g., to buy steroids to support their involvement in bodybuilding – Klein identifies how the 'sport' fosters 'behaviour and values that underscore virility and macho posturing' (1990: 139) while simultaneously creating heterosexual identity issues that fuel existing homophobic tendencies.

Tim Curry's analysis of 'Fraternal Bonding in the Locker Room' has been one of the most significant studies of contemporary and everyday constructions of hegemonic masculinity in sport. Curry's observational research highlights how conversations in this context degrade women through 'talk that promotes rape culture' (1994/2002: 178). Male athletes learn to avoid public expressions of compassion and to construct a sense of self grounded in competitiveness. Close bonds do exist but are contingent on athletic participation and are thus easily dissolved. Humour is used as a way of reinforcing hegemonic masculinity, disparaging homosexuality and securing the ideological link between sport and (hyper-)masculinity. Similarly, Sabo and Panepinto look at how the hierarchical relations between coaches and athletes are a 'nexus of patriarchal ritual that reproduces hegemonic forms of masculinity as well as competitive behaviour and achievement ideologies' (1990: 125). Crosset would subsequently examine male athletes' sexual violence against women (2000). In an important reversal to previous works, this body of research sees men and masculinity as the problem.

Further deconstructing the notion of a unified masculinity is research that focuses on the experiences of homosexual males in sport. Brian Pronger (1991) identified the 'ironic' meaning which many gay male athletes take from sport where the erotic experience of being in a male changing/locker room is juxtaposed with the compulsion to hide their sexuality and thus conform to the broader cultural norms. Price and Parker's (2003) study of a gay male rugby team similarly shows that members go to considerable efforts to portray themselves as 'just like' any other (heterosexual) sports team and to this end there is a tendency to suppress camp, 'feminine' and overtly (homo-)sexual behaviours for hegemonic masculine behavioural styles. Players comply with behavioural restrictions in order to maintain acceptance in the sports setting. Eric Anderson (2002) further argues that homosexuality is seen as disrupting the 'natural' link between males and muscles and females and passivity. There are fewer openly gay male than lesbian athletes, he argues, because the verbal and physical abuse the former experience is more extreme. Even when gay athletes 'come out', few behavioural adjustments are made by those in the heterosexual subculture of (male) sport and explicitly homophobic practices continue. Anderson argues that gay athletes experience heightened discrimination due to the paradox they are seen to present: conforming to gender norms through muscularity but violating others through same-sex desires. If males can do both, then sport as a prime site for the generation of hegemonic masculinity and male privilege is threatened and thus, as this literature suggests, is sport's *raison d'être*.

Physicality, sexuality and the body

In focusing on physicality, sexuality and the body as sites for defining gender, research has addressed a number of conforming and resistant practices. Aerobics, for instance, largely conforms to dominant notions of femininity and is, therefore, part of women's 'legitimate' range of physical activities. These activities flourished as part of the 1970s 'fitness boom' and have been partly responsible for the considerable increases in female sports participation in recent years. Sociologists of sport, however, have questioned the de-facto empowerment available to women through highlighting some of the contradictions of the activity. Research (e.g., MacNeil 1988) has critiqued the sexualization of aerobics in the media that led the liberating potential to be reworked according to traditional gender ideologies. MacNeil also critiqued the commodification of femininity through aerobics that led to a stress on appearance over performance. Markula (1995) drew explicitly on Foucault to expand the analysis of aerobics (and is therefore more accurately described as a post-structural feminist), arguing that in attempting to conform to feminine ideals – 'firm but shapely, fit but sexy, strong but thin' – aerobics participation stemmed from *surveillance* and became a *disciplining* practice in Foucault's sense. Women enjoyed being physically active in a safe environment that provided opportunities to devote time to themselves and socialize with other women but at the same time recognized that the ideal is unachievable and therefore 'find the whole process ridiculous' (Markula 1995: 450). A central theme in this work is to note the contradictions between the image and the practice, the enabling and constraining consequences of sports participation.

Posing a greater challenge to dominant notions of femininity is female involvement in sports which have traditionally been seen as the preserve of males. Crosset's *Outsiders in the Clubhouse* (1995) is a study of the Ladies Professional Golf Association. Inequitable practices for male and female golfers have historically included segregated clubhouses and tees (based on assumptions of differential physical strength) and dress and etiquette codes that mark gender difference. Crosset sought to 'capture … the experience of life on the tour, its tensions and conflicts with the broader culture' (1995: 1) and found that female players experienced 'a sense of freedom, equality, and justice not found off the course' (1995: 226). While in many ways privileged, the players struggled against patriarchal values and were frustrated by a media and public that judged them according to their appearance and sexuality. Similarly, Theberge's *Higher Goals,* based on ethnographic research with a women's ice hockey team in Canada, attempted 'to examine questions of gender and physicality in the context of a cultural practice that is intimately connected to notions of masculinity and national identity' (2000b: x). In a context where resources are unevenly distributed, and where there is a preoccupation with homophobia and an organizational mixture of integration with and separation from the male game, females who play ice hockey are treated 'like little sisters who don't belong' (Theberge 2000b: 1). Theberge identifies a number of paradoxes posed by female ice hockey:

- challenges to the myth of female frailty;
- the harmonization of images of femininity and athleticism;
- female adoption of male and masculine practices such as violence, elitism and commercialism.

Examining the social organization of women's hockey, internal dynamics of life on the team and the everyday world of the elite women's game, Theberge finds that the team is an important site for the construction and confirmation of empowering athletic identities. Yet, through the gendering of physical practice (e.g., male administrative control, playing under rules that prohibit violent [male] practices such as 'checking') the sport fails to challenge the hegemonic position of men's ice hockey as the 'real' version of the game. Studies of female boxers similarly conclude that while challenging the existing gender order through a redefinition of boxing from an exclusively male practice, and while able to construct a variety of feminine identities in this context, the pervasive influence of traditional modes of femininity makes the position of the female boxer ambivalent (Mennesson 2000).

Post-structuralism, gender and the sociology of sport

In concluding this discussion of gender in the sociology of sport, studies which are more explicitly positioned as post-structuralist should be considered. Post-structuralist feminism emphasizes the difference and diversity in the subjective experiences of individuals, arguing that 'the very term "women" has little significance in the fragmented and changing world that we live in today' (Scraton and Flintoff 2002: 40). Post-structuralism argues that the truth-claims of so-called experts are merely competing narratives and thus reject the kind of totalizing theories which seek to understand the social world within one explanatory framework (such as, amongst others, radical feminism).

As noted above, the ideas of Foucault are influential here. Another important influence in this regard is Judith Butler's 'heterosexual matrix' which examines the interrelationship between and the performance of sex, gender and sexuality (Butler 1990).

Butler notes that it is customary to use sex as a biological category (men and women), gender to describe culturally prescribed behaviour (masculine and feminine) and sexuality to refer to one's choice of sexual partner (heterosexual or homosexual). Butler argues, however, that while cultural assumptions lead us to believe that the three are causally related – that a man will be masculine and heterosexual – such categories are rather more fluid such that social reality cannot be reduced to binary categories (e.g., hetero- or homosexual). With sex, like gender, being socially constructed, Butler argues that feminists have been mistaken and that 'sex … [has] been gender all along' (1990: 11). The deconstruction of sex, gender and sexuality in this way has been termed 'queer' theory because it both seeks to 'make (very) visible previously denied and silenced "identities" and sexualities' (Caudwell 2006: 2) and question (or queer) definitional boundaries (e.g., between the sexes). As recently as 2002 it could be argued that 'post-structural feminist analyses of sport are as yet relatively underdeveloped' (Scraton and Flintoff 2002: 40).

Perhaps the most comprehensive statement on diversity and difference is Hargreaves's *Heroines of Sport* (2000). Though described by Hargreaves as 'feminist cultural studies with critical autobiography' (2000: 4) the influence of post-structuralism is also apparent. The book responds to criticism that existing feminist scholarship is exclusionary by investigating historically marginalized groups. Such work is important because liberal sports feminism 'has failed systematically to challenge the established and destructive principles of mainstream sport' with female sports stars 'constructed via the same imperatives of the sports industry and the same ideologies of aggressive and exploitative competition that construct the male sport hero' (Hargreaves 2000: 4). Analysis of the sporting experiences of black women in South Africa, Muslim and Aboriginal women, and lesbian and disabled women is an attempt to address this and to illustrate how identities are complex, diverse and fluid.

Another important application relates to the sex testing of athletes which, Cavanaugh and Sykes (2006) argue, confirms the post-structuralist position regarding the diversity of sex and gender. They note that these tests have only been applicable to female athletes and, in fact, do not test sex but 'femaleness'. If a person is not female, the assumption is that they must be male, but the inadequacy of such tests (and the case of Semenya discussed at the start of this chapter is a case in point) have led to their widespread withdrawal. Furthermore, Cavanaugh and Sykes note that those people who are intersex – hermaphrodite – have atypical chromosome counts, testosterone levels, genital and/or skeletal configurations and have been subject to humiliating inquiry and disqualified from competition in order to protect the 'purity' of women's sport and thus the binary categorization of sex. The fluidity of sex is illustrated through an examination of the IOC's policies regarding transsexuals. The so-called Stockholm Consensus states that transsexuals may compete if they are post-operative, have legal and governmental recognition of gender confirmed by their country of citizenry, have hormonal therapy to minimize 'gender-related advantages' and live for a minimum of two years in their newly assigned gender. Cavanaugh and Sykes argue that this is simply a continuation of the trend of policing gender. The participation of transsexuals is based on the underlying rationale that it would be unfair for a male to become female and compete against females and that there need be no policy for female-to-male transsexuals as this would not constitute an unfair advantage (and/or an implicit assumption that transsexual men are not 'real' men).

Caudwell's (2006) anthology *Sport, Sexualities and Queer/Theory* provides the most wide-ranging feminist post-structuralist statement in the sociology of sport. The book charts the development of queer theory and describes its potential for the study of sport, including:

- 'exposing the constructedness of sexuality;
- exposing the illusion/fiction of sexual identity;
- avoiding normative and essentializing identities;
- resisting regimes of the "normal";
- violating compulsory sex/gender relations;
- dismantling binary gender relations;
- and undermining heteronormative hegemonic discourses' (2006: 2).

Chapters examine the use of queer/theory in interpreting research from studies of elite sport in Norway, men's softball in Canada, tennis in England and the Gay Games. They also examine how the body is given meaning in sport settings such as rowing and football and through the regulation of transgendered athletes and the experience of pain. Caudwell concludes that there is a need for further work on intersectionality and the acknowledgement that whiteness and heteronormativity are 'inseparable from Western capitalist sport cultures' (2006: 7). It is likely that work of this type will dominate gender research in the sociology of sport for the foreseeable future.

Sociology of gender and sport

Given the traditions of sport as a male preserve, it was not a sphere of study which was seen as immediately relevant by feminist theorists. Indeed, Messner and Sabo note that 'one is hard put to find any consideration of sport in mainstream feminist classics written before the 1980s' (1990: 2). Hall notes the difficulties of relating this literature to her sport-related research (1996: 2). Even with the later development of feminist cultural studies, a distinct divide remained. In Hall's experience, 'women's studies programs in general have not embraced sport and leisure, nor have they been perceived as particularly inviting to physical education and sport studies students' (1993: 54). In Hall's view, 'the problem … is that those with either a background in cultural studies or just entering the field … are not interested in sport, whereas those interested in sport have neither the theoretical preparation nor methodological expertise to do the work' (1993: 58). How accurate are these evaluations and to what extent do they remain true today?

Probably the first sport-related work written by a sociologist of gender was Paul Willis's 'Women in Sport in Ideology'. At the time Willis was conducting research on the transition of working-class boys to employment, which would subsequently form the basis of the seminal study of masculinity, *Learning to Labour* (Willis 1977).

'Women in Sport in Ideology' started life as a conference paper (Willis 1974) and has been re-published (Willis 1982/1994) and much cited since. Willis argued that the 'commonsense' view of sport is 'inflected through "patriarchal" ideology' (1994: 34). Building on widespread beliefs about the innate difference between the sexes, the inferiority of females becomes a reality through the sexualization of women's sport (e.g., by the media). This in turn leads to the assumption that male sport is the 'natural' form of the activity. That a male should produce the first study of this type underlines both the dominance of males within sociology at this time and the antipathy that appeared to exist between feminists and the study of sport.

In contrast, the publication of a special issue of *Women's Studies International Forum* in 1987 was described as 'one more demonstration that sport is at last coming into its own as a topic for mainstream theoretical analysis' (Bryson 1987/1994: 47). A pioneer of Australian sociology, Bryson contributed the most celebrated article to the edition. Bryson (1994: 47) argued that 'we ignore sport at our peril' for it constitutes a key institution through which 'male hegemony is constructed and reconstructed'. Bryson drew on a government-commissioned study of female athletes and the media for data. She argued that one could demonstrate how sport contributes to masculine hegemony through the media's definitions of sport, through male administrators' direct control of women's sport and through norms that led women's sport to be ignored and/or trivialized. Sport not only linked maleness with highly valued physical skills, it needed 'to be analyzed along with rape, pornography and domestic violence as one of the means through which men monopolize physical force' (Bryson 1994: 60).

The subsequent uptake of sport by sociologists of gender has, however, been mixed. Where Messner and Sabo had been 'hard put' to find feminist analyses of sport before the 1980s, one could argue that relatively little has changed. Amongst feminist theorists there are, however, two notable examples: Catharine Mackinnon and Judith Lorber. (NB: bell hooks also makes occasional reference to the role of sport in the construction of black masculinities [see Chapter 4]; an 'honourable mention' also goes to John Hood-Williams [1995] for his work on sex testing in sport.) Mackinnon's *Feminism Unmodified* (1987) includes the transcript of a 1982 conference paper called 'Women, Self-Possession, and Sport'. A practising martial artist, Mackinnon critiques liberal feminist work on women and sport (though noticeably no references are given) and forwards an essentially radical feminist analysis which, in replicating debates over theoretical boundaries discussed above, she redefines as simply feminist. She argues that the meaning of sport should be transformed so that, *pace* Lenskyj (1986), women are not excluded from participation and socialized into passivity and weakness and are not forced to choose between being female or successful athletes. This is important to the larger feminist project, Mackinnon argues, because 'women *as women* have a survival stake in reclaiming our bodies in our physical relations with other people' (1987: 123).

Lorber's *Paradoxes of Gender* is an eclectic mix of feminist theories that seeks to question the naturalness and inevitability of gender. Gender is defined 'as a process of social construction, a system of stratification, and an institution that structures every aspect of our lives' (Lorber 1994: 5), and the 'paradoxes' of the book's title highlight

Lorber's belief that much of what is generally believed about gender does not hold up to scrutiny. One aspect of this is the 'epistemologically spurious' reliance on 'only two sex and gender categories in the biological and social sciences' (Lorber 1994: 39). Lorber uses sport as an illustrative example of the gendering and social construction of bodies. Citing extensively from the sociology of sport literature, Lorber highlights how sports have been designed by and for men, how female sport attracts lower levels of investment and media exposure and how male and female athletes are presented in qualitatively different ways. This culminates in bodies being constructed in distinct and hierarchical ways: men as powerful, women as sexual.

While sport is prominent in work on men and masculinity, it generally attracts limited coverage in the sociology of gender literature that focuses on women. 'Gender readers' are a good illustration of this neglect. While the following exceptions do include reference to sport, they also reveal certain characteristics of the field's orientation in this regard. In Saltzman Chafetz's *Handbook of the Sociology of Gender,* Mikaela Dufur (1999) argues that sport is both a 'useful' and 'exciting' context in which to study gender relations. Dufur broadly divides the existing literature into two branches:

1 the construction of masculinity and femininity through sport;
2 the discrimination against and limited opportunities for women in sport.

The former, she argues, extends understanding through addressing the fluidity of gender relations and gender symbolism but, with notable exceptions (Klein 1993; Curry 1994/2002) 'is less proficient in testing theory' and in creating new theories of gender relations (Dufur 1999: 589). The latter area Dufur depicts, as sociologists of sport themselves have, as relatively atheoretical. Dufur is thus quite critical of work in the field and concludes that 'the study of sport and gender cannot fulfil its promise until sports scholars [NB: not feminists or gender scholars] address theoretical and methodological shortcomings' (1999: 595).

Second, 'gender readers' suggest that the empirical interests of sociologists of gender do not mirror those of sociologists of sport interested in gender. For instance, Jackson and Scott's *Gender: A Sociological Reader* (2002) contains one sport-related chapter, Mansfield and McGinn's (1993) analysis of female bodybuilders, 'Pumping Irony' (see Chapter 6 for a discussion of female bodybuilding). This inclusion is indicative of the remarkable level of interest in bodybuilding amongst sociologists of gender. In addition to Mansfield and McGinn, one could cite the work of Balsamo (1994), Bolin (1992), Grosz (1994), Holmlund (1989), Ian (1991), Kuhn (1988), Miller and Penz (1991) and Shultze (1990). Hall (1996: 59–63), in her review of this work, identifies three strands of analysis addressing:

1 the way female bodybuilders' self-image is influenced by participating in such a 'gender-inappropriate' activity;
2 ethnographic studies of both competitive and recreational bodybuilders;
3 cultural critiques of the 'texts' of bodybuilding that appear in magazines, photographs and films.

Much of the appeal of bodybuilding as an empirical focus lies in the threat that female bodybuilding poses to socially constructed ideas about the relationship between muscle and masculinity. Researchers explore this contradiction and examine the practices (e.g., judging criteria) that '"tame" professional female bodybuilders and make sense of their bodies by pulling them back toward a normalizing regime' (Hall 1996: 61). Bolin (1992) in particular identifies the differences between male and female bodybuilders' attitudes towards muscle and fat, and Miller and Penz (1991) identify the counter-ideologies that female bodybuilders produce to legitimize their presence in this gender transgressive domain. Such is the interest in bodybuilding amongst sociologists of gender that there is also an anthology published on the subject, Pamela Moore's *Building Bodies* (1997). Although 'a good example of what is possible around the body in other areas of women's sport and leisure' (Hall 1996: 63), the research concentration on this activity stands in contrast to the more limited attention that sociologists of sport have paid to bodybuilding (e.g., Obel 1996) and may reflect a greater interest in the sociology of the body than the sociology of sport.

Third, 'gender readers' illustrate how interest in sport is disproportionately skewed towards studies of men and masculinity. Typical in this regard are Ferree *et al.*'s *Revisioning Gender* (1999) and Richardson and Robinson's *Introducing Gender and Women's Studies* (2008). The former includes a chapter by Dworkin and Messner (1999) which uses research on men and sport to highlight the centrality of race and class in studies of gender before arguing that the commercial orientation of elite sport ultimately dictates that it remains gender segregated and thus reaffirms conventional understandings of masculinity and femininity. The latter is even more marked in that almost all references to sport in the book appear in the chapter titled, 'Men, Masculinities and Feminism' (Robinson 2008). Robinson charts the development of studies of men and masculinity, arguing that from initial 'sex role' and biological determinism work, three key ideas arose:

1 masculinities are multiple;
2 men and masculinities should be studied historically and cross-culturally;
3 power relations between men and women and men and men are central to a broader understanding of gender relations.

Robinson cites Edwards's (2006) three main waves of 'men's studies' which are essentially coterminous with the three stages of the study of gender in the sociology of sport outlined earlier, namely:

1 categoric and distributive approaches;
2 the relational approach of feminist cultural studies;
3 post-structuralist approaches.

Sport is cited as one of eight topics which have 'sustained critical attention in the context of hegemonic masculinities and heterosexuality' (Robinson 2008: 63). The chapter focuses on men and sport as a case study, in recognition of Connell's argument that 'images of ideal masculinity are constructed and promoted most systematically through competitive sport' (Connell 1987, cited in Robinson 2008: 64).

Indeed, the interpenetration of the sociology of sport and studies of men and masculinities is one of the more remarkable characteristics of the gender and sport literature, with sport prominent amongst the anthologies that marked the emergence of 'men's studies'. Kaufman's *Beyond Patriarchy* (1987) contained a chapter by sociologist of sport Bruce Kidd on 'Sport and Masculinity', and Kimmel's *Changing Men* (1987) contained both a chapter by Gary Alan Fine reporting aspects of his study of gender-role socialization in Little League baseball and a chapter by Messner charting the importance of sport for male identity at various stages of the life course. The latter argued that 'from boyhood through to adulthood, sports often act as a central aspect of individual life structure of the male' (Messner 1987: 65). Such was the demand for work on sport that a revision of this chapter appeared in Brod's *The Making of Masculinities* (1987). Indeed, Haywood and Mac an Ghaill (2003) justify their decision to omit discussion of sport (as well as health and crime) from their text because such areas 'are well represented in the sociological literature'. The analysis of sport is thus deeply ingrained in this branch of gender studies.

At its most pronounced, we see a particularly fluid interchange between those we might initially have classified as sociologists of sport and those working within men's studies. For instance, Messner has authored texts that discuss masculinity more generally (2000). Eric Anderson followed a similar path, publishing *Inclusive Masculinity* (2009) a few years after his first book *In the Game: Gay Athletes and the Cult of Masculinity* (2005). The reverse is also true. Kimmel (1990) has written about the role of baseball in the reconstitution of American masculinity around the turn of the twentieth century, and he and Messner have collaborated on edited texts (Kimmel and Messner 2006). Whitehead and Barrett's *The Masculinities Reader* (2001) includes a chapter by Messner on non-sport-related material and a chapter by Richard Majors (2001) on 'cool pose' and black masculinity. David Coad's *The Metrosexual: Gender, Sexuality, and Sport* (2008) is another a good example. Coad argues that metrosexuality originally developed through reference to homosexual lifestyle (consumption-oriented, pleasure-seeking urbanites concerned with aesthetic appearance) rather than sexuality but that the link to sport was essential because, 'rather than give pride of place to nonathletic aesthetes', it enabled metrosexuality '[to hold] up the sportsman as a hero and a behavioural model' (Coad 2008: 24). David Beckham was the perfect metrosexual role model because of the belief that he did not need to prove his manhood and thus metrosexuality could be attached to heteronormativity and lose its asexual/homosexual links (see Chapter 7).

What makes this all the more remarkable is the juxtaposition of this trend with the (lack of) interpenetration of the sociology of sport and studies of women and femininity. This point is recognized by Hargreaves and Vertinsky who bemoan 'mainstream' feminists' neglect of the work of 'sport feminists' (2007a: 20) particularly in relation to studies of the body and physical culture. No feminist sociologist of sport has yet produced a 'mainstream' text on gender, and no 'mainstream' feminist sociologist has yet produced a text focused on female sport participation. Scraton and Flintoff's

Gender and Sport: A Reader (2002) further illustrates this point. The collection includes two chapters by sociologists of gender (as opposed to sociologists of sport). One, by Connell (2002), includes a range of citations of sport as examples of many different aspects of masculinity. The second, by Mary Maynard (2002), discusses the concept of 'difference' as a way of introducing a section on race and gender but makes no mention of sport at all. It is similarly interesting that Kath Woodward, who has written extensively on gender issues, initially demonstrated an interest in sport through research on boxing and masculinity (Woodward 2002).

Conclusion

This overview provides considerable support for Theberge's (2000a) contention that the study of gender is one of the most dynamic areas within the sociology of sport. There is clear movement towards a greater commitment to more theoretically oriented studies. Such studies have also seen the use of *particular* feminist theories evolve in the context of sport-related research. In contrast to my comments in previous chapters regarding the role of social theory, North American sociologists have been relatively prominent in the incorporation and development of feminist theory in relation to sport. But feminist sociologies of sport are not, as Ingham and Donnelly suggest, 'a victim of fashions' (1997: 394). Rather one could argue that sociologists of sport who conduct research into gender embrace the subdiscipline's 'professional project' by seeking legitimacy in the eyes of the 'mainstream' through the adoption and embrace of theoretical innovations. In their rejection of the positivist epistemology which underpinned the sociology of sport at its emergence, and in the explicit welcoming of multidisciplinary work (as long as that work has a central focus on gender), feminist sociologists of sport deviate from this project. Such trends are, however, congruent with contemporary sociology and the sociology of sport more generally. We revisit these issues in Chapter 10.

Despite these endeavours, the work of sociologists of sport has had a limited impact on the sociology of gender. Birrell's claim that feminist theory and sport is an area which 'draws on and *contributes to* the development of feminist theories outside the field' (2000: 61, emphasis added) is probably only true in relation to feminist informed men's studies. The epistemological principles of feminist sociology contribute to this relative failure, for the belief that men cannot understand the subjective experiences of females (and logically vice versa) means that the productive vein of research on men and sport is not embraced by female sociologists of gender. Ironically, work on sport by sociologists of gender bears a striking resemblance to the early sociology of sport, dominated by men writing about men.

There are, at least, two further consequences of these trends within the study of gender and sport. First, theoretical developments are problematic in that 'the issues central to the concerns of post-structural analyses are … considered to be somewhat distant from the everyday realities of many people's lives' (Scraton and Flintoff 2002: 40). In contrast to the research of Hall, Boutilier and San Giovanni, etc., which was inspired by personal experiences, sport-related research by sociologists of gender has relatively limited relevance for the vast majority of female participants in sport. This is most apparent in relation to the dominance of studies of bodybuilding. Second, the degree to which these studies directly feed into the kind of political change which initially inspired research on gender and sport has diminished. It is particularly the case that sport-related studies of men and masculinity have not been translated into policy and social change. In response to Theberge's claim that the study of gender is also one of the most important areas within the sociology of sport, one might suggest that in some senses it is becoming *less* important.

Yet, as illustrated by the Caster Semenya example that opened this chapter, sport remains a particularly powerful medium for illustrating the gendered nature of contemporary society. Sport is implicated in, and reaffirming of, the division of the human population into categories based on bodily constitution. These issues are developed in the next chapter.

6

SPORT AND THE BODY

In 2007, the International Amateur Athletics Federation altered its rules, prohibiting the use of various technical devices during competition. Oscar Pistorius, a South African double amputee Paralympian, was subsequently told that according to these regulations he could not compete in the 2008 Beijing Olympic Games. While the ruling was overturned by the Court of Arbitration for Sport, ultimately Pistorius failed to achieve the qualifying time. The case, however, illustrates how practices in the field of sport have the potential to challenge our understanding of what the body is and the way in which (elite) sport participation implicates and impacts upon the body in hitherto unimagined ways.

While race and gender are areas of study essentially defined by bodily characteristics, up until the 1980s, sociology (of sport) rarely explicitly analysed 'an obvious and prominent fact about human beings: they have bodies and they are bodies' (Turner 1984: 1). In *The Body and Society*, a book which many have since described as a defining moment in the development of the sociology of the body, Bryan Turner sought to describe the largely disembodied character of sociology and to suggest ways in which the body could become a more central focus of sociological enquiry. Subsequent texts (notably Featherstone *et al.* 1991; Scott and Morgan 1993 and Shilling 1993) and journals (*Theory, Culture and Society* [1982–], then *Body and Society* [1995–]) have helped shape this into one of the most prominent fields in contemporary sociology. The initial aim, in contrast perhaps to the development of the sociology of sport, was not so much to establish a new sociological subdiscipline but rather to develop 'a new way of "looking" at sociology and doing sociology' (Synott 1993: 6).

Sociologists of sport welcomed this new sociological agenda. An obvious and prominent fact about sport is that, by definition (see Chapters 1 and 2), it centres upon the physical body. As John Hargreaves (1987: 141) notes, 'Although the degree of physical input varies from sport to sport, the primary focus of attention in sport overall is the body and its attributes ... it is the body that constitutes the most striking symbol as well as constituting the material core of sporting activity.'

Maguire (1993: 33) noted the sociology of sport's 'unique position to emphasize to the parent discipline the importance of the body'. Potentially, 'not only would the subject of the body become more central to the concerns of sociology, but the marginal status of the sociology of sport could be shed.' This chapter examines the impact of sport on the sociology of the body and the development of an embodied approach to the sociological analysis of sport. Has an understanding of sport helped the body to become more central to sociological investigation? Have we seen the development of a more embodied sociology of sport? What have been the consequences of the interpenetration of these two areas?

The emergence of the sociology of the body

In the introduction to *The Body and Society* – 'Body Paradoxes' – Turner outlines some of the difficulties people have in starting to think sociologically about the body. He states, 'The body is at once the most solid, the most elusive, illusory, concrete, metaphorical, ever present and ever distant thing – a site, an instrument, an environment, a singularity and a multiplicity' (1984: 8). Synott similarly notes:

> The body social is many things: the prime symbol of the self, but also of society; it is something that we have, yet also what we are; it is both subject and object at the same time; it is individual ... as unique as a fingerprint ... yet it is also common to all humanity ... [It] is both an individual creation, physically and phenomenologically, and a cultural product; it is personal, and also state property.
>
> *(1993: 4)*

Yet sociology has neglected the body as a focus of research. This has been attributed to the influence on Western thought of the Cartesian mind–body dualism, the knowledge monopoly medicine has traditionally enjoyed over the body, the threat biological reductionism poses to a discipline focused on the social and the fact that the body has been most prominent in fields such as socio-biology and social Darwinism which have been linked to ideas of racial difference. Thus, examination of the body takes sociology onto particularly challenging terrain, examining phenomena at the interface of the 'natural' and the social. Historical and cross-cultural comparison illustrates how the body and its various aspects are defined differently across time and space. Contemporary technologies render the body increasingly malleable, suggesting that the body is a lifestyle accessory to be sculpted, shaped and stylized (Featherstone 1991). For some the body is wholly socially constructed (e.g., Synott 1993) but for others (e.g., Shilling 1993) our understanding is necessarily limited if we neglect the material, physical and biological dimensions of the body.

Sociological investigation of the body extends beyond this fundamental question of nature vs. nurture. The body is central to defining identities. For Shilling (1993: 3), the body provides the sense of security to individuals that religions and grand political narratives once did. The body is also centrally implicated in the balance between agency and structure or the degree to which our life chances are determined for us (e.g., by class, gender, race, nationality, economic system) and the degree to which we, as individuals, are able to shape our own life experiences. The body also signals the boundaries between the public and the private, for social norms determine that some parts remain permanently on show while others are invariably hidden. And sociological study of the body illuminates issues of social control with parallels between the regimen of the body and regime of a society (Turner 1984: 2) and a 'complex interplay of societal regulation and individual self-surveillance' (Scott and Morgan 1993: viii). Turner notes that the government of the body underpins classical sociological questions of social order. He notes, 'Every society is confronted by four tasks: the reproduction of populations in time, the regulation of bodies in space, the restraint of the "interior" body through discipline, and the representation of the "exterior" body in social space' (Turner 1984: 2).

The emergence of the sociology of the body has been attributed to various theoretical and social developments. Scott and Morgan (1993) cite feminism, sociological studies of health and illness and cultural studies (though they single out Foucault as a major influence on the field). Frank (1990: 132) cites a combination of theoretical stimuli – Foucault and feminism (and in particular, critiques of the control of female bodies through the institution of medicine) – and social developments he summarizes as the 'contradictory impulses of modernity'. Shilling clarifies these contradictory impulses: an 'unprecedented degree of control over bodies', combined with an enhanced level of doubt about 'our knowledge of what bodies are and how we should control them' (1993: 3). Shilling further argues that bodies have become 'projects' in contemporary societies, with an expectation that these projects will be worked on by the individual. The reasons for these developments, he argues, range from the rise of feminism and the ageing profile of Western populations to the changing character of human understanding of the body which is connected to its rationalization in modernity (1993: 15). There is therefore a synergy between theoretical and social developments which have forced the body onto the sociological research agenda. As Cregan notes, the development of the sociology of the body not only marks the social trend towards intensified scrutiny of our own and other people's bodies, it has, ironically, been a part of that intensification (2006: 5).

Sociologists of the body also largely demonstrate a high degree of consensus over the central areas of empirical analysis. Turner (1984) examines a variety of what he calls 'disorders' which illustrate the problems of bodily control. These focus on gender, the secularization of body management and discipline and the way in which health and illness disrupt our view of the relationship between the body and the person. In 'Bringing Bodies Back In', Frank suggested a fourfold typology for organizing 'academic imaginations' (1990: 134).[1] The *medical body* refers to medicine's knowledge monopoly over the body and the challenge posed to that monopoly by research which shows a disparity between patients' and physicians' perceptions of physical conditions. Such differences were particularly evident in relation to women (whose bodies, as we have seen, have historically been dominated by [male] medicine) and those defined as disabled. The *sexual body* refers to social and sociological debates about reproductive technologies and the role of sex in power relations as a vehicle for both dominance and liberation. The *disciplined body* refers to the techniques available to, or required of, people to shape their bodies or make them conform in particular ways, either in terms of emotion or movement. Workers' bodies are disciplined for production, and disciplined bodies are a means to the achievement of distinction (c.f. Bourdieu 1984). The *talking body* refers to the transparent way bodies reveal who 'we' are: male–female, black–white, middle class–working class.

The role of sport in the sociology of the body

Sport has played a relatively significant role in the development of the sociology of the body. For Turner, there has been a gradual awakening to the significance of sport. In the first edition of *The Body and Society,* he notes that a knowledge of 'gymnastics' is one of half a dozen areas that lie beyond his 'competence', and, furthermore, he fails to see sport – in contrast to medical sociology, patriarchy, religion, consumer culture and social control – as an area in which 'the question of the human body is especially prominent' (Turner 1984: 6). By the second edition, however, Turner was to describe embodiment as 'fundamental to much of the sociology of sport' and was to praise the work of Wacquant as providing an empirical basis for an understanding of how the body is shaped and managed through training and exercise (1996: 32–3). The third edition (Turner 2008) contains a chapter on 'Bodies in Motion', which, while largely based on Turner's collaborative work with Steven Wainwright on ballet, suggests explicit parallels between dancing and the sport of boxing.

Featherstone's engagement with sport, by contrast, was rather more apparent from the beginning. Featherstone (1987) has argued for a relational theory of leisure across the life course in which biological characteristics and changes are viewed as mediated by individuals' access to different types and amounts of capital (e.g., economic, social, physical). His subsequent collection, *The Body: Social Process and Cultural Theory* (Featherstone *et al.* 1991), includes a chapter on the parallels between martial arts and liberal education (Levine 1991). The book, which mainly consisted of articles previously published in *Theory, Culture and Society*, features a revision of Frank's earlier typology (identifying communicative, disciplining, dominating and mirroring bodies) which draws more explicitly on sporting examples and concludes with Berthelot's citation of the sociology of sport as an exemplar of sociology's general neglect of the body (1991: 400). In a later anthology, Featherstone (2000) again highlights the significance of practices such as gymnastics and bodybuilding and includes contributions from Lee Monaghan on the latter and Roberta Sassatelli on gym cultures.

Amongst the early sociology of the body texts, sport is perhaps most prominent in Shilling's *The Body and Social Theory* (1993). Shilling cites sports science, 'keep fit', the relationship between exercise and health and bodybuilding as apposite examples of his core theme of 'the body as a project'. Yet Shilling's text is essentially an attempt to provide a critical overview of some of the main theoretical perspectives relevant to a sociology of the body, and, in devoting significant attention to the work of Bourdieu and Elias (see Chapter 3), sport features throughout the text.

Examination of the journals which have been particularly significant in galvanizing this area of research also demonstrates the relative prominence of sport in the sociology of the body. The first twelve editions of *Theory, Culture and Society* contained twelve articles on sport, authored by some leading sociologists of sport (e.g., Eric Dunning, Jennifer Hargreaves and Alan Ingham), as well as non-sport specialists. The role of sport in *Body and Society* was explicit in Featherstone and Turner's (1995) opening editorial which outlined a research programme for the sociology of the body including:

- the symbolic importance of the body and the active role of the body in social life (in particular its role in sex and gender relations);
- the changing relationship of the body and technology;
- the continuing relevance of medical sociology;
- *and* the analysis of sport.

Articles in this journal have focused on bodies in aerobics, climbing, dancing, martial arts and swimming, as well as examining sport-related issues such as sex testing, the social construction of racialized bodies, the interface between sport and genetics and the body in such diverse contexts as gym cultures and Japanese society. Again authors have been drawn from both within the sociology of sport and without.

Readers and anthologies of the sociology of the body offer an additional gauge of the interpenetration of these fields. Atkinson's (2005) and Price and Shildrick's (1999) readers contain nothing on sport and exercise while Hancock *et al.* (2000) make occasional mention of sport, exercise and fitness. Nettleton and Watson (1998), Fraser and Greco (2004) and Moore and Kosut (2010) include just single readings on bodybuilding, the commercialization of keep fit and the media portrayal of disability sports respectively. Yet amongst the nine chapters in Scott and Morgan's *Body Matters* (1993) are studies of dance and (female) bodybuilding cultures. Malacrida and Low's (2008) reader contains a section titled 'sporting bodies', and of the four sections in Watson and Cunningham-Burley's *Reframing the Body* (2001), 'Bodies in the Gym' contains chapters on bodybuilding, gym cultures and weight-training.

Sociologists of the body have also produced book-length studies focusing on sporting bodies. Monaghan's (2001) ethnographic study of bodybuilding in South Wales provides a grounded analysis of embodiment, identity, gender and risk. Drawing on the work of Anthony Giddens, Ulrich Beck, Chris Shilling and Bryan Turner, Monaghan also embraces sport-related literature, taking the work of sport anthropologist Alan Klein (1986) as a point of departure. Monaghan positions his work as an antidote to the somewhat abstracted and over-generalized character of much of the sociology of the body literature, and he seeks to counter notions that participation in bodybuilding is simply a 'crisis' response to the insecurities generated by hegemonic masculinity. He concludes that, in contrast to its perceived irrationality, bodybuilding should be understood as 'an ongoing practical accomplishment' which provides a 'coherent and meaningful' lifestyle in which self-imposed risks are constructed as manageable through everyday social reality (2001: 181).

In *Body Language: The Meaning of Modern Sport,* Andrew Blake seeks to 'illuminate the relationships through which the sporting body operates' (1996: 23). His text covers the historical development of sport, geographical consideration of sport and the nation, the nature of spectatorship and media representations of sport. The body, however, is only actually central to one chapter, 'The Body Language: Designing the Performer'. Here Blake discusses how athletes' bodies are adorned by sponsors, how developments in sports equipment alter interest in sport and what he terms the 'Faust' and 'Frankenstein' effects, namely the pursuit of victory which entails the (dangerous) use of performance-enhancing drugs, and the manipulation of humanism through cyborgification of sports bodies. In contrast to Monaghan, Blake's engagement with the literature from the sociology of sport is limited.

Perhaps most notable, however, is Wacquant's work on boxing (e.g., 1992, 1995, 2004) which stems from a study initially designed to understand black, urban ghetto life in Chicago. Wacquant initially joined a gym to gain access to this social world, but found his experiences of the physicality of boxing provided something of an epiphany. He argues that putting his body on the line in training and competition earned him respect and access which would otherwise have proved impossible. Moreover, it was through this embodied research process that he came to recognize that the researcher is, first and foremost, flesh, bones and muscles. He thus became committed to a 'carnal sociology' (2004: viii), a sociology not only *of* the body but *from* the body.

In *Body and Soul,* Wacquant (2004) discusses links between the street and the ring that show the ghetto world is not simply chaotic and unruly. Wacquant locates boxing as important for developing status, meaning and relationships as well as producing and reproducing distinct corporeal cultures. The text outlines in minute detail a day leading up to a competitive bout to expose the contradictions of boxing:

> the drab and obsessive routine of the gym workout, of the endless and thankless preparation, inseparably physical and moral, that preludes the all-too-brief appearances in the limelight, the minute and mundane rites of daily life in the gym that produce and reproduce the belief feeding this very peculiar corporeal, material and symbolic economy that is the pugilistic world.
>
> *(2004: 6)*

Blending sociology, ethnography and fiction, Wacquant describes the preparation for, and performance in, his one competitive bout. Here he shows how commitment to the development of the body is both all-encompassing and a distinct corporeal excellence. Boxers are active in moulding and creating their bodies, but their body work also 'inhabits' them.

In concluding this section, special note should be made of the work of Shilling, whose sustained belief in the significance of sport stands out amongst those who have made major contributions to the development of the sociology of the body. In his fourth book, *The Body in Culture, Technology and Society* (2005) Shilling attempts an overview of writings on sport and the body. He discusses how some sports developed out of defence and subsistence activities but have since become increasingly rationalized, 'season-informed' and 'performance driven'. Rationalization has increased the value of sports for governments and commercial organizations, and subsequently sporting bodies have become totems of nationalism and vehicles for commercial promotions. Sporting bodies are sites for the demonstration of human limitation (through injury) and potential (through chemical experimentation). But sporting bodies have also become important for the generation of emotional experience, of individual and group identities and, correlatively, for gender and ethnic inequalities. These examples support Shilling's general theoretical point that 'the body should be read as a multidimensional medium for the constitution of society' (2005: 209)

Furthermore, Shilling has written on the relevance of Durkheim's work for the understanding of the embodied nature of (physical) education, viewing pupils' bodies as the 'physical *location* on which society inscribes its effects … a material *source* of social categories and relations, and a sensual *means* by which people are attached to or dislocated from social forms' (2004: xvii). He is co-author of a study of female body-builders as 'gender outlaws', outlining the motivations and rewards that 'compensate' participants for their social stigmatization (Shilling and Bunsell 2009). Finally, Shilling (2010) has contributed to a special issue of *Sport, Education and Society*, exploring the 'society-body-schooling nexus', locating a range of empirical studies of the body in educational contexts within broader theoretical debates and issues in the sociology of the body. His commitment to an embodied sociology informed by an understanding of sport is therefore unparalleled.

Shilling's sustained commitment to sport as an area for the advancement of his work on the sociology of the body can be explained with reference to a number of factors. First, Shilling started out as a sociologist of education at Southampton University. Here he came into contact with physical educationalists and John Evans in particular. Shilling's sports orientation was also no doubt fuelled by his two main theoretical influences, Bourdieu and Elias (see Chapter 3). Indeed, Shilling's website notes that he welcomes Ph.D. applicants interested not only in the body and social theory but also in sport and those using the theories of Norbert Elias. He also has a deep personal interest in sport as both a supporter of Arsenal Football Club and a regular practitioner of *tai chi*.

The body in the sociology of sport

As noted above, the emergence of an embodied sociology was quickly incorporated into sports studies such that the subdiscipline became significantly contoured by these trends. After the initial incursions of Klaus Heinemann (1980) and Jean Harvey (1986) a group of review essays appeared in the early 1990s (Theberge 1991; Loy *et al.* 1993; Maguire 1993) which argued that the body had largely been neglected in the sociology of sport. Each further noted that this omission was ironic given the centrality of the body in sport. The reasons for this omission replicated those of the 'mainstream' and showed how the sociology of sport had embraced the discipline's methodological orthodoxy. Additionally, the influence of physical education with its scientized, performance-oriented and somewhat mechanical approach to the body was identified as negatively impacting on the bodily orientation of the sociology of sport. Sociologists of sport had been influenced both by their desire for legitimacy within 'mainstream' sociology as well as by their attempt to distance the subdiscipline from its physical education roots.

The significance of the body within the sociology of sport is now such that most textbooks provide reviews of the area that reflect the trends within and stimuli to the 'mainstream' sociology of the body. Craig and Jones (2008), for instance, discuss how sport is a way of disciplining, controlling and constraining the body. They illustrate this with reference to questions of medicalized bodies and the treatment of injury, as well as the role of the body in constructing race, class and gender. In particular they examine trends towards the increasing role of the body in consumer society and the commercialization of sport and exercise. Maguire *et al.* (2002) discuss the nature–nurture interface of emotions, aspects of medicalized bodies through the case study of pain and injury and the relationship between sport as an emotional experience and the establishment of identities through the concept of a quest for exciting significance. Jarvie's (2006) chapter draws most directly upon the sociology of the body, explicitly linking discussion of the sporting body to the theoretical perspectives of Elias (civilized bodies), Bourdieu (body, class and physical capital) and Foucault (the body, power and knowledge). Jarvie further focuses on the relationship between the body, social identities and difference, recognizing the alternatives to dominant Western body cultures.

The impetus for a more embodied sociology of sport was attributed to many of the same social and sociological developments that sociologists of the body identified. Theberge (1991), for instance, cited the work of post-structuralist feminists and work on sport, gender and power more generally as generating interest in the body. Loy *et al.* (1993) cited Frank's (1991) work but argued further that interest in the sporting body had been stimulated by developments in medical sociology, the sociology of the emotions and an embrace of the ideas of Erving Goffman, Pierre Bourdieu and Norbert Elias. Social developments such as an ageing population, changes in consumer culture and controversies surrounding AIDS, women's reproductive rights and men's sexual violence towards women were also identified.

Theberge's overview focused solely on gender-related research such as medical rationales for the exclusion of females from sport, ideological aspects of sport that offer apparently neutral accounts of the construction of gender (and the physical inferiority of females in particular) and the structural bases of disciplinary power (e.g., the organization of physical education, the media portrayal of female athletes). Loy *et al.* and Maguire undertook broader surveys of existing and potential areas of sociological research on sport and the body. Both drew on Frank's updated typology of communicative, disciplined, dominating and mirroring bodies, though where Loy *et al.* used it as a heuristic device for organizing their review of research related to the body in sport, Maguire sought to revise this typology in line with his advocacy of Eliasian sociology allied to an empirical focus on sport.

Loy *et al.* cite works such as Polsky's study of poolroom hustlers (1967), Donnelly and Young's (1988) analysis of the construction and confirmation of identities in rugby and climbing subcultures and Weinberg and Arond's (1952) study of the careers of professional boxers as examples of *communicative* sporting bodies. These studies illustrate how sportspeople use body techniques for impression management and thus also communicate aspects of group membership and social location. Loy *et al.* also cite Wacquant's (1992) work on boxing and Bolin's on bodybuilding (1992) as illustrative of how *disciplined* bodies are voluntarily moulded, and Hargreaves (1986), Harvey and Sparks (1991) and Elias and Dunning (1986a) to show how bodies are disciplined through physical education and sport. Together these reveal the 'dynamic relationship between power, knowledge and corporeal existence' (Loy *et al.* 1993: 352). Under *dominating* bodies, Loy *et al.* discuss the subjugation of female bodies through sport and cite Bourdieu's (1978) work on social class relations and sporting bodies. Finally, with regard to the *mirroring* body, Loy *et al.* relate work on the commercialization of sport (Hargreaves 1986; Brohm 1978; Rigauer 1969/1981) to particular impacts on the body and discuss work on postmodernity and hyperconsumption to illustrate how sport (through the things we buy to adorn it) relates to the way the body reflects our social relations and social status.

Maguire (1993) similarly illustrates Frank's typology using sporting examples but develops a critique that establishes an agenda for the sociology of sport and the body. In so doing, Maguire takes issue with Frank's work. Arguing that a sociology of the body must theorize institutions from the 'body up', Frank is accused of favouring an agency-based theoretical model that emphasizes individual rather than social bodies and thus obscures the essential interdependence of the individual and society. Frank's work also appears locked into a social constructionist model and thus reproduces the nature–nurture dualism. Maguire, citing Elias's concept of the hinge, argues that a more adequate conceptual framework would incorporate the interweaving of the biological, psychological and cultural. He further argues that Frank's model is more applicable to sport and that sport has more relevance for the model than Frank himself recognizes. Maguire concludes that Elias's work might be applied to overcome these deficiencies and proposes that an analysis of sport and the body 'in the round' would incorporate such areas as stratifying bodies, biomedical bodies, disciplined bodies, commodified bodies and symbolic bodies.

Being the most recent, Cole's (2000) review of the field of body studies in the sociology of sport is probably also the most comprehensive. In contrast to earlier overviews, Cole suggests that the previously identified neglect of the body in the sociology of sport draws attention to the historical specificity of perception/knowledge. She argues that recent interest in the body stems less from scholarly intervention and more from the changing social conditions and capitalist-driven demands on the body (the privatization of health and citizenship, workplace changes). Cole then identifies three themes in the literature. 'Sporting Bodies and the Modern Process' refers to the historical use of physical activities to counter external threats, including the nineteenth-century examples of gymnastics in France, bodily production through the Games Cult and Cult of Athleticism in English public schools and the use of sport in America to counter the perceived crisis in masculinity posed by urban industrialization (see Chapter 5). This theme includes the role of science and the body in modern sport, incorporating the development of sports science and the implications for defining normality and truth about bodies through, e.g., drug and sex tests. 'Embodied Deviance and Sport' addresses bodybuilding's role in propagating the idea that transgressive bodies reveal the contests that maintain 'proper' boundaries between what is and is not natural and the representation of celebrities in revealing political discourses and moral norms. 'Sporting Bodies in Consumer Culture' focuses on the political and social processes behind the apparently individual and economic developments of health, exercise and beauty body cultures, as well as the role of celebrities in allocating moral responsibility for the pursuit of particular body shapes to the individual and exemplifying both what is achievable and normal.

These review essays illustrate that the sociology of sport has responded to the same theoretical and social trends which have stimulated the sociology of the body more generally. Specifically, the influence of feminism/gender, the sociology of health/medicine and the theoretical perspectives of Bourdieu, Elias and Foucault have inspired some of the key developments in the sociology of the sporting body. The remainder of this chapter details the influence of these ideas on an embodied sociology of sport.

Particularly illustrative of the influence of gender and feminism is research which focuses upon aerobics and other 'exercise to music' activities. The work of MacNeil (1988) and Markula (1995) which identified the contradiction between the empowering and repressive effects of participation was discussed in Chapter 5. In addition to this, the Eliasian-inspired work of Maguire and Mansfield (1998) is notable. They link women's participation in aerobics with Elias's idea that the theory of civilizing processes entails:

- a historical trend towards a tighter control over the appearance and function of bodies;
- the internalization of social rules governing the rationalization of emotional and bodily discipline;
- the increasing role of shame and embarrassment as regulators of behaviour.

Gender concerns have inspired a similar interrogation of the relationship between sports participation and male bodies. Sparkes and Silvennoinen's *Talking Bodies: Men's Narratives of the Body and Sport* contains analyses of men's subjective experiences of sport and the body, their 'multiple senses of self and shifting identities' (1999: 6), and the relationships they form with their bodies and with the bodies of others. Using narrative or autobiographical techniques the contributions speak to the role of the body in transformations and crises in male identity and show the significance of sport in shaping masculinity, and thus also male bodies.

The increasing focus on the body in the sociology of sport has also helped to develop links with the sociology of medicine and health and illness. As Roderick (2006) notes, from the early 1990s sociologists began to contest the dominance of natural scientists and psychologists over the study of injury experiences and medical treatment of athletes. Roderick highlights how research looking at the relationship between medicine and the sporting body has examined the subculture of sport, aspects of masculinity, female athletes' experiences, the management of pain and injury and the relationship between pain and injury and risk (Hoberman 1992; Messner 1992; Nixon 1992; Curry 1993; Young 1993; Young *et al.* 1994). A number of these areas are covered in Howe's *Sport, Professionalism and Pain* (2004).[2]

An overview of this research can be gained from Young's *Sporting Bodies, Damaged Selves* (2004) and Loland *et al.*'s *Pain and Injury in Sport* (2006). Young's text discusses:

- *pain cultures*: the causes and contexts of sports injuries and pain, particularly the way sport is organized and how this leads athletes to view pain and injury in particular ways;
- *pain zones*: the lived experiences of pain and injury, particularly the employment of coping strategies, self-care/ethnopharmacology and the management of risk;
- *pain parameters*: the social responses to pain and injury including, for instance, the provision of medical care, health and public policy agendas and economic and legal issues.

Loland *et al.*'s text combines philosophical and sociological ideas about the relationship between pain and injury and performance, the management of pain and injury and the deliberate infliction and meaning of pain and injury. Two (of five) sections are primarily sociological, addressing the athlete experience of pain and injury and the medical management of pain and injury (similar to *pain zones* and *pain cultures* in Young 2004). Duncan's (2008) guest editorship of a special issue of the *SSJ* on 'The Social Construction of Fat' is further evidence of the increasing interpenetration of the sociology of sport and medical understanding of the body, as is Malcolm and Safai's anthology, *The Social Organization of Sports Medicine* (forthcoming).

Two further monographs embracing an embodied sociology of sport are of note, the first because of its theoretical orientation and the second because it illustrates the interdisciplinarity of this movement. A wide range of journal articles have drawn upon Bourdieu for an embodied understanding of the sporting body (e.g., White and Wilson 1999; Thorpe 2009) but Smith-Maguire's (2008) overview of the intersections between the producers and consumers of 'fitness' and the broader social processes that define physical culture practices is perhaps the most detailed example of the approach. Suggesting that, in contemporary societies, the body has become a 'project', Smith-Maguire examines fitness sites (e.g., health clubs), media (e.g., magazines, manuals and videos), goods (equipment and apparel) and services (personal training, classes) and argues that 'Through fitness, participants negotiate social demands and thereby produce their own bodily status' (2008: 22). Smith-Maguire further suggests that the fitness movement has emerged out of the twin processes of individualization and consumption. Identity, health and social mobility become defined as the duties and responsibilities of the individual, and the production of bodies and selves demonstrates the individual's 'fit[ness] for consumption – fit to consume; fit to be consumed' (Smith-Maguire 2008: 190). Smith-Maguire concludes by linking these developments to the paradoxical relationship of fitness and fatness, that is to say, the parallel trends of this developing body culture and increasing concerns about levels of obesity, which, in turn, is identified as a major health-risk factor. She sees the commercial fitness field as representing the commodification and reproduction of 'the already deeply entrenched class-based stratification of health and health risks' (Smith-Maguire 2008: 204), and argues that the fit/fat paradox is, in many ways, the rational outcome of seeking individualized solutions to social, structural problems.

Body Cultures: Essays on Sport, Space and Identity consists of the writings of German-born Denmark-based academic Henning Eichberg (1998), collated, edited and introduced by two geographers: John Bale and Chris Philo. The central premise of Eichberg's work is that modern sports (and modern societies) have been characterized by a kind of rationalization – or 'geometricization' – with measurement (e.g., of time, length, height) and the disciplining of space (e.g., stadia, the environment) prominent trends. Eichberg further stresses that bodies are 'profoundly implicated' (Bale and Philo 1998: 11) in making the social world and thus that the consequences of these broader trends should be related to embodied human experience. There has been, he suggests, a 'territorialization' of the human body, its spatial confinement and social disciplining within sport. Crucial to understanding the entirety of Eichberg's approach, however, is recognition of the importance he attaches to trends that run counter to this rationalization. So, for instance, he is cognisant of the impact of environmental movements and of a feminist-inspired critique about assuming that male and female bodies experience the masculinist character of contemporary sport in identical ways. He also notes that, contrary to the homogenizing trends of globalization, the demonstration of national or cultural identities through non-Western body cultural practices such as dance and indigenous games is significant. He introduces the notion of the 'trialectic', 'in order to demonstrate that the prevailing notion of sport is only one way in which the moving, physical body can be configured in modernity' (Bale and Philo 1998: 16).

Bale and Philo (1998: 17) bemoan Eichberg's lack of recognition amongst Anglo-American researchers, but perhaps most significant are their comments about the difficulty in accurately placing Eichberg's work in any particular discipline. Trained as a historian, his work has become increasingly interdisciplinary. His appeal to the editors (as geographers) as well as his philosophical orientations and interest to sociologists of sport illustrates a blurring of traditional disciplinary boundaries. In arguing that 'to restrict his influence … solely to sports studies would be misleading' (1998: 3), Bale and Philo note the presence of a number of substantive non-sport themes in Eichberg's work. His emphasis on body culture rather than sport is rooted in his recognition of the multiplicity of configurations of the human body.

Hargreaves and Vertinsky's *Physical Culture, Power, and the Body* (2007b) currently stands as the only 'sport'-specific reader on the body. Critical of the 'highly theoretical and generalized' work within the sociology of the body, their focus is on an area they feel has been neglected: namely, the body-in-movement (2007a: 20). They are further critical of the dominance of empirical studies of 'male' sports such as boxing and bodybuilding and of 'mainstream' feminists' neglect of the work of 'sport feminists' (see Chapter 5). Through studies of technology, medicine, disability, gender and race/ethnicity they demonstrate that bodies are socially constructed within the context of broader and (normally) unequal power relations. Paralleling stimuli of the sociology of the body noted above, Hargreaves and Vertinsky point to the theoretical influences of Bourdieu (habitus), Giddens (identity project), Foucault (bio-power) and Butler (performativity). The various contributions show how the personal and the social are linked, 'how identity is constructed within the body, and how representations of the body specifically in physical culture are assigned meaning and influence identity' (Hargreaves and Vertinsky 2007a: 8). This is clearly illustrated in Leslie Haywood's (2007) discussion of gender discourses which construct girls in terms of 'can do' and thus gender roles as matters of personal responsibility and self-policing, and through Sparkes and Smith's (2007) examination of the life histories of former rugby players who suffer spinal-cord injuries. Problematizing the biological determinism of gender and race differences, Hargreaves and Vertinsky analyse the nature–nurture interface and explore the complex and contradictory character of the body (see discussion of Turner's 'Body Paradoxes' on p. 86) through, for instance, the example of Muslim women who demonstrate that bodies are not simply passive recipients of social power.

Conclusion

The Hargreaves and Vertinsky text encapsulates a number of broader trends that are worthy of note. For instance, echoing Eichberg's body of work, the collaboration of a sociologist (Hargreaves) and historian (Vertinsky) illustrates the disciplinary boundary-blurring increasingly evident in the sociology of sport in recent times (see Chapters 8 and 10). Most interesting for present purposes, however, is what the text suggests about the relationship between sports studies and the sociology of the body and the impact that the emergence of the sociology of the body has had on the sport subdiscipline(s).

It is clear from the analysis above that those primarily interested in the sociology of the body have paid relatively more attention to the sociology of sport than their counterparts in many other sociological subdisciplines. Michael Atkinson, who many would consider a sociologist of sport, but whose Ph.D. and first book *Tattooed* (2003) was widely acclaimed within sociology of the body circles, shows this to be a two-way process (a similar case might be made for Smith-Maguire). However, there has been a recent decline in sport-related research in *Theory, Culture and Society* and (to a lesser extent) *Body and Society*, which, allied to the still marginal or tenuous position of sport in readers and anthologies of the body, and the neglect of sport by feminist scholars of the body, suggests some ambivalence. That Hargreaves and Vertinsky draw authors from both the sociology of sport and what might be called 'mainstream' sociology of the body (most notably Wacquant) is indicative of a level of interpenetration. But such interplay is often not sustained. Indeed it seems more commonly to be the case that sociologists of the body have become established via the study of sport (notably Wacquant and Monaghan) but have since moved on to non-sport-related areas. On the one hand, this might be cause for optimism. For instance, Snyder and Spreitzer (1974/1980: 31) note that 'the more developed specialities such as medical sociology involve more practitioners who are just passing through and just happen to touch down for an episodic research effort on the content of that given speciality' (e.g., Talcott Parsons, Robert Merton, Howard Becker) and suggest that such circulation is desirable and beneficial for sociology's subdisciplines. Conversely, there is little evidence to suggest that the movement of sport from the sociological periphery which Maguire (1993) predicted might be a consequence of the development of a more embodied sociology has come to fruition. Indeed, the opposite might be more true, with people leaving the sociology of sport for other subdisciplines.

A partial explanation for this unfulfilled promise can also be detected in the Hargreaves and Vertinsky text. Significantly, this book illustrates a movement away from research on 'sport' as narrowly defined at the conception of the subdiscipline (see Chapter 2), prioritizing instead the field of 'physical culture'. This they define as 'those activities where the body itself … is the very purpose, the raison d'être of the activity' (2007a: 1), and thus the collection includes analyses of both dance and striptease in addition to activities which have more traditionally been defined as sport. Indeed, reflection back on the contents of this chapter illustrates that much of what has been of central interest to sociologists of the body has not really been sport. The studies of bodybuilding, of gym culture, of dance and even Shilling's interest in the body and physical education are rather tangential to the research mainstays of sociologists of sport as traditionally conceived. It is particularly telling, for instance, that despite numerous studies of bodybuilding by sociologists of the body, the closest comparison which sociologists of sport can offer is the work of sports anthropologist Alan Klein (1986) and Camilla Obel (1996). We will return to these issues in Chapter 10.

7

SPORT AND CELEBRITY

An even more recent development in sociology is the critical exploration of celebrity, stardom and fame. In their editorial marking the launch of the journal *Celebrity Studies,* Su Holmes and Sean Redmond (2010) reflect on the largely unfavourable media response to their initiative which they attribute to fears about the 'dumbing down' of higher education. Indeed, as one British broadsheet journalist predicted, 'we can expect plenty of pseudo-academic mumbo jumbo'. However, in linking these fears to reports that 'David Beckham Studies' were amongst the 'Mickey Mouse' degrees for which future government funding would be under threat in the UK, they inadvertently highlight the relationship this chapter centrally seeks to examine, specifically: To what extent has sport been influential in the development of this field? How have sociologists of sport responded to this developing academic trend? And how has the work of sociologists of sport been received within the 'celebrity studies' community? More broadly, to what extent has the growth of this area enabled sociologists of sport to make an impact on other areas of sociology?

The next section examines the area of celebrity studies, identifying its definitions and roots, the social functions attributed to contemporary celebrity culture and the recommended modes and scope of analysis. Following this I examine the role of sport within the celebrity-studies literature before moving to review the literature on sports celebrities and the examinations of celebrity written by sociologists of sport. Particular attention is devoted to research about David Beckham. The conclusion offers a broad assessment of the relationship and interpenetration of these two fields of study.

Celebrity studies

As we saw in Chapter 2, definitional debates are characteristic of the formation of academic fields and in this respect the study of celebrity and stardom is no exception.

For conciseness, there is much merit in Boorstin's (1961) definition of a celebrity as 'a person who is known for his well-knownness'. Similarly, Rein *et al.* (1997: 14) talk of a celebrity as 'a name which, once made by the news, now makes the news itself', while Geraghty (2000: 187) suggests that for a celebrity fame overwhelmingly rests upon lifestyle rather than profession. Rojek argues that individuals become celebrities when their private lives become more significant than their public roles. He goes on to define celebrity as 'the attribution of glamourous or notorious status to an individual within the public sphere' (Rojek 2001: 10), which can more simply be relayed via the equation 'celebrity = impact on public consciousness'.

To further clarify the term, celebrity is often contrasted with two related terms: stardom and heroism. The notion of the 'star' betrays the area's roots in film studies and the examination of the cinema industry's purposeful intervention into the management of the interaction between the on- and off-screen image of actors (Redmond and Holmes 2007: 8). Crucially this alerts us to both the constructed character of celebrity and the distinction between the public and the private, the mediated and the 'real' person. The hero, by contrast, is someone whose well-knownness is seen to be based on their own accomplishments. Heroes perform 'good deeds' in the fields of politics, science, warfare or exploration and thus their public personas may require little further construction (Cashmore 2006: 50). Again, this contrast alerts us to the potential absence of talent or ability in the definition of celebrity. Marshall's (1997: 7) genealogical analysis leads him to suggest that while terms such as 'hero', 'star' and 'leader' relate to individuals with specific social functions, the term 'celebrity' has been used historically to depict an emerging, and largely disparaged, representation of social value which certain individuals are said to hold for the public sphere. As Turner (2004: 4) notes, contemporary celebrity epitomizes 'the inauthenticity or constructedness of mass-mediated popular culture' which is generally viewed as a symptom of broader social decline.

Most commentators agree that celebrities have become ubiquitous in recent years, yet the processes by which this has occurred have led the distinction between the above categories to become blurred. Redmond and Holmes (2007: 6) note that the multimedia and inter- and cross-textual appeal of contemporary celebrities 'has fuelled a debate about the flattening of distinctions between stars, celebrities and personalities'. Evans and Hesmondhalgh (2005: 4) raise the question of whether the declining distinction between the star and the celebrity represents a significant historical shift away from more elite, enduring and specialist 'stars' towards more mundane and fleeting celebrities. Caution needs to be expressed about the extent of this change, however, for in the public imagination there remains an implicitly accepted 'hierarchy of cultural values … with the concept of "star" positioned above the concept of "celebrity"' (Redmond and Holmes 2007: 8). As we will see, this point has particular relevance for the study of sports celebrity.

Analytically, most agree that it makes sense to interrogate these phenomena together because distinguishing between the 'talented' and the 'talentless' is a highly subjective process. In light of this, Rojek (2001: 17–20) identifies three broad types of celebrity:

1 ascribed (through family relations);
2 achieved (through the meritocratic recognition of specific accomplishments);
3 attributed (when cultural intermediaries single out an individual as exceptional).

To this he adds the category of 'celetoid', a short-lived, hyper-visible and often unwitting media star, a category that signals 'the need to address the heightened intensity and the apparent arbitrariness of the modern media's concentration on the celebrity' (Turner 2004: 22). In this way, Rojek usefully shifts attention from the attributes of individuals to the broader social processes of celebrity production.

Stripped of such moralistic evaluation, celebrity studies therefore focus on the individual as a way of making sense of the social world. Schickel (1997: xi) sees famous people as symbols 'used to simplify complex matters of the mind and spirit; they are used to subvert rationalism in politics, in every realm of everyday life'. The production of what he calls *Intimate Strangers* confuses the public and private spheres and thus blurs the line between state and personal responsibility. For Turner (2004: 9), celebrity 'is a genre of representation and a discursive effect; it is a commodity traded by the promotions, publicity, and media industries that produce these representations and their effects; and it is a cultural formation that has a social function.' This quote neatly summarizes the convergence of various realms of celebrity analysis. There are those, whom Marshall (1997: 51) identifies as mainly drawn from the dominant culture, who intentionally and instrumentally create celebrities and those, largely drawn from the subordinate classes, who are the audience for and the consumers of that celebrity image. Celebrities promote social values such as individuality, freedom and meritocracy and provide stability in times of rapid social change, but their audiences are active in receiving and interpreting these images. While the audience gives the celebrity their power, 'the celebrity is a locus of formative social power' (Marshall 1997: 51). In this respect, celebrity is 'linked to the development of mass democracies and concerted efforts to contain the power of the mass in those democracies' (Marshall 1997: 241). The global reach of individual celebrities and the speed with which their fame spreads illustrates the degree of interconnectedness of the contemporary world and the so-called compression of time and space.

While all societies have, and have had, individuals who are publicly exalted, the celebrity phenomenon is largely seen as a product of modernity and the development of mass-circulation media in particular (Turner 2004). The development of photography, which led to the 'dissemination of the face' (Gamson 1994: 21) was also influential, as was the invention of a public-relations industry at the beginning of the twentieth century. Indeed, Schickel (1997: 23) simply argues that 'there was no such thing as celebrity prior to the twentieth century.' Writers are also largely agreed that not only were film stars the first modern celebrities (Marshall 1997) but also that film studies provided the first extended analysis of the contemporary phenomenon (Redmond and Holmes 2007). Gamson (1994) for instance argues that Hollywood established the techniques that underpin the modern celebrity industry, and Schickel (1997) definitively dates the origin of celebrity to 24 June 1916 when Mary Pickford signed the first million-dollar film contract. Although the search for single origins is somewhat misguided (as illustrated in Chapter 2), there is broad agreement that deCordova's (1990) seminal work on the development of *Picture Personalities* as a means to stimulate demand for films starring particular actors has enabled us to identify the epicentre of these developments as 'the American motion picture industry at the beginning of the twentieth century' (Turner 2004: 12; see also Marshall 1997).

Sociologists of sport might baulk at these analyses for if celebrity studies was as dependent on the sociology of sport as it is on film studies, the orthodox historical account of the emergence of celebrity culture would look rather different. Whannel (2002: 82) notes that the emergence of the mass media coincided with that of modern spectator sport (i.e. from around 1870), while Andrews and Jackson (2001a) further argue that the establishment of specialist sports sections in American newspapers in the 1890s were driven by consumer demand and the desire to increase circulation. Sports, moreover, centrally feature individuals or groups with whom spectators form an emotional attachment, thereby blurring the public and private spheres (Whannel 2002). Both Whannel (2002) and Andrews and Jackson (2001a) mention W. G. Grace as one of sport's earliest notable figures, as well as others such as Jack Johnson who became a boxing world champion in 1908 and latterly Jack Dempsey (boxing), Babe Ruth (baseball), Bobby Jones (golf) and Fred Perry (tennis). The case for sport celebrities pre-dating their counterparts in cinema could, however, be stated even more strongly. Grace's fame is said to have been matched only by Queen Victoria, Prime Minister W. E. Gladstone and Florence Nightingale (Trelford 1998). Richard Holt (1989: 102–3) refers to Grace as the first national sporting 'hero' but, crucially, his 'great deeds' were augmented by active image management. Regularly featured in the press, *Punch* magazine campaigned to have Grace knighted. Grace stimulated demand for his consumption, organizing cricket matches and international tours. He endorsed advertisers' products as he sought to capitalize on the fame accrued from his sporting achievements. Subsequent revelations about his infringement of amateur regulations and surreptitious playing practices which ran counter to his identity as the embodiment of sportsmanship expose the degree to which his private and public personas were split and actively managed. Testimony to the international reach of Grace is C. L. R. James's (1963) account of worshipping Grace from afar during his childhood in Trinidad. One could make a similar case for Albert Spalding, 'baseball star and sporting goods magnet' (Kirsch 1989: 51), who successfully combined playing and managing professional baseball teams with eponymous merchandising. Spalding also sought to propagate the Abner Doubleday origin myth of baseball, which, by establishing the game's American roots, increased the market for his products. None of this is to suggest a different origin point for the establishment of the modern concept of celebrity, merely to query a consensus which appears to be built on the exclusion of sport.

Not only do existing accounts reduce the emergence of celebrity to a particular sphere of social life, focus on the film industry fuels a kind of technological reductionism; that is to say, the growth of celebrity culture becomes simplistically linked to the development of the mass media. More adequate are approaches that encompass broader social processes. In this vein, Cashmore (2006) concludes his book on celebrity by considering three explanations for the rise of celebrity culture:

1 the decline of religion;
2 the creation of para-social relations through the media;
3 the interests of capitalist production.

The relationship between celebrity and religion is largely drawn from the work of Rojek who suggests that 'post-God celebrity is now one of the mainstays of organising recognition and belonging in secular society' (2001: 58). Citing psychologists who have drawn parallels between the fanaticism of religion and celebrity culture, the essence of this argument is that celebrities have replaced the sense of identity people previously drew from being members of a religious community. Second, the creation of para-social relations is predicated on a similar belief that human interdependence has fundamentally changed in modern societies, such that people now are more atomized, individualized and privatized. In the absence of 'real' social relations people develop an identification with celebrities which is *imagined* to have a degree of intimacy. These para-social relations account for the obsession with the personal that is mediated through television, magazines and, increasingly, the internet and is envisaged to hold some kind of compensatory function. Not only are celebrities substitutes for 'real' people that we 'really' meet, they give people a shared interest and *lingua franca* by which relations are built with people whom we *do* meet in person. Third, the rise of celebrity culture has been attributed to what Rojek calls the 'commodification of everyday life' (2001: 13). Celebrities are vehicles by which producers market their products. Through identification with celebrities, a new level of demand is created, in part for the particular goods for which our favoured celebrities appear to have a predilection, but more generally aspirant for the lifestyle which the 'social elite' possess and which celebrity culture vividly displays to us. Invoking the notion of bread and circuses (i.e. pacifying the masses by keeping them fed and entertained), Cashmore describes this process as acting as a form of distraction and thus reinforcing existing social relations. He argues that Marshall's thesis is merely a slightly more sophisticated version of this, in that the notions of 'identity, individuality, and the self that are explored through these readings of celebrity' (Marshall 1997: 3) are prescribed as essential aspects of capitalist democracy and consumerism which ultimately obscure broader social processes (such as inequality) through a focus on the personal.

Seen in this light, celebrities can be said to perform various functions. For Marshall (1997: 241–7), there are four. Celebrities, he argues:

1 show (not necessarily truthfully) the extent of agency in contemporary society, that is to say the degree to which individuals can invoke change;
2 act as 'brands' which give security through familiarity and thus provide stability during times of rapid social change;

3 suggest that there are no barriers that the individual cannot overcome and thus that society is meritocratic;
4 contribute to the psychologization of the public sphere, reducing the cultural meaning of events and undermining ideological movements.

Turner (2004) likewise suggests that celebrities generate cultural identities, surrogate or para-social relations, provide an integrating function holding society together through common identification and legitimate the process of capitalist exchange and commodification.

Consequently, studies of celebrity should attempt to investigate a number of realms. Marshall (1997) argues that in investigating celebrity as a form of cultural power, we need to look at it as a form of rationalization in which alternative cultures are ideologically subordinated to consumer capitalism, as signs/texts which expose a system of culturally specific meanings and as a relationship between audience and subject in which identities are constantly negotiated through the representation of individuals and collectives. Celebrities represent 'subject positions that audiences can adopt or adapt in the formation of social identities' (Marshall 1997: 65). Citing the work of Turner (2010), Holmes and Redmond (2010) express this agenda slightly differently. For them, key areas include 'the myriad of economic networks which make up the celebrity industry; the economic and cultural contours of the celebrity-as-commodity; celebrity in a global context; and the relationship between celebrity and its audiences' (Holmes and Redmond 2010: 6). Amongst existing work, Turner argues, too much focuses on the representational or discursive level of celebrity, and too little focuses on audience reception. Too little work, moreover, has engaged with the celebrity industry and especially the journalists who are fundamental to public perceptions of such individuals.

The role of sport in celebrity studies

In a number of ways celebrity studies lends itself to a relatively thorough empirical integration of sport-related work. Both the sociology of sport and celebrity studies 'defamiliarise the everyday, and … make apparent the cultural politics and power relations which sit at the centre of the "taken for granted"' (Holmes and Redmond 2010: 3). Both are largely interdisciplinary, and both are relatively new areas of study (though in contrast to the somewhat hyper-orthodox roots of the sociology of sport in the 1960s, celebrity studies has, arguably, largely developed since the cultural turn in the social sciences [Andrews and Jackson 2001a]). More specifically, the increasing prominence of the sports star was one of the cultural trends that inspired some of the seminal works in celebrity studies. For instance, Leo Lowenthal's 'The Triumph of Mass Idols' (Lowenthal 2006) specifically highlights the prominence of sportspeople as biographical subjects of newspapers, while Dyer comments that in the portrayals of many male film stars – Clark Gable, Humphrey Bogart, Paul Newman, Steve McQueen – 'sporting activity is a major, perhaps the major, element in their image' (Dyer 1987, cited in Whannel 2002: 50). Most significantly, perhaps, members of both communities experience accusations of being a 'low-brow area of derisible scholarship' (Holmes and Redmond 2010: 2). These elements of overlap suggest that the respective academic communities might mutually benefit from collaboration and be sensitive to their respective claims for recognition. To what extent then have these two fields interacted? To what extent does celebrity studies take sport seriously?

There is evidence to suggest that the area of celebrity studies has been more significantly influenced by the sociology of sport than many sociological subdisciplines or interdisciplinary areas. One interesting characteristic of celebrity studies is the prominence of scholars (namely Rojek and Cashmore) who have backgrounds of working with sport. However, few recognize this as a distinguishing trait of Rojek and Cashmore's analyses (the former is largely lauded for his work on celebrity and religion) and a more ambivalent attitude towards sport is generally displayed. Typical of this are Evans and Hesmondhalgh (2005) whose book *Understanding Media: Inside Celebrity* contains no more than four references to two sports celebrities, footballers David Beckham and George Best. Marshall explicitly focuses only on film, television and popular music. Despite his admission that areas such as sport would be 'equally valid starting points' (Marshall 1997: 65), he justifies his exclusion of sport on the (not wholly convincing) basis that television, film and pop music have clear and openly acknowledged industrial strategies for making celebrities, have celebrity forms which have been appropriated into the political sphere, are highly interdependent, thus enabling a systemic conception of celebrity, and have clearly identifiable audience-consumers. (Certainly the last three of these appear to be equally true of sport; see the discussion of Rojek [2006] on p. 106.) Marshall's one mention of Michael Jordan relates to Oprah Winfrey's celebrity status which stems from having guests *like* Jordan on her television show. While he has written specifically on the Beatles (Marshall 1999/2006), his analysis does not encompass the person often referred to as the fifth Beatle: George Best.

This ambivalence is also expressed in the three celebrity 'readers' that have been produced. Rojek's (2009) *Celebrity: Critical Concepts in Sociology* places sport most prominently, giving it equal weighting with film, television and pop music as one of four genres with discrete sections. It also includes Real's (1975) work on the Superbowl in a section on 'Audiences' and Chung's (2003) work comparing Korean sports and pop stars in 'Counter-Genres'. By contrast, and despite his claim that it is important to illustrate how celebrities transcend media and genres (Marshall 2006), just two of the forty-one readings in Marshall's reader involve sport: Rahman's (2004) work on David Beckham, and Cole and Andrews's (2001) work on Tiger Woods. Most peculiar in its treatment of sport is the Redmond and Holmes (2007) reader. Dedicated to George Best, it opens with Redmond's 'Star confessional' about his boyhood attachment to the football celebrity, yet contains nothing explicitly addressing sport and only three articles which make even passing mention of sport.

Amongst the 'celebrity studies' writers who effectively integrate sport into their analysis is Graeme Turner. Turner describes the 'sports star celebrity' as 'a particularly interesting case' (2004: 18). He uses sporting examples throughout his text, identifies sport as centrally implicated in processes of media convergence through the vertical integration of film, television and sports franchises, and argues that the ability to 'cross-promote' sportspeople (athletes can become actors and models, but actors cannot become athletes) places them centrally in the globalized 'Economy of Celebrity'. Furthermore, Turner discusses the distinct cultural function of sport celebrity, often having a link with nationalism and national identity that celebrities from other genres rarely match. Citing Whannel (2001), he notes that their exaltation as 'role models' leaves them particularly vulnerable to a cycle of 'celebration, transgression, punishment, redemption'. Most unusually amongst celebrity-studies writers, Turner embraces theoretical concepts developed within the sociology of sport and in particular Whannel's notion of vortextuality (the increased range of media and the heightened speed of circulation of information which leads all public interest to be drawn to a single point).

In *Celebrity,* Rojek displays a familiarity with, and knowledge of, sport and sports celebrities that few writers match. Perhaps even more so than in the case of Turner, sporting examples permeate his text. In particular he uses athletes as examples of 'achieved' celebrity (Rojek 2001: 18). He has also written specifically on 'sports celebrity', citing the growth of satellite television, the increased cultural cachet of sport via the health and fitness 'boom', the prominence of sport in social discourses about (so-called crises in) masculinity and the growing economic significance of the sports sector as reasons for the 'elevation of sports celebrity in popular culture … [which] has been nothing short of astonishing' (Rojek 2006: 682–3). Rojek highlights the fluidity of movement between the genres of sport, pop music, business and fashion, the clamour by politicians to be associated with elite athletes, the 'wholesome allure' of the sports celebrity and the geographical mobility, incredible wealth and physical capital of soccer stars in particular. These factors make athletes archetypal 'cosmopolitan flexible accumulators' (Rojek 2006: 685) and potentially fruitful subjects of analysis in celebrity studies. They also implicitly challenge Marshall's rationale for his non-sport focus.

By comparison, Cashmore's engagement with sport is somewhat disappointing. It may be that having authored two celebrity biographies (on Beckham and Mike Tyson [2002, 2005a]) his book *Celebrity/Culture* is an attempt to expand his analysis to embrace other genres of celebrity, but ultimately there is something rather unsatisfactory about his treatment of sportspeople. Sporting examples appear throughout the text but the absence of sport in Cashmore's chapter 'Commodifying/Race' is especially surprising given the prominence of Michael Jordan in sociology of sport studies of celebrity and indeed Cashmore's (1982) own previous work on sport and race. Unlike celebrities from other genres, Cashmore's sportspeople are largely confined to a discrete chapter. Here Cashmore suggests that whereas George Best and Joe Namath were unusual in their time, now 'virtually any athlete who has public visibility is handed endorsement contracts, requests for talk show appearances, and possibly a media retinue of their own' (Cashmore 2006: 229). He suggests that while the health and fitness movement and the ability of sport to provide relatively cheap television to a demographic group highly desired by advertisers are significant reasons for the growing ubiquity of athlete-celebrities, the latter's primary 'selling point' is their conservative character. Stating that 'the global celebrity athlete whose status is based on marketing rather than sporting accomplishments' (Cashmore 2006: 241) is increasingly common, he further suggests that in recent times sport has undergone a process whereby, 'the rogue elements ... were domesticated. There was no place for rebels or political protestors. Resistance was turned into stylistic affectation' (Cashmore 2006: 238). Undermining this analysis is the fact that, as we will see, others identify the authenticity of sports celebrities as their distinguishing characteristic. Moreover, outside of this chapter, references to sports celebrities most frequently appear in Cashmore's chapter, 'Thriving/On Scandal'!

Celebrity and the sociology of sport

Amongst sociology of sport studies of celebrity, David Andrews's (1996a) *SSJ* article, 'The Fact(s) of Michael Jordan's Blackness', is seminal. Andrews focused on four distinct aspects of Jordan's racial signification:

1 his conformity to traditional racial stereotypes;
2 the consistent underplaying of Jordan's 'blackness' in an attempt to create an 'all American' image and therefore appeal to basketball's predominantly white audience;
3 the growing prominence of 'blackness' as his image became tarnished by personal and commercial scandal;
4 the location of Jordan within a broader discourse of the moral laxity of African Americans.

While this was not the first sociology of sport publication to focus on a particular celebrity (others competing for this 'honour' include Critcher [1979] and Ingham *et al.* [1979]), most significantly this article led Andrews (1996b) to edit a special issue of the *SSJ*, *Deconstructing Michael Jordan: Reconstructing Postindustrial America.* Not only did this provide a highly visible body of theoretically rigorous work on celebrity, it also became the best-selling single issue in the journal's history and attracted contributions from significant figures from media and cultural studies (namely Norman Denzin and Douglas Kellner).

Three key texts have built on these foundations: Andrews and Jackson's *Sports Stars: The Cultural Politics of Sporting Celebrity* (2001b), Whannel's *Media Sport Stars: Masculinities and Moralities* (2002) and Barry Smart's *The Sport Star: Modern Sport and the Cultural Economy of Sporting Celebrity* (2005). *Sports Stars* 'is underpinned by the notion of sport celebrity as a product of commercial culture, imbued with symbolic values, which seek to stimulate desire and identification among the consuming populace' (Andrews and Jackson 2001a: 9). Andrews and Jackson (2001a: 7–8) argue that sport celebrities are distinct from their counterparts in other cultural realms for three reasons:

1 because sport is deemed to be fundamentally meritocratic, sport stars are argued to be 'worthy' of fan adulation;
2 because sport has a social prominence and a link to nationhood that gives these celebrities a heightened presence and affection;
3 because sport stars have an appearance of authenticity that those in other genres cannot match (though this also leads to a particular vulnerability as performance will inevitably decline, and thus the basis of celebrity status is undermined).

Featuring individuals from a range of sports (athletics, baseball, basketball, cricket, football, tennis) and territories (Argentina, Australia, Britain, the Caribbean, Japan, Kenya, Pakistan, Switzerland, and the USA), Andrews and Jackson stress that in addition to 'national resonance', celebrities have 'multiple representative subject positions' (2001a: 10) so that reducing them to specific identity categories is problematic. That said, most of the contributions centrally focus on a specific identity issue: race/ethnicity (chapters on Michael Jordan, Dennis Rodman, Andre Agassi, Tiger Woods, Venus Williams and Ian Wright), national identity and cultural differences (chapters on Diego Maradona, Wayne Gretzky and Hideo Nomo), post-colonialism (chapters on Nyandika Maiyoro and Kip Keino, Cathy Freeman, Imran Khan and Brian Lara) and masculinity (chapter on David Beckham). Only Giulianotti and Gerrard's (2001) analysis of Paul Gascoigne specifically focuses on the incoherence and contradictory nature of celebrity discourses. While the breadth of the text is impressive, the depth of treatment of celebrity is rather limited as all the chapters essentially examine 'sport celebrities as contextually informed discursive subjectivities' (Andrews and Jackson 2001a: 10). In addition, there is something of a disjuncture between Andrews and Jackson's introduction, which is located in and informed by the broader literature on celebrity outlined earlier in this chapter, and (with the exception of Giardina's (2001) chapter on Hingis) the marked absence of similar references in the rest of the text. Thus, although the text represents a significant advance in terms of the study of sport celebrities, it is limited in its theoretical relevance to celebrity studies more generally.

Contrast this with Whannel's *Media Sport Stars*. Based on the premise that sport is a potentially productive field for the study of celebrity, Whannel points out that the study of celebrity is both highly context-specific (in terms of an individual's appeal in particular national cultures) and liable to quickly change as celebrities come and go, or become characterized by different narratives. Crucially, however, Whannel argues that 'The image of sports stars, questions of morality, of youth and of masculinity are all bound up together' (2002: 1). He further suggests that the 'construction of stardom' is not a neutral process but 'takes place on prestructured ground' (Whannel 2002: 12). In this respect he identifies three broader debates:

1 late-twentieth-century debates about (a crisis in) masculinity;
2 the rapid development and impact of the media, especially the tabloid revolution, new men's magazines, advertising, satellite/digital/internet and games, particularly in relation to the commercialization of sport;
3 the perception in both sport and society more generally of a decline of heroism, and its replacement with a notion of stardom which is based on representation and image production.

Through a series of case studies, Whannel further demonstrates how the narrative of sports stars has changed. Charting the presentation of 'good boy' sports stars such as Joe DiMaggio and Stanley Matthews in the 1950s, 'pretty boy' sports stars George Best and Muhammad Ali in the 1960s, and 'bad boys' Alex Higgins and Ian Botham in the 1970s, Whannel concludes that 'the growing professionalization of sport, and the greatly increased financial rewards, have together produced greater pressure for dedication and commitment' (2002: 145). Concurrently, tabloidization of the news has led to a culture of surveillance with less tolerance of transgressions and increased emphasis on the importance of 'recovery' from falls from grace. Consequently, the 'images of sports stars are mobilized within specific moral discourses' (Whannel 2002: 161) and a new form of sport star narrative has become predominant. In sum, 'Sport stars [a]re expected to be good role models, moral exemplars and [a]re castigated for failing in this role and setting a bad example' (Whannel 2002: 213). This particular narrative resonates with broader social concerns about morality and masculinity, the changing structure of the media industry and the development of consumer capitalism.

The strength of Whannel's book is that it combines a detailed understanding of both the literatures on celebrity and the social development of media production with a broad knowledge of sport. Not only does Whannel provide an analysis that enables him to draw links across and between different celebrities, he develops a historical dimension to the study of celebrity by highlighting how narratives have changed over time. In contrast to the Andrews and Jackson book, where contributions are largely self-contained analyses of individuals' single subjective positions, this text describes and explains why and how narratives of sport stars change. The lack of conceptual depth of contributions in the Andrews and Jackson book means that they can only, at best, reaffirm or further illustrate theoretical points, whereas Whannel's argument generates theoretical developments and more fundamentally shifts our understanding of sport celebrity. It also comes closest to matching the kind of broad research agenda proposed by Marshall (1997) and Turner (2010) that stresses the multiple realms which need to be considered in the study of celebrity. It is perhaps for this reason that *Media Sport Stars*, rather than *Sports Stars*, is relatively influential in celebrity studies. This is particularly evident in Turner's (2004) work, and more implicitly in Cashmore's (2006), for while the latter does not cite Whannel, there are clear parallels between his focus on the increasingly conservative nature of the contemporary sports celebrity and Whannel's earlier analysis.

Finally, mention should be made of Barry Smart's (2005) *The Sport Star*. This book is unusual in that although it is solely dedicated to sport, it is authored by someone who is essentially a social theoretician, having published a range of texts on social theory and individual theorists such as Foucault, before developing work on consumer culture. Prior to this book – and indeed since – Smart has published little or nothing on sport. Yet the book makes the case for the cultural centrality of sport, arguing that 'sport represents one of the most significant remaining institutional sites for popular cultural recognition and acclaim of exceptional performance and prowess, if not the most prominent context in which the deeds of participants continue to retain authenticity' (2005: 9). Relying mainly on Rojek for theoretical guidance, he charts the development of sport (codification, origins, professionalization, commercialization, etc.) before presenting two case-study chapters – corporate culture and branding (which focuses mainly on Woods and Jordan) and cultures of sport stardom (mainly Beckham and Kournikova). His engagement with the sociology of sport literature is thorough but his main conclusions – that the commercialization of sports has helped to make sports celebrities and that corporations are attracted to sports celebrities because (through performance, or achieved celebrity) they have authenticity – does not advance our understanding much beyond Andrews and Jackson's (2001b) work. In further arguing that athletes' relationships with corporate bodies threaten their very authenticity and thus, paradoxically, celebrity status, Smart effectively concurs with Andrews's (1996a) earlier analysis of Michael Jordan's career trajectory.

These three books have formed the foundations on which the study of sporting celebrity has blossomed. Notable examples include Theresa Walton's analysis of American runner Steve Prefontaine in which she argues that Nike's posthumous use of his celebrity image 'provides relief for the dual cultural crises of masculinity and Whiteness in the sport arena' (2004: 73). The transformation of his image 'from working class rebel with a cause … to a commodified hero' (Walton 2004: 80), she argues, both benefits Nike and supports late capitalist consumer culture. Markovitz (2006) has discussed how the rape case involving American basketball player Kobe Bryant was influenced by social memories of racist/anti-racist discourses of racist violence and feminist discourses of sexist injustice. Bairner's (2004) work cites George Best as British football's first media sports star and emphasizes the player's ability to unite people (or Manchester United supporters at least) across Northern Ireland's sectarian divide, while Nalapat and Parker offer Indian cricketer Sachin Tendulkar as a counter to the 'geographical and cultural myopia' (2005: 434) of the analysis of sports celebrity, arguing that Tendulkar's celebrity status is underpinned by his ability to be 'all things to all people' and thus satisfy a range of political, religious and nationalistic viewpoints. Harris and Clayton discuss the relationship between Welsh rugby player Gavin Henson and issues of masculinity and conclude that 'Henson remains a highly visible representation of the transgression of hegemonic masculinity and the continual, dialectic process of (re)defining of gender identities' (2007a: 161). Falcous and Silk's (2006) analysis of Muslim-Australian Aboriginal boxer Anthony Mundine, and Burdsey's (2007b) analysis of the British-Muslim boxer Amir Khan both focus on post-9/11 representations of Muslims in sport. All of these texts, however, essentially examine the celebrity as a text, as a signifier of meaning. Moreover, they revolve around the same few discourses – race, nationalism and gender identities – and make reference to those bodies of literature rather than studies of celebrity culture. For this reason, Chung's (2003) work comparing Korean sport and pop stars advances our understanding rather further as it illuminates the particular characteristics of the sport celebrity genre. Similarly, Melnick and Jackson's (2002) analysis of the attitudes of New Zealand youths towards American athletes addresses the global reach of celebrities and contributes to our limited understanding of the effects of celebrity representation on public consciousness. Finally, Darnell and Sparks's (2005) research on Canadian triathlete Simon Whitfield, and in particular their interview data with journalists about the processes behind his rise to celebrity status in Canada following his gold medal at the Sydney Olympics, forwards knowledge of the economic networks that make up the celebrity industry. Through these latter texts in particular sociologists of sport have begun to address the kind of expanded agenda for celebrity studies for which celebrity studies writers have called.

Beckham studies

Studies of David Beckham merit special attention. Unlike the other sports celebrities discussed (Jordan is an exception to this), Beckham's celebrity phenomenon has been addressed by a number of writers. Beckham, moreover, has drawn the attention of those both within and outside the sociology of sport subdiscipline. Prominent here is Cashmore's (2002) book-length study in which he argues that Beckham's rise to celebrity status owes much to the specific time and space in which he arose. Relevant factors include the growing power of players (augmented by their agents) relative to clubs, the increasing dominance of the elite clubs within English football which led to the formation of the Premier League, the parallel development of satellite television in England and the increased competition for football broadcasting rights, the increased competition between newspapers (and tabloids in particular), which expanded their coverage of sport, and broader processes interlinking consumer culture and sport. Beckham emerged at a time when mediated football was becoming increasingly culturally central in England, when English (club) football was becoming globally ascendant and during something of a 'celebrity vacuum' in the UK following the death of Princess Diana, at a time of heightened demand for the creation of new 'para-social relations'. However, it was Beckham, rather than other footballers, who emerged in this context because he played for England's most successful club and international football's biggest 'brand', Manchester United, married pop star and former Spice Girl Victoria Adams, which afforded him access to a sophisticated network of public-relations advisers, and formed a relationship with Adidas that facilitated his sporting career including, subsequently, enabling his move to Real Madrid.

In collaboration with Andrew Parker, Cashmore has also written about Beckham's relationship to discourses of masculinity (Cashmore and Parker 2003). Citing various aspects of his media coverage – focus on his looks, his interest in fashion and cosmetics, his football talent, his acceptance of his appeal as a gay icon, his supposed subservience to wife Victoria and an ability to rise above sexual inferences, his decision to miss football training to spend time with his sick child – Cashmore and Parker argue that Beckham is in many ways the antithesis of traditional values of football and working-class masculinity. Rather, his celebrity is based on 'a version of masculinity that contradicts, confuses, and conflates all in one' (Cashmore and Parker 2003: 225). Whannel (2001, 2002) uses Beckham, and in particular the Beckham wedding, to illustrate his concept of vortextuality and concludes that Beckham is the epitome of a postmodern celebrity. He 'appears rootless: he can be dressed in anything because surface appearance is all'. He is a 'post-"new lad" man' (Whannel 2002: 212). Harris and Clayton (2007b) have also examined how the representation of Beckham relates to masculinity discourses, but specifically the discourse of masculinity and English national identity. In addition to this is the work of Momin Rahman (2004), who writes from a gender and sexuality studies background. Rahman examines the degree to which the representation of Beckham signifies a shift in masculinity discourse and concludes that 'traditional cultural hegemonic forms of masculinity are transforming' but that this is not necessarily indicative of 'a significant or completed shift in the social gender order' (2004: 230).

There are relatively few substantive differences between these authors: the analyses based in the sociology of sport are indistinct from those informed by other subdisciplinary backgrounds. However, studies of Beckham show other interesting features of inter-subdisciplinary relations. Rahman cites Cashmore's book on Beckham but is apparently unaware of (or chooses to ignore) his work (with Parker) on Beckham and masculinity, or the work of Whannel. Peculiarly, Rahman's analysis is based on a reading of lifestyle magazines and an explicit exclusion of sport-related coverage of Beckham, an approach which seems to deliberately extract the celebrity from his broader context. There is clearly a disdain for, or ignorance of, sport and sport-related scholarship. Conversely, Harris and Clayton cite Whannel and Cashmore and Parker but seem unaware of Rahman's work. The literature on Beckham therefore shows that while the analysis in these two academic worlds is similar, their integration and mutual recognition is relatively poor.

Conclusion

In reviewing this work, it can be seen that celebrity studies has had a significant impact upon the sociology of sport. This impact is clearer in relation to inspiring particular case studies than it is in terms of theoretical development. Inasmuch as the subdiscipline has been dominated by discrete investigations of individual sport celebrities, knowledge advances have been limited, and generally lacking broader resonance. What broader applicability they do have feeds back into the sociology of sport – understandings, for example, of sport and race, sport and gender, sport and nationalism – rather than into the parent discipline or parallel subdisciplines (celebrity studies, gender studies, etc.). Few sociologists of sport (if you exclude Cashmore and Rojek from this category) have attempted to embrace a broader agenda of celebrity studies, and relatively few demonstrate an awareness of the broader literature in the field.

It can also be concluded that, probably as a consequence of the degree of public exposure athletes experience and thus the compelling case they make for analysis, sport has had an unusually high impact on celebrity studies. Yet one might question whether the impact that sport has had has reached its full potential. My comments above would suggest that, in part, work within the sociology of sport has not lent itself to broader engagement. Yet it is also the case, I think, that traditional prejudices about sport as an area of academic study have affected the degree of interpenetration. The disregard of the historical emergence of sports celebrities is one example. The lack of dialogue between sport and non-sport specialists in relation to Beckham is another. Ironically, given that the area of celebrity studies is underpinned by the explicit belief that evaluations of the worth of particular cultural activities should not lead us to eschew their investigation or to underestimate their social significance, there is evidence to suggest that sport has been viewed either as an area of marginal academic interest, or as an area which can be ignored.

What we find within celebrity studies then is a curious juxtaposition that returns us to definitional debates in the field. While the sociological neglect of sport more generally is often a product of perceptions of its lack of cultural value – not the 'serious' stuff of life, the antithesis of work – there is reason to suggest that one rationale for sport's neglect in celebrity studies is because the cultural value of sporting celebrities actually 'elevates' them above the 'talentless' individuals who otherwise dominate contemporary celebrity culture. As noted, Rojek largely considers sports celebrities to be examples of 'achieved celebrity'. In introducing Cole and Andrews's (2001) work on Tiger Woods, Marshall (2006: 11) comments that 'Sport is perhaps the transitional cultural activity in its mediated form that moves between the idea of the hero and the celebrity.' Smart's work is based on the premise that athletes are distinct as a group of celebrities in that their status is underpinned by authenticity. Turner largely accepts these claims for the distinctiveness of sport – referring to the 'sports star celebrity' (2004: 18) – before concluding that of greater importance is the similarity of 'mass mediated processes of celebritisation' (2004: 19) which work across genres. Ironically, given his previous research interests, only Cashmore amongst these authors replicates traditional views about the low cultural worth of sport, endorsing the view of Len Shearman who claimed that 'We have forsaken our traditional heroes and replaced them with actors and athletes … where we once admired people who do great things, now we admire people who play people who do great things' (Shearman 1992, cited in Cashmore 2006: 50). Empirically, the only sport celebrity who has so far been the subject of sustained analysis, and whose 'talent' and achievements have been questioned, is the former Russian tennis player Anna Kournikova (Harris and Clayton 2002; Smart 2005). The only athlete described as being 'as known for his well-knownness as for any concrete sporting achievement' (Andrews and Jackson 2001a: 13) is David Beckham. Most tellingly, the titles of all three books devoted to the study of sport and celebrity prioritize the word 'star', an implicit recognition of the discomfort caused by equating athletes with the more fleeting or mundane characters in celebrity culture.

Perhaps then there is something distinct about sport. Perhaps sportspeople cannot be fully integrated into celebrity studies. But this is not to say that an understanding of sports stars is irrelevant to the broader field. Indeed, in developing a more detailed understanding of why celebrities have become increasingly prominent in contemporary societies, an understanding of their closest competitor for media exposure is clearly desirable. There is, I think, a compelling case that the study of athletes has a potential to add to our broader understanding of celebrity which, as yet, has only partially been fulfilled.

Part III
The *external* impact of the sociology of sport

8

SOCIOLOGY OF SPORT AND SPORTS HISTORY[1]

In the remaining chapters the focus moves beyond the discipline of sociology and examines the impact of the sociology of sport further afield. Among the various sports-related subdisciplines, sociologists of sport most closely align to, and interact with, sports historians. Increasingly sports historians and sociologists of sport have come to have 'complementary scholarly interests' (as the BSASSG calls them), not only in terms of overlapping subject matter but also in terms of analytical approach. This chapter outlines some of the key aspects of the relationship between these two subdisciplines. After setting out the intellectual grounds for the disciplinary overlap, the chapter assesses the contribution sociologists have made to the historical understanding of sport. I then argue that there have been two distinct ways in which these sociological incursions have been received by sports historians. The chapter concludes with an assessment of the impact sociology, and the sociology of sport in particular, has had on sports history, arguing that the organizational weaknesses of, and crises within, the latter have enabled sociology to be the dominant partner in the relationship.

Sociology, history and historical sociology

It is perhaps not surprising that sports history should be the subdiscipline most closely aligned to the sociology of sport for the intellectual distinction between the two has long been disputed. The common-sense distinction between sociology and history is temporal: the former is focused on the present, while the latter is concerned with the past. Logically, of course, this does not bear scrutiny for the evidence upon which all those working in the humanities and social sciences draw is fixed in time, and thus located in the past. Some historians extend their historical analyses up to the present day. In relation to sport the time-oriented distinction between history and sociology has been most explicitly blurred by the publication of *Sport in Britain, 1945–2000* authored by two leading sports historians (Holt and Mason 2000) and by a book, *Sport Histories,* edited by three sociologists (Dunning *et al.* 2004a).

A further similarity between history and sociology lies in the mode of analysis, for there is a high degree of consensus, both within and between the subdisciplines, on the desirability of contextualization. Coakley (2007: 4) argues that, 'sociology helps us examine social life *in context.*' In *Sport, Culture and Society,* Jarvie argues that 'sport must be properly located within the social, cultural and historical context in which it moves or is located' (Jarvie 2006: 61). Douglas Booth (2005: 11) similarly argues that sports historians can broadly be categorized as re-constructionists (those who believe they can examine the past as it actually was), constructionists (those who believe evidence needs to be interpreted using penetrating questions like how and why) and deconstructionists (those who reflect on a past they see as fragmented and partial). He suggests that the constructionist approach generally holds sway and thus 'nothing is more fundamental in the lexicon and methodology of history than context' (Booth 2005: 18). Martin Polley (2007: 8–9) proposes an alternative past-narrative-analysis tripartite framework for categorizing sports history (and encompasses Booth's constructionists and deconstructionists):

1 *past*: the evidence of events involving people in the past;
2 *narrative*: the use of that evidence to tell a story;
3 *analysis*: examining sport in its 'full cultural context' relative to the society in which it took place.

Polley argues that this is the approach with which 'academic historians would feel most comfortable' (2007: 8). Thus, despite differences, the broad analytical aims and temporal focus of history and sociology can appear indistinct.

Consequently, there is much merit in the argument that the distinction between sociology and history can be too sharply drawn. Both sports historians and sociologists of sport have spoken of the need to reject the uncritical acceptance of common-sense understandings and destroy sporting myths. Consequently, the historical sociologist Philip Abrams has argued that, 'there can be no relationship between [sociology and history] because in terms of their fundamental pre-occupations, history and sociology are and always have been the same thing' (1982: x). In a similar vein, though with the notable caveat of specifying particular types of history and sociology, the historian Peter Burke has advocated that the distinction between social history and historical sociology should become irrelevant (1980). Dutch sociologist Johan Goudsblom has similarly observed, 'the divorce of history and sociology is detrimental to both: it makes historians needlessly allergic to the very idea of structures, and sociologists afraid of dealing with single events' (1977: 136).

Yet (sub)disciplines are socially rather than logically constructed, and the sociology of sport and sports history clearly exist as distinctive areas of study. The most obvious manifestation of difference is the existence of distinct professional associations. Just like the sociology of sport, sports history has national, continental and international organizing bodies. Before looking at how the origins and composition of these organizations enable and constrain sports historians in their relations with sociologists of sport, it is important to assess the impact sociologists have had on our understanding of the history of sport.

Sociological contributions to sports history

From the outset, sociologists of sport produced work which was historically oriented. This literature is now substantial and thus this review will be necessarily selective. The theoretical framework employed constitutes my basis for organizing these contributions. Three main sociological approaches to historical research can be identified:

1 figurational sociology;
2 Marxism;
3 feminism.

What contribution did sociologists make to the historical understanding of sport, and how were these cross-disciplinary 'incursions' received?

The first, perhaps the most significant and ultimately the most controversial contributions have came from figurational sociologists. Dunning and Sheard's *Barbarians, Gentlemen and Players* (1979) is a key text here (see Chapter 3 for a discussion), though prior to this both Dunning and his mentor Elias had already published work on the development of football (e.g., Dunning 1963; Elias and Dunning 1971), and the development of sport in Ancient Greece and Rome (Elias 1971). Other significant contributions by figurational sociologists include research on the historical development of football hooliganism and Jarvie's work on the development of sport in Scotland. The figurational sociologists of the 'Leicester School' enjoyed 'hegemony in football sociology' in the late 1980s (Giulianotti 1999: 44), and a central motif of this approach was the detailed empirical research published in *The Roots of Football Hooliganism* (Dunning *et al.* 1988). The text illustrated the historical variability of the phenomenon and the reactions to it from sports organizations, the media and state officials. Though rarely explicitly figurational, Jarvie's *Highland Games* (1991b) was the product of a doctoral study supervised by Dunning and bears many of the organizational hallmarks of *Barbarians, Gentlemen and Players*, identifying four stages or phases of development of Highland Games that parallel broader social structural transformations in Scotland. The study highlights Scotland's dependency on England, the uneven development of the British Isles and how the development of Scottish national identity has been heavily dependent upon the English dominated British state. Indicative of the strength of the commitment of figurational sociologists to historical study, Dunning *et al.* (2004b: 199) have argued that compared to 'any other identifiable theoretical framework within the sociology of sport, figurational sociology has facilitated a more consistent and thoroughgoing developmental approach.'

While perhaps attracting more criticism from sports historians than that of any other group of sociologists, this work has also attracted considerable praise. Mangan, for instance, describes *Barbarians, Gentlemen and Players* as an 'innovative', 'irradiant' and 'pioneering' work (2005: vii), while Collins argues that *Barbarians, Gentlemen and Players* 'helped to establish the history of sport as a serious and scholarly activity' (2005: 289). Holt further describes *Barbarians, Gentlemen and Players* as 'probably the most detailed and important contribution to the discussion of British amateurism' (1992/2003: 274), and Polley (2003: 57) notes that Dunning and Sheard's schema distinguishing modern sports from their folk antecedents, 'has been very influential in all British sports historiography' providing 'for a decade … the orthodox description of the dramatic changes that occurred in sport during the nineteenth century'. Elsewhere, Polley suggests that both *Barbarians, Gentlemen and Players* and *The Roots of Football Hooliganism* were 'seminal … in linking sociology and history' (2007: 47). Jarvie is similarly praised as exemplifying how figurational sociologists can 'work comfortably in both history and sociology camps' (Polley 2003: 60). Though little influenced by figurational sociology, Jarvie and Walker's (1994) *Scottish Sport and the Making of the Nation* has been described as 'one of the most imaginative of recent studies of British sport' (Hill 1996: 16), important in stimulating historical research into the connections between ideologies (specifically national identities) and historical processes (Struna 2000).

The second group of writers can be categorized together under the broad theoretical umbrella of Marxism/neo-Marxism/cultural studies. This category includes the works of Rick Gruneau (1983/1999), John Hargreaves (1986), John Sugden and Alan Bairner (1993), and John Sugden and Alan Tomlinson (1998).

Gruneau (1983/1999) provides an account of the emergence and development of sports in Western capitalist societies which emphasizes problems of 'class inequality and domination' (Gruneau 1983/1999: 16). Canadian leisure reflected class differences, and Gruneau's research illustrates the different capacities of social classes to structure the organization and meanings of sports; where aristocratic ideals and developing bourgeois values of disciplined enjoyment of colonial games flourished, the 'undisciplined' play practices of the working classes were crushed. Amateurism was a 'regulative strategy' serving to reinforce the dominance of the ruling classes (Gruneau 1983/1999: 134), and entrepreneurial capitalism provided a foundation for the emergence of commercial sport. While state programmes for sport reflected the interests of middle-class volunteers, commercial entrepreneurs and state bureaucrats, there is evidence of resistance with a growing number of opportunities for increasingly diverse groups of people to play a greater range of sports. Holt compliments Gruneau's synthesis of developmental case-study and 'highly sophisticated theoretical discussion' (1989: 363), while Pope refers to Gruneau's text as 'the key work' that 'inspired a new generation of sport historians to analyze their subject as a medium of class, gender, racial domination, and resistance' (1998: ii).

John Hargreaves's *Sport, Power and Culture* similarly focuses on class inequality and domination, and, more specifically, the concept of hegemony as a means by which to understand how sport served as a site for 'accommodating' the British working class into the dominant social order (1986: 2). Hargreaves argues that, during the nineteenth century, popular sports forms founded upon traditional values of community and kinship, catharsis and entertainment, were replaced by sports based on bourgeois ideals of discipline, sobriety, self-reliance and hygienic/therapeutic technologies.

Sport was used as a tool for educating and disciplining the masses. Through education, religion and youth and community groups (e.g., the YMCA and Boy Scouts), attempts were made to incorporate the working class into the bourgeois model of social life. Hence Hargreaves argues that bourgeois hegemony emerged and developed through twin processes – *re-composition* and *accommodation* of the working class – and that sport was an important tool through which this was achieved. Despite a number of reservations about the work, Holt describes this book as 'the first general history of modern British sport' (1998: 21). Jeff Hill more enthusiastically describes *Sport, Power and Culture* as 'the most systematic attempt to place the development of sport in a *theoretical* perspective' (1996: 6; emphasis in original).

Sugden and Bairner's *Sport, Sectarianism and Society in a Divided Ireland* (1993) was so well received by sports historians that the British Society of Sports History (BSSH) awarded it the inaugural Lord Aberdare Literary Prize for Sports History. In what the authors describe as a political sociology of sport, Sugden and Bairner illustrate how sport, rather than being divorced from politics, is particularly susceptible to political manipulation, not only reflecting but also helping to sustain broader social conflicts. Thus, aspects of civil society (such as sport) cannot simply or automatically be mobilized by the state for its own ends. Ironically, the state's facilitation of sports participation actually fuels the sectarian differences which in turn threaten to undermine the state. Finally, mention should be made of Sugden and Tomlinson's *FIFA and the Contest for World Football* (1998). The content of this book is discussed at greater length in Chapter 9, but for present purposes it is enough to note that the authors argue for a 'critical interpretive framework' for researching sport which places particular emphasis on what is referred to as the 'dynamic historical dimension' of sport.

The third group of sociologists to have exerted a significant influence on sports history have been feminists. Though Struna (2000: 193) identifies the work of M. Ann Hall and Nancy Theberge as significant in this regard (see Chapter 5 for a discussion of their work), of greatest significance is Jennifer Hargreaves's *Sporting Females* (1994). Combining the concept of hegemony with a feminist sensibility, Hargreaves illustrates that from the late nineteenth to the middle of the twentieth century women's sports reflected and reinforced popular views about women as physically inferior to men. An ideology of the natural weakness of women pervaded the principles and practices of physical education, exercise and sport for females in Great Britain during the period. In spite of such narrow definitions of femininity, some women, most often middle-class ladies, experienced new forms of corporeal freedom through active participation in sports such as tennis and croquet and in physical activities such as medical gymnastics. Yet female emancipation through sport existed at the same time as persistent opposition. Hargreaves further explores the gendered history of the Olympic Games and examines contemporary gender relations and sporting masculinities and femininities. Notwithstanding the enduring legacies of nineteenth-century versions of femininity, since the middle of the twentieth century processes of contestation and change have resulted in increasing opportunities for female participation in a range of sporting activities and a degree of diversity in what counts as 'acceptable' in terms of female appearance, behaviour and emotion.

In 1994, reflecting on a decade that had witnessed the 'burgeoning' of scholarship on sports history and gender relations (Vertinsky 1994: 23), Patricia Vertinsky highlighted Hargreaves as one of the feminist social scientists whose voice was a significant catalyst to this development (1994: 10). (See also Struna 2000: 193.) In 1998, Holt described the book as 'a new and important synthesis' (1998: 13), and Alan Metcalfe (1998) argued that *Sporting Females* was British sports history's 'first real attempt to deal with the whole question of gender'. While Jeff Hill identified *Sporting Females* as a stark illustration of 'the importance of theory' (1996: 13), Polley simply described it as 'seminal' (2003: 60).

Sports historians' critical reception of sociological research

While I have so far highlighted instances where historians have praised the historical work of sociologists of sport, this research has been neither universally nor unequivocally embraced. In this section I want to argue that there have been two distinct ways in which sports historians have critically received sociological work: an initial approach that stressed the distinctiveness of the disciplines in terms of the role of theory and a second phase during which historians have focused on questions of empirical 'fact' and the interpretation of evidence. The change in the nature of these critiques indicates a convergence of the subdisciplines in recent years.

Traditionally, a key distinction between sociology and history has been identified in relation to the role of theory. As Richard Holt notes, 'Sociologists frequently complain that historians lack a conceptual framework for their research, whilst historians tend to feel social theorists require them to compress the diversity of the past into artificially rigid categories and dispense with empirical verification of their theories' (1989: 357).

To a degree, as Mansfield and Malcolm (2010) have argued, the distinction identified by Holt is based on stereotype, for the respective criticisms (and indeed the basis on which historians and sociologists commend work in their own discipline) are not reserved for those in the opposing discipline (see, for instance, Ingham's [1979] criticisms of sociologists and Guttmann's [2008] assessment of historians' criticisms of his work). However, it was on this basis that, at the end of the 1980s, historians started to query the value of sociological interpretations of the past. It may be that this stemmed from the relative maturing of the subdisciplines – that their relative strengths pushed them apart – but perhaps also significant was the political crisis over football hooliganism in the UK, for it was in this context that debates were initially raised, as historians expanded their analysis to include the contemporary sporting scene. Notable in this regard were Mason's *Sport in Britain* (1988) and Holt's *Sport and the British* (1989). Both texts included 'forays' into territory traditionally seen as the preserve of the sociologist and therefore behoved these historians to address competing explanations. Both – Mason implicitly (1988: 69) and Holt explicitly (1989: 357) – acknowledged the interdependence of history and sociology and the desirability of cross-fertilization, but the critiques they posted largely had the effect of asserting the superiority of sports history, and thus that subdiscipline's independence.

Mason addressed two sociological works, Thorstein Veblen's *The Theory of the Leisure Class* (1899) and Bero Rigauer's *Sport und Arbeit* (1969). He provides only a tacit critique of Veblen, citing the 'lively workers' sports movement in Europe ... before the First World War' (Mason 1988: 71) as a counter to Veblen's orientation towards the elite. He treats Rigauer more harshly, arguing that the 'rigidity of Rigauer's theory ... eventually undermines it' (Mason 1988: 75) and suggests that Rigauer fails to account for the scope for human agency, the role of sport as a vehicle for resistance to domination and the incongruity between the supposed exploitative nature of sport under capitalism and the greater propensity of the bourgeoisie to participate in such activities. Mason consequently damns (sociological) theorizing about sport with faint praise, dismissing it as 'a worthwhile exercise if for no other reason than that it compels at least some of those heavily involved in sport to look closely at the assumptions which they make about it', before proceeding to a 'much more concrete' and, by implication, more adequate level of analysis (1988: 77).

Horne *et al.* (1999: 75) have countered Mason's critique with some hostility. They argue that elsewhere Mason has 'referred somewhat condescendingly' to sociological theorization of contemporary trends, has reduced the sociologist to 'a figure of fun, a naïve gossip' and, in failing to acknowledge his own reliance on such theories, produces a 'bogus' and 'disingenuous' critique. Further criticism could be made of Mason's selection of theories to review. First, one could argue that in overlooking the aforementioned texts which have had a greater impact on sports history he has been selective in his choice of evidence. It seems somewhat obtuse to focus on Veblen's work about late-nineteenth-century American society in a book titled *Sport in Britain*. Second, Mason fails to acknowledge the (then) recent publication of critiques of Rigauer's work by leading British sociologists of sport (Hargreaves 1986; Dunning 1986c) which highlight similar deficiencies. He thus unfairly represents sociological theories of sport by constructing a 'straw man'.

Unlike Mason, Holt embraces various sociological analyses of sport and especially those which are historically oriented. More importantly Holt's discussion differs in the extent of its praise of sociology. He states that within sociological theory 'there are some good things to be found' (Holt 1989: 357–8), and that 'theoretical formulations have served mainly to make explicit a concept [class relations] of which historians were already implicitly aware' (1989: 365). He also identifies a 'convergence' between his own work and the classic problems in the sociology of the city and further stresses that historians should recognize that their selection of research themes rests on 'hard to pin down', 'more or less shrewd "hunches"' (Holt 1989: 358). Historians, he concludes, should acknowledge that 'smuggled into any general interpretation there will be ... a fair degree of subjectivity in the choice of organizing ideas' (Holt 1989: 367), and he is critical of the 'tendency for some historians' to want to apply sociological concepts uncritically and reject them when this becomes problematic (1989: 358).

Despite such positive comments, Holt remains critical of sociology, in particular the use of obscure terminology, the 'theoretical neatness' of John Hargreaves's work (in particular) which 'leads to problems when dealing with the complex historical reality' (1989: 363) and what he sees as the pitfalls of the use of Gramsci's concept of hegemony. While not wishing to embrace Holt's critique in its entirety, it is interesting to note that since he wrote this piece the sociology of sport has developed in such a way as to embrace many of the areas Holt identified as lacking. In retrospect, Holt's comments regarding the importance of sexual identity (and masculinity), local and regional identities and the role of sport as a source of sociability (c.f. Bourdieu) seem particularly prescient, for such themes have become increasingly prominent in both sports history and the sociology of sport in recent years. There is no doubt that Holt remains committed to a position that extols the merits of history relative to sociology because of the latter's tendency to make unsubstantiated 'assertions' (1989: 358), its use of theory to produce a 'blanket "explanation"' (1989: 364) and its production of '"one-dimensional" [interpretations], lacking context' (1989: 361), but there is a relatively healthy respect for sociological concepts and a belief that a dialogue is productive for sports historians. Maguire recognizes this 'laudable' call for dialogue, regretting only that such comments are 'tucked away in an appendix' (1995: 6).

In contrast to earlier debates about the role of theory, more recent debates between sociologists and sports historians have focused upon more detailed examinations of 'empirical fact' and their interpretation in light of the broader historical context. Critiques of this kind include Reid's (1988) 'Folk Football, the Aristocracy, and Cultural Change', Lewis's (1996) critique of the 'Leicester School's' developmental analysis of football hooliganism and a collection of critiques in the last decade of the work of Dunning *et al.* (Goulstone 2000; Harvey 2001, 2002, 2004; Collins 2005) and Malcolm (Vamplew 2007).

Reid (1988) argues that there is little evidence to support Dunning and Sheard's (1979) contention that the aristocracy withdrew from folk football and became more status-exclusive in the late eighteenth and early nineteenth centuries, thus precipitating the emergence of 'new' sport forms. Lewis argued that football crowd disorder in nineteenth-century Lancashire was far more significantly related to gambling than previously believed and that, allied to other temporal differences to crowd disorder, this undermined what he terms Dunning *et al.*'s 'continuity thesis' of spectator violence. Goulstone argues that Dunning and Sheard's 'public school status-rivalry' thesis is undermined by new historical evidence which showed that:

- modern notions of equality in football stemmed from working-class forms of the game, in which gambling was a central component; and
- the bifurcation of football codes could be seen in folk forms of football that predate codification in the public schools.

Harvey similarly critiqued the 'public school status-rivalry' thesis, providing historical data regarding 'modern forms' of football played in the Sheffield area in the nineteenth century, which developed independently of the public schools. Collins suggests:

- that Dunning and Sheard overstate the originality of their work in relation to the Webb Ellis myth;
- that civic rivalries rather than public-school rivalries drove the bifurcation of football and rugby;

- that Dunning and Sheard falsely depict rugby as being viewed as more violent than football at the end of the nineteenth century;
- that the use of the theory of civilizing processes (in Dunning *et al.*'s work on football and rugby but also in Malcolm [2004] and Sheard's [2004] work on cricket and boxing respectively), leads to teleological historical analyses.

Finally, Vamplew argues that Malcolm's work on cricket (1999, 2002, 2004), especially that relating to the theory of civilizing processes, is flawed by the use of 'unchecked' secondary sources which lead to misinterpretation and factual error, and because there are limited empirical examples to support the argument.

To a greater or lesser extent, each of these critiques has been responded to (Murphy *et al.* 1998; Dunning 2001; Dunning and Curry 2002; Curry *et al.* 2006; Malcolm 2008). There is insufficient space here to provide an assessment of the various strengths and weaknesses of these positions. Rather, for present purposes, what is more interesting about these debates is the emergence of common themes. Goulstone, Harvey, Collins and Vamplew all suggest that there are areas where these sociologists make assertions which are not backed up by evidence. Collins, Harvey and Vamplew question the sources used, suggest that their opponents have misrepresented evidence, undertaken a selective reading of evidence or ignored contrary evidence. Collins points to Dunning and Sheard's 'failure to understand the importance of context in examining historical events' (2005: 296). Most interesting of all perhaps is that all these critiques relate to the work of figurational sociologists who, as noted above, claim to have had a more significant impact on sports history than any other group of sociologists.

The counter-critiques also share similar themes. All the historians are accused of the inaccurate representation of the work they are critiquing. Lewis in particular is singled out for ignoring some of the evidence used in the original argument and for overlooking the use of cautionary, conditioning and relativistic wording (Murphy *et al.* 1998). Curry *et al.* similarly accuse Collins of putting words into their mouths (2006: 114), while Dunning argues that the 'misrepresentation' in Harvey's work undermines one's confidence in his scholarship (Dunning 2001: 90). Malcolm (2008) suggests that Vamplew ignores the most significant parts of his argument relating to rule changes and is unable to illustrate that Malcolm's use of secondary sources leads to incorrect conclusions. Lewis, Harvey and Collins respectively are criticized for overstating evidence, overstating the originality of their argument and failing to acknowledge the originality of the work that they are critiquing. Reid and Lewis are accused of presenting as their own arguments, those which are almost identical to the original being critiqued. All are accused of using limited or problematic sources and of factual inaccuracies. The key difference between historians' critiques and sociologists' counter-critiques is that the latter often complain that their adversaries have failed to fully understand their broader theoretical perspective. A key similarity is that the sociologists counter-accuse the historians of failing to understand and take account of the context in which their primary evidence was generated.

One of the most interesting features of historians' critical reception of sociological work, therefore, is that whereas in the late 1980s historians and sociologists of sport essentially argued from divergent positions, more recent debates contain a commonly accepted core premise: *pace* Booth and Polley and Coakley and Jarvie, the need to analyse sport in its wider cultural context. The existence of such common ground in these critical dialogues is indicative of a significant degree of (sub)disciplinary convergence. This in turn throws into sharper relief the more recent phase of criticism. Are the divisions as deep as they previously were, or is there something about the historical work of figurational sociologists which is radically different from that which other sociologists, and (some) other historians produce? Is it possible to construct a sociological argument that explains why figurational sociologists have come to form the central focus of tension between sports history and the sociology of sport? In the final section of this chapter I attempt to explain why sports historians' critiques of sociologists' research has changed in character and why it is that in the context of convergence between the subdisciplines there remains a deep division focused upon one theoretical perspective.

The impact of the sociology of sport on sports history

The convergence of the sociology of sport and sports history in recent years can be illustrated by the tangible impact of the former on the latter and the reliance on the latter by most exponents of the former. In addition to historians' praise for historically oriented sociological work, and the changing nature of cross-disciplinary critiques, historians have become increasingly explicit about their debt to sociology, and social theory in particular. Guttmann (1984: 6), for instance, has written, 'I do not think I could have written *From Ritual to Record* if I had not been excited, provoked, fascinated, and annoyed by European theorists.' Hill cites the influence of Barthes, Bourdieu, Derrida, Baudrillard, Geertz (an anthropologist) and Gramsci in his work (2002: 2–3), and Johnes has acknowledged his own debt to postmodernism, and the influence of Gramsci more generally within sports history (2004: 150). A further indication is the emergence in recent years of texts jointly edited by historians and sociologists. In addition to the aforementioned *Scottish Sport and the Making of the Nation* (Jarvie and Walker 1994), we might cite Brian Stoddart and Hilary Beckles's *Liberation Cricket* (1995) and Jennifer Hargreaves and Patricia Vertinsky's *Physical Culture, Power and the Body* (2007b). But perhaps the most significant marker of this impact is the way in which historians who produce overviews of the field (see for instance Struna 2000; Polley 2003) are reluctant to distinguish between research stemming from the respective subdisciplines. Nancy Struna, for instance, includes Jarvie in a list of works containing leading sports historians Tony Mangan, William Baker, Richard Holt and Chuck Korr (2000: 196). Polley (2007: 69) simply cites John Hargreaves' work as an example of a historian 'working within the traditions of Marxism and history from below'. Illustrative of the 'openness' of history in this respect, Ross McKibbin even refers to geographer John Bale as a 'pioneer' of sports history (2002: 192). While Holt notes that 'sports history partly grew out of a new social history fed by the boom in sociology' (1998: 11), the impact of sociologists on sports history has not only been significant, to a large degree it has become normalized within the subdiscipline.

An appreciation of the development of sports history helps to illuminate why this has been the case. The long tradition of writing sports history includes many people whom Tony Mason has called 'fans with typewriters' (cited in Hill 1996: 2). Many were 'amateur enthusiasts', following a '"chronicle and numbers" approach' (Vamplew 2000: 179), accumulating 'facts and anecdotes unrelated to the larger historical framework' (Baker 1983: 53). Equally descriptive and limited in terms of the broader relevance of their work were those physical educators who developed an interest in the history of their profession, but failed to 'explain causes … [or pay] attention to theory' (Booth 1997: 195).

Both in North America and Britain physical educators played a significant role in establishing professional bodies for sports history. All the leading figures in the 1972 foundation of the North American Society for Sport History (NASSH) were employed in physical education departments, as indeed have been fifteen of the organization's first twenty presidents.[2] Similarly the BSSH, founded in 1982 by Richard Cox (himself essentially a physical educator), largely emerged out of the History of Physical Education Study Group of the History of Education Society (Cox 2000: 48). Yet physical educators did not want to work in isolation, and those who established the NASSH looked to the history 'mainstream' for collaborators (four of the last eleven NASSH presidents have come from outside physical education). For the BSSH, the interest of non-physical educators provided a significant catalyst, with Tony Mangan and Tony Mason elected as the organization's first two chairmen (followed by Richard Cox and Grant Jarvie). In his 1983 review of the state of British sports history, Baker could claim that

> the academy has come to see that the history of sport is far too important to be left in the hands of sportsmen and journalists *cum* amateur historians … British sport history now thrives as a self-conscious discipline attuned to economic causation, to class distinction and conflicts, to the masses as well as the elites, to cultural continuity and change.
>
> *(1983: 54)*

The last of the major national organizations to emerge, the Australian Society for Sports History (ASSH), appointed a political scientist (Colin Tatz) as its first president in 1983.

In 2004, Martin Johnes noted that, in contrast to an up-and-coming generation of academics who had sports history doctorates, 'the background of most sport historians, especially those over forty-years-of-age, working in UK universities is within the wider discipline of history' (2004: 146). Moreover, the awards that the professional bodies bestowed illustrated a belief that the work emanating from the 'mainstream' represented the highest standard. Only five of the eighteen NASSH Book Award winners have come from the physical education domain. Though more eclectic in its choice, up to 2007 the BSSH had awarded the Lord Aberdare Literary Prize for Sports History to six people in history departments compared to three in physical education departments. Other winners include Sugden and Bairner (see p. 121), Mike Marqusee (journalist and political activist) and John Bale (geographer).[3]

By the mid to late 1990s the cultural turn toward postmodernism was being seen as generating a crisis in the subdiscipline. Though Mangan argued for 'cautious optimism balanced by careful realism' (1999: 61), the more prominent argument was that the 'postmodern challenge' (Phillips 2001) could lead to 'an end to sports history as we know it' (Nauright 1999: 5). One effect of these debates was to highlight the differences between the 'old school' and 'new school', physical education and the 'mainstream' and the amateur and the academic sides of the subdiscipline, with, in each case, the latter identifying the former as the cause of sports history's weakness. Nauright, for example, argued that one of the core problems lay with the 'atheoretical, and sometimes un- or anti-intellectual' (1999: 6) aspects of sports history. Hill (1996: 14) argued that sports history in Britain had 'clung grimly to a methodological conservatism' and consequently exhibited two outstanding characteristics: empiricism and 'reflectivism' (defined as the tendency to view sport as merely reflecting other, more important, social issues). Various solutions were proposed. Steve Pope argued the sports-history community was too cosy and pointed towards the 'conspicuous reticence for thorough, searching review and evaluation' (1998: i). Hill (1996: 15–16) suggested that postmodern influences could be 'usefully embraced' and that the focus on 'meaning' and 'identity', 'could yield significant new insights for sports history'. Nauright (1999: 6) warned colleagues against closing ranks and treating sociological theory as a threat and argued that sports history needed to develop links with other sport-related disciplines in order to survive. Douglas Booth argued that in addition to 'a dose of intellectual rigour' sports history needed 'an injection of relevance' to broaden its appeal within the sports sciences (1997: 192).

This developmental trajectory explains not only why the sociology of sport has had such an influence on sports history but why some aspects of sociology and figurational sociology in particular continue to receive a hostile reception. While the influence of social history enabled sociological theory to penetrate sports history, sports historians' clamour for recognition from the broader discipline meant that they were relatively receptive to *particular types* of theory. As Holt concludes in his review of British and European sports history, 'the influence of social and cultural studies as pioneered by [E. P.] Thompson, [Raymond] Williams and [Richard] Hoggart is striking' (1998: 21). (Hill 1996: 6 makes a similar point.) Where Malcolmson (1973), who produced the seminal *Popular Recreations in English Society, 1700–1800*, was trained by Thompson, Cunningham's (1980) equally seminal *Leisure in the Industrial Revolution, c.1780–c.1880* both challenges and embraces Thompson's ideas (Baker 1983: 57). The focus, therefore, was on 'sport "from below"', an approach that sought to 'gain a perspective on working class culture and social relationships that could not be acquired by studying dominant national forms of sport' (Hill 1996: 3). The middle classes were subsequently 'overlooked … and still not fully understood' (Holt 1998: 11). This research theme was seen to 'fit' with the work of sociologists such as Gruneau and Hargreaves who used Marxism/neo-Marxism/cultural studies (Holt 1989: 365), for they also 'tended to despise middle class culture' (Holt 1998: 11–12). In sharp contrast, figurational sociologists have focused on the social elites who codified sports in their own style and for their own ends. Historian critics of figurational sociology often invoke evidence of sport 'from below'. This 'class conflict' is most explicit in the work of Tony Collins who claims that there is an 'inherent tendency to lay blame for violence at the door of those opposed to the dominant classes' (2005: 303). Part of the inspiration for (some) historians' critiques of figurational sociological research is an a priori commitment to the study of particular social classes.

From Thompson's 'explicit agenda of seeking to study minority groups and overlooked people' (Polley 2007: 45), it was a short step to a feminist epistemological position which 'confront(ed) the taken-for-granted notions of sport that are often inscribed in empirical accounts of sporting activity' (Hill 1996: 13). When Catriona Parratt (1998) 'proposed an agenda for a new scholarship in women's sports history which proceeded from women's experiences and which placed women at its center' (Vertinsky 1994: 10), she made an explicit call for the commonality of sex to be prioritized over disciplinary differences. The 'natural enemies' of feminist sports historians were not, therefore, sociologists, but researchers who exhibited a male bias.

This theoretical empathy towards class and gender may have 'blinded' sports historians to some of the weaknesses of the historical work of some sociologists and, in comparison, heightened awareness of their own differences with others. This can be seen in relation to the role of primary data, the de-centring of sport and ontology. Of those sociological texts reviewed in this chapter for their impact on sports history, *Barbarians, Gentlemen and Players* is the most directly amenable to that litmus test for (many) historians, archival research. It may be for this reason that, as Collins argues, there has been 'very little historical analysis or criticism of this book' (2005: 290). While Vamplew criticizes Malcolm's work for its reliance on secondary sources, the longer-standing and more influential works of John Hargreaves, Jennifer Hargreaves and indeed Rick Gruneau, though similarly reliant on secondary sources, have escaped such criticism. Vamplew's attempt to depict this methodology as characteristic of figurational sociology more generally is therefore problematic (Malcolm 2008). Ironically, figurational sociologists rather than historians have been critical of John Hargreaves's and Rick Gruneau's reliance on secondary sources, arguing that 'if one examines the work of hegemony theorists closely and searches for detailed historical analysis of the development of either particular sports or sports in general, then one looks in vain' (Dunning *et al.* 2004b: 199).

Second, sports historians have also expressed concern over the degree to which sports history has become like 'watching "Hamlet without the Prince" … [where] context becomes all and sport is seen only in terms of something outside of itself' (Holt 1998: 17; see also McKibbin 2002; Johnes 2004). While sports historians have not levelled this criticism at John Hargreaves, figurational sociologists have. Dunning *et al.* (2004b: 195) cite Hargreaves's 'failure to understand that a concern with the "rule and law of sports" is not simply a matter for the sports enthusiast but that it is also central to understanding the development of modern sports'. In contrast, figurational sociologists draw attention to Elias's (1986b) stress on the importance of investigating the specific manifestation of sports forms, rules and conventions and what they indicate about the intentions, interests and sensibilities of those who codified what became modern sports (see, e.g., Bloyce 2004).

Third, particularly in light of the postmodernist critique of history, sports historians have tended to overlook the ontological similarities between themselves and figurational sociologists. Figurational sociologists have posited the same kind of critique of the postmodern 'descent into discourse' (see, e.g., Dunning 2004) as some sports historians (e.g., Nauright 1999). Though doubtless reluctant to use such terms, sports historians are epistemologically much more closely aligned to the figurational position of 'involvement and detachment' than to postmodernist cultural relativism, and the empirical inclinations that dominate much of the 'mainstream' of sports history are closer to the figurational emphasis on the importance of gathering primary data (Maguire 1995: 4) than to the 'notion of history as a form of fictional literature' favoured by postmodernists (Phillips 2001: 331). In these three regards, therefore, there is a significant degree of overlap between figurational sociology and the now 'mainstream' sports history approaches.

It may be that personalities are a significant cause of the rift between figurational sociologists and sports historians, and it may also be that the controversial nature of Elias's theory of civilizing processes is a further source of tension. But if figurational sociologists correctly assess that their commitment to a historical approach and archival research is more sustained than other sociologists of sport, then a further reason for sports historians' critical reception of figurational sociology can be identified. Figurational sociologists have been at the forefront of arguments for the 'blending or fusion' of history and sociology (Dunning *et al.* 1993: 6; see also Maguire 1995: 3). This has stimulated something of a 'turf war', where sports historians have 'expressed resentment at being "preached at" by those who were seen to argue that "history was illegitimate unless sociologically driven"' (Rowe and Lawrence 1996: 14). In part this brings us back to the system of professions and the notion of the professional project discussed in Chapter 1. As the French historian Roger Chartier has argued, while the rift between history and sociology may often be 'formulated in terms of conceptual and methodological differences', it is also 'embodied in struggles for predominance, both between and inside the disciplines and in the intellectual sphere in general' (cited in Maguire 1995: 6). Thus, while the most recent sports historians' critiques of sociological work are more cross-theoretical than cross-disciplinary, the divisions might be as much a manifestation of the desire to reassert disciplinary boundaries and the relative independence of sports history as they are of intellectual differences.

Conclusion

The remit of this chapter has been to focus on the impact of the sociology of sport on sports history rather than vice versa. Had it been written from a historical perspective it would have looked very different. For every positive evaluation of a sociological work by a historian, one could provide parallel praise from a sociologist for, in particular, the work of Douglas Booth (1998), Richard Holt (1989), Stephen Jones (1986, 1988), Tony Mangan (1981), Kathleen McCrone (1988), Steve Pope (1997) and Patricia Vertinsky (1990). Perhaps the best indication of the impact of history on the sociology of sport, however, is the almost uniform way in which the textbooks of the latter contain chapters on history (Cashmore 2005b; Coakley 2007; Horne *et al.* 1999; Houlihan 2003; Jarvie 2006; Scambler 2005). While historians may be critical of the quality of some of these (e.g., Johnes's [2005] criticisms of Cashmore), as indeed sociologists are critical of the 'tokenistic fashion' with which some sociology of sport textbooks address historical matters (Horne *et al.* 1999: 73), they are nevertheless evidence that sociologists view history as providing an essential dimension of their analysis (see also Chapter 10).

The subdisciplines' respective impacts upon each other are, however, qualitatively different. While sports history can be said to have *entered* large parts of the sociology of sport domain, or indeed been *embraced* by it, sociological theory (as much, it must be said, through social history as the sociology of sport) has *colonized* sports history. Where history adds to sociology, social theory now defines significant proportions of sports history. Moreover, while sports history has become more theory-oriented, sociologists of sport are no longer producing historically oriented accounts in anything like the number or significance they once were.[4] As historians have pointed out (Pope 1998), sociology of sport is not without its crises, but, as discussed in Chapter 10, the malleability of sociology enables it to survive these challenges relatively unscathed. In contrast, there is a sense in which the challenges facing sports history can only be solved by going beyond their traditional domain, be it an expansion into the wider field of leisure (Johnes 2005), the more widespread use of social theories 'fashioned outside our discipline' (Hill 1996: 19; Metcalfe 1998) or forging new relationships and collaborating with other sports-related subdisciplines in a broader sports-studies project (Booth 1997; Nauright 1999). In recent years one of the most notable developments has been a literary turn (Hill 2006; Bateman 2009). As Johnes notes, 'Sport History … needs to secure its location within two disciplines, to ensure it engages with and is taken notice of by both' (2004: 158).

There are perhaps three reasons why the sociology of sport has had a greater impact on sports history than vice versa:

1 sports historians' insecurity within the broader discipline;
2 the weaknesses within the subdiscipline;
3 the field's continued disunity which is itself a legacy of its past.

In 1998, for instance, Alan Metcalfe (1998) argued that sports history remained 'on the periphery of the discipline of history', while five years later Jeff Hill continued this theme, speaking of 'bringing sports history out of the cold and into the common weal of history' (2003: 360). Similarly, Johnes has expressed concerns about the ghettoization of sports history and has claimed that it 'has yet to provide any evidence that sport history is highly valued by the wider historical discipline' (2004: 148). Previous chapters have charted the insecurities of sociologists of sport, but, to my reading, they appear less pronounced.

The weaknesses of sports history stem from members' occupational insecurity and relatively limited publishing opportunities. While Hill, for instance, talks of a 'dearth of sports history courses in British Universities' compared with North America (1996: 2),

Metcalfe notes that sports history programmes are disappearing in an 'increasingly ahistorical' North American society (1998). Booth's citation of a number of posting on the ISHPES email discussion forum indicates that these concerns are more broadly international (1997). Consequently, 'where mainstream departments offer sports history, it is usually because individuals have carved out a niche' (Booth 1997: 202). Hill makes a similar point. Where employed in 'mainstream' departments, sports historians are often 'lone historians nurturing their individual interest, working their passage as historians of sport by fulfilling other teaching roles in the mainstream syllabus' (Hill 2003: 356). Alternatively, sports historians may work in sports studies departments, but again, Hill warns, 'not always in a relationship of equality' (2003: 356). Consequently, both Booth (1997: 191) and Johnes have talked about the difficulties sports historians face in obtaining employment. Johnes argues that there is 'little explicit demand from sport science for historians, but there is some demand for those who study the socio-cultural aspects of sport' (2004: 149). Tellingly, he concludes that 'the Ph.D. student of sport history who engages with the literature of sport sociology and sport studies … will find broader employment opportunities' (Johnes 2004: 149).

To some extent the number of peer-review English-language journals that regularly publish work on sports history is incongruous with the scarcity of occupational opportunities. Johnes (2004: 146) cites twelve such journals, whereas the sociology of sport can, perhaps, claim eight.[5] Yet, as Johnes goes on to argue, the proliferation of journals has led some to question their quality. Crucial in this regard is the fact that international bodies for sports history – ICOSH, HISPA and latterly ISHPES – have been unable to publish regular journals and thus failed in 'THE most important function of organizations – the promotion of publications' (Metcalfe 1998; emphasis in original). Johnes argues that 'the sport history journal market is … complicated by factionalism, where some publications are perceived to be overly influenced by the whims of their editors' (2004: 147). This has exacerbated the trend for leading sports historians to send their best work to journals outside the subdiscipline which sometimes reduces their impact within.

The final reason why the sociology of sport has had such an impact on sports history is because of the continued disunity in the field. Headline membership figures present an apparently healthy picture (see Table 8.1). The membership of the NASSH is roughly equivalent to its sociological counterpart (NASSS); the membership of the BSSH is considerably greater than that of the BSASSG; and in Australia the ASSH has no equivalent sociology group. While the membership of the ISHPES is considerably smaller than that of the ISSA, this is perhaps offset by the relative strengths of the European confederations. But in Britain and Australia the national organizations are bolstered by the presence of a significant number of non-academic historians who, typically, constitute a two-thirds majority of the membership. As Johnes (2004: 148) notes, the BSSH has reformed its publications to meet the separate needs of these two distinct groups. Tellingly, whilst NASSH and ASSH journals have both aired debates about the state of the subdiscipline and potential future directions, the main BSSH journal, *Sport in History*, has been strangely silent, with British sports historians (Hill 1996; Johnes 2004) airing their concerns elsewhere.

TABLE 8.1 The organization of sports history.

Name	*Established*	*Membership*	*Proportion with academic positions*	*Split between history and sports departments*	*Journal*
British Society for Sports History (BSSH)	1982	approx. 200	33%	20–5%:75–80%	*The Sports Historian* (1982–2002) *Sport in History* (2003–)
Australian Society for Sport History (ASSH)	1983	170	33%	20%:80%	*Sporting Traditions* (1984–)
North American Society for Sport History (NASSH)	1972	402	90–5%	< 50%: > 50%	*Journal of Sport History* (1974–)
European Committee for Sports History (CESH)	1995	72	58%	15%:85%	*European Studies in Sports History* (2008–)
International Society for the History of Physical Education and Sport (ISHPES)	1989, following the merger of ICOSH (the International Committee for the History of Physical Education and Sport, founded 1967) and HISPA (the International Association for the History of Physical Education and Sport, founded 1973)	72	95%	n/a	–

Sources: I am grateful to the following people for providing me, via email, with information about their respective organizations: Frank Galligan and Mike Huggins, BSSH (3 May 2011; 15 April 2008); Gary Osmond and Tara Magdalinski, ASSH (6 May 2011); Jean Saint-Martin, ISHPES Honorary Secretary (20 March 2008); Ronald A. Smith, NASSH Secretary Treasurer (4 May 2011); Daphne Bolz, CESH General Secretary (23 May 2008). For additional data on the BSSH see Cox (2000).

A second division relates to the historical legacy of a membership divided between history and physical education backgrounds. While figures are not available for the CESH, NASSH membership is estimated to be 'more than half' in physical education departments and 'less than half' in history. In Britain and Australia the split is nearer 80:20, and, indeed, the recent retitling of the BSSH's journal, from *The Sports Historian*, reflects a further division within the subdiscipline, namely an orientation away from sport and physical education and towards the history 'mainstream' (Johnes 2004: 157). Metcalfe (1998) points towards the paradoxical situation where 'although the leaders at the cutting edge are social historians, the majority, the workers, still come from physical education backgrounds'. Occasionally these divisions have been exposed. In contrast, sociology of sport has few 'amateur' practitioners and has tended to unify around a sociological (rather than physical education) orientation.

Sociologists of sport (with the exception of figurational sociologists) can therefore consider their engagement with sports history as something of a 'success' in that it is an indication of the relative strength of their field. Many sociological contributions to sports history have been well received by historians and have enabled the penetration of social theory into the field. This has, to some extent, redefined sports history and especially those aspects of the subdiscipline which the community itself seems to value most highly. Historians' critiques of sociology have therefore changed and now take a form which is partly driven by theoretical rather than disciplinary differences, but possibly also by territorial defensiveness. There is little doubt that sports history has also been influential in shaping the sociology of sport, but the various status insecurities and the disunity of the former have enabled sociology to assume an ascendant position.

9

SOCIOLOGY OF SPORT AND PUBLIC ENGAGEMENT

In the run-up to the 1997 general election at which Tony Blair would become British Prime Minister, I received a telephone call from a journalist called Ciaran Fitzgerald. Looking for a non-election story, he asked about current research, and I sent him a paper – my first journal article – which had recently been accepted for publication in the *Sociology of Sport Journal* (Malcolm 1997). That Sunday I awoke to find my research featured on the front page of the *Sunday Times* and being discussed on national television and radio. My argument that there were social rather than biological reasons why Black British and British Asian cricketers were disproportionately 'stacked' into particular playing positions was contested by leading players and coaches who explained the pattern according to the 'loose limbs' and 'wristy' stroke play of some 'racial' groups. My work had become 'public' before it had an academic impact.

The debate about the relationship between academics and the public is long-standing. In relation to the subdiscipline, Harry Edwards's role in the Olympic Project for Human Rights and the Black Power salute at the 1968 Mexico Olympic Games represents probably the first example of the sociology of sport informing a public debate and subsequent political activism. In the UK, debates about football hooliganism pushed, or enabled, some sociologists of sport to address a broader audience. The debate was recently reinvigorated by Michael Burawoy's 2004 American Sociological Association Presidential Address, 'For Public Sociology' (Burawoy 2005). This keynote led to various special issues of sociology journals addressing the role of the sociologist as a public intellectual (defined as someone who 'writes for the general public, or at least for a broader than merely academic or specialist audience, on "public affairs"' [Posner 2003: 23, cited in Bairner 2009]). Jarvie (2007) and Bairner (2009) have addressed these debates with reference to the sociology of sport. The spectrum of academic–public engagement extends from subject specific media appearances or writing for a popular audience, to being invited, once one's public intellectual credentials are established, to speak on a whole range of issues on the public agenda, much like British historian David Starkey is today.

Given that a sociology of the sociology of sport should examine the subdiscipline's public reception, this chapter provides an examination of the characteristics and consequences of intellectual engagements between sociologists of sport and their publics. Instances of academic–public engagement are numerous and, as the opening example illustrates, largely ad hoc. The empirical examples discussed here are therefore necessarily selective. However, through an analysis of three types of engagement – where sociologists of sport have published texts that make their academic ideas available for lay consumption; where edited collections attempt to bridge the divide by combining the works of sociologists and other social critics of sport; and where popular writers have assessed the contributions of sociologists of sport – I argue that the public work of sociologists of sport has largely had negative consequences for the standing of the subdiscipline. First, however, we need to consider the rationale for sociologists to engage with a lay audience and the potential costs and benefits for the academics who do so.

Why engage with the public?

As we saw in Chapter 2, the sociology of sport emerged amidst a debate in which the value-free orientation of the science of sociology became dominant over the traditional 'sport is good' evangelism of physical education. Since the 1960s, however, and especially in relation to race and gender issues, the movement towards a more politically oriented sociology of sport has gained momentum. This has been stimulated by both the continued commitment of sociologists to the transformative potential of sport and the increasing tendency to view sport not as a reflection of, or reproducing, society but as a sphere of resistance to broader social structures and processes (Donnelly 2003: 21). While Jarvie (2007: 411) welcomes the frequency with which articles 'about the importance of combining scholarship and commitment' have appeared in the *IRSS*, this position remains contested. Dunning (2004: 18), for instance, has argued that placing 'the need for action above, rather than together with, the need for understanding' is one of the two major threats to the 'balance' of the subdiscipline. Underpinning this viewpoint is the belief that politically or policy-oriented sociology is likely to produce less valid sociological knowledge.

In addition to the desire to invoke social change there are professional and moral rationales for seeking to engage with the public or popular readership. The professional rationale has two components. As noted in Chapter 1, some, like Andrew Yiannakis, have argued that dissemination enables academic ideas to be tested and refined 'in the world of sport' (1989: 5). Second, one might argue that the legitimacy of the subdiscipline will partly rest upon the ability of its practitioners to solve, or at the very least address, the problems of the broader sporting world. As we saw in Chapter 2, pressing social issues provided part of the stimulus for the development of the sociology of sport in the 1960s. The continuation of public funding partly rests on the perception that knowledge generated in the subdiscipline is 'useful'.

The moral rationale for academic engagement with non-academic audiences stems from the claim that the skills which sociologists develop through training give them a uniquely informed view of the world. As Talcott Parsons argued, the 'widespread idea that the common man is his own social scientist: that any ordinary intelligent person is qualified to understand the operation of social processes … is very far from the truth' (cited in Haney 2008: 34). With respect to sport, Jarvie argues that the public intellectual has 'the capacity to see above and beyond existing debates, to get off the tramlines of discussion' (2007: 422). For researchers to claim informed insight on the one hand while simultaneously denying the practical consequences of these insights to the citizens that fund them would be morally unjustifiable. Indeed, as recipients of public funding, the knowledge generated by sociology of sport researchers is in some senses public property. In Weber's (1991) sense, engaging with a lay readership is comparable with working 'for' one's vocation.

Such altruistic reasons may, however, be mixed with more selfish motivations. Appearances on television and radio, writing for newspapers and specialist magazines and producing books which publishers intend for a market beyond academia opens up new and relatively large sources of income for sociologists of sport. Such ventures may also, but not necessarily, be recognized and economically rewarded within the profession. Public engagement may also enable the academic to mix with the socially and politically powerful. This potential for ego enhancement has a peculiar dynamic for sociologists of sport, for the world of professional sport is both glamorous and closed and many sociologists of sport combine the role of investigator and fan. By engaging with the broader sporting world the sociologist of sport may gain access not just to a rich research environment but also to a social world beyond the reach of most sports fans. Through popular writing, sociologists of sport may, therefore, also live 'off' their profession.

Undertaking such work, however, is not without potential costs to the individual as colleagues may be suspicious of the motives of public intellectuals in sport. As noted in Chapter 1, Ingham and Donnelly (1990: 62) expressed 'little sympathy' with those who exploit their publicly funded positions to establish private business ventures and consultancies. Moreover, because sociological writing is qualitatively different from popular writing, the literary expression required to communicate beyond academia may serve to obscure nuances or simplify complex ideas and thus undermine the scholarly integrity of work, as, for example, occurred with David Riesman, 'the first major postwar popularizer of sociology' (Haney 2008: 212). Conversely, the continued use of sociology's technical language may be seen by those outside the field as an 'attempt to disguise the triviality of research subjects and conclusions' (Haney 2008: 11) and thus invoke criticisms.

Indeed, it has been argued that the status of sociology will *necessarily* be diminished by engagement with the public. Barnes (1981) notes that the work of the public intellectual is to facilitate the absorption of sociological ideas into popular thought. Once absorbed, and possibly modified, an unintended consequence becomes more dominant; that is to say, the scientific achievements of sociology become 'buried as common sense' (Barnes 1981: 22). Thus, 'building an edifice of professional sociological achievement is like building on quicksand' (Barnes 1981: 22). Barnes sees denigration in the popular media and by colleagues in other disciplines as not only a permanent feature of sociology but as 'evidence for the maturity of the society in which sociology has been institutionalised' (1981: 22).

To what extent, then, has the engagement of sociologists of sport with public audiences been driven by the different rationales noted above? What have been the characteristics and consequences of such public intellectual work?

Disseminating sociological ideas through popular writing

The critical and commercial success of Nick Hornby's *Fever Pitch* (1992) alerted UK publishers to a broader potential of popular writing on sport than had previously been imagined. Publication coincided with the launch of the English Premiership and the unprecedented commercialization of football. Though formally in opposition to these commercializing processes (Haynes 1995), the football fanzine movement was similarly a product of late-Thatcherite and post-Fordist economics (King 1997). Entrepreneurial fans used fanzines to campaign about the status of the game and subsequently found that they could also make a profit from their football knowledge while also enhancing their status. Sociologists of sport contributed to the early phases of the fanzine movement, regularly appearing in the national fanzine *When Saturday Comes* (*WSC*) in particular. The *WSC* website, for instance, lists four sociologists of sport amongst its list of writers, including Adam Brown (twelve articles), Tim Crabbe (two articles), John Sugden (five articles), Alan Tomlinson (nine articles), Stephen Wagg (eight articles) and John Williams (twenty articles).[1]

Mainstream was one of the first publishers to recognize and exploit this potential market. Mainstream has published books written by former hooligans, journalists, players, managers, etc., but most interestingly for present purposes, Mainstream also identified the commercial potential of books written by sociologists of sport. This section compares and contrasts two bodies of work authored by sociologists of sport and published by Mainstream: the work of John Sugden and Alan Tomlinson, and that of John Williams and various co-authors.

Sugden and Tomlinson have published three books with Mainstream:

1 *Great Balls of Fire: How Big Money Is Hijacking World Football* (Sugden and Tomlinson 1999a);
2 *Scum Airways: Inside Football's Underground Economy* (Sugden 2002);
3 *Badfellas: FIFA Family at War* (Sugden and Tomlinson 2003).

The authors explicitly describe these publications as attempts to disseminate sociological ideas to lay audiences. The stimulus for *Great Balls of Fire*, they state, came from journalist friends who suggested that they make their academic work more widely available. Sugden and Tomlinson describe the process of conversion as 'much more difficult' than anticipated (1999a: 9), while Sugden (2002: 10–11) refers to the challenging but 'nonetheless liberating' experience of doing away with the conventions of academic writing. In recognition of the fact that such ventures are not always welcomed or rewarded in academia, Sugden explicitly refers to *Scum Airways*' likely exclusion from future Research Assessment Exercise submissions.[2]

Sugden and Tomlinson's sociological ideas on football are most clearly expressed in *FIFA and the Contest for World Football: Who Rules the People's Game?* published by the academic publisher Polity Press in 1998. The book charts the global growth of football through (1) an examination of intra-organizational relations involving different national and continental federations and power struggles between different FIFA personnel and (2) inter-organizational relations between FIFA and other sports governing bodies, the sports industry, football's financial partners and politicians. Empirical evidence comes from interviews with prominent figures in world football and archive and documentary research. It draws particularly on the literatures on globalization and national identity formation (citing Robertson, Hobsbawm, Giddens, etc.) and concludes by comparing FIFA to international institutions such as the UN and examining the role of football in cultural reproduction and resistance to dominant global processes. The authors note, for instance, that 'adequate theorization of FIFA's impact must consider the extent to which football can be viewed as a symbol of economic and cultural imperialism; and the role FIFA has played in the brokerage of forms of neo-imperialism' (1998: 223).

Appearing a year later, *Great Balls of Fire* draws on much of the empirical evidence that appeared in *FIFA and the Contest for World Football* but presents it in a 'more accessible and populist' style (1999a: 9). The text focuses more on the lack of 'transparency, democracy or accountability' in FIFA (1999a: 7) whereas *FIFA and the Contest for World Football* is pitched as 'a commentary on the international dynamics of the twentieth century' (1998: 3). Using more 'catchy' chapter titles – 'The Politics of the Belly' as opposed to 'FIFA and Africa' – there is considerable overlap in the central areas of analysis, though the more theoretically orientated conclusion to *FIFA and the Contest for World Football* is replaced by a speculative discussion of the possible future of the game should commercialization processes remain unchecked. Believing that 'information is power', Sugden and Tomlinson's aim in writing *Great Balls of Fire* is to 'return' the game to its popular roots by fuelling resistance to the commodification of football (1999a: 8).

Badfellas and *Scum Airways* are essentially extensions of this body of work. The former uses similar data to address the global expansion and internal dealings of the FIFA 'family', while *Scum Airways* uses ethnographic research to make links between financial corruption in FIFA and the ticket fraud that fuels football's underground economy. There are discussions of masculinity, nationalism, racism, social mobility and risk and pleasure-seeking in working-class (youth) cultures. The book also compares and contrasts observational research with undercover journalism, discusses some of the problems of the research method and research ethics issues and thus bears out Sugden's claim that the book is 'profoundly sociological' (2002: 11).

John Williams has been even more prolific for Mainstream, authoring or co-authoring seven books in seven years (Williams 2001a, 2002a, 2003, 2010; Williams and Kennedy 2004; Williams and Hopkins 2005; Williams and Llopis 2006, 2007). The number of texts Williams has published with Mainstream suggests that they have been relatively successful commercially. Williams became prominent as an academic writing and speaking about football hooliganism in the late 1970s and 1980s (Williams *et al.* 1984; Dunning *et al.* 1988; Murphy *et al.* 1990), but during recent years the sole book Williams has produced with an academic publisher has been *Passing Rhythms: Liverpool FC and the Transformation of Football*, co-edited with Cathy Long and Stephen Hopkins and published by Berg in 2001. What is the relationship between Williams's academic work and his writing for popular audiences?

Being a co-edited text, *Passing Rhythms* does not provide an exact parallel to Sugden and Tomlinson's *FIFA and the Contest for World Football*, but ultimately provides the fullest statement of Williams's sociological orientation. The aim of *Passing Rhythms* is 'to consider the deeper significance of the relationship between professional football and other local cultural practices' (2001: 2). The introduction attempts to establish a sociological framework for the text, citing authors such as Scott Lash, John Urry and Raymond Williams, but the degree to which this is achieved is limited by the contributors assembled. *Passing Rhythms* combines the work of academics (Liz Crolley and Raymond Boyle as well as Williams and Hopkins) with populist sports writers and those working in the football industry (Dave Hill and Andrew Ward, and Rick Parry, Colin Moneypenny and Long respectively). This latter group exhibit a limited engagement with or commitment to sociology. Williams's own chapters are similarly inconsistent in their sociological engagement, ranging from an attempt to illustrate Raymond Williams's notion of 'structures of feeling' in relation to Liverpool football to a descriptive history of the city and football club which draws on a combination of academic and popular sources.

Given the absence of sociological engagement in *Passing Rhythms*, it is unsurprising that Williams's Mainstream publications do little to disseminate sociological ideas about sport to a broader public. For instance, Williams describes *Into the Red* as 'a fan's eye view … set against some of the wider developments' in football (2001a: 16). The book covers a number of social issues which sociologists of sport have also addressed – the commercialization of football, the policing of fans, expressions of Englishness, attitudes towards women's football, race relations – but unlike Sugden and Tomlinson's work these analyses are not rooted in a distinctively sociological approach. There is, for instance, no evidence of empirical research based on the kinds of specialist skills and techniques (mainly interviewing and ethnography) which sociologists claim lead to an advanced understanding of social phenomena. Indeed, one could argue that over time Williams's publications with Mainstream become progressively *less* sociological, for he latterly co-authors texts with journalists and former players and increasingly focuses on playing events and personalities rather than broader social changes.

What conclusions can be drawn from comparing the work of Sugden and Tomlinson and Williams? The subject matter, empirical underpinning and theoretical orientation of *Great Balls of Fire*, etc., clearly identify those texts as sociological works. The combination of content and the omission of specialist terminology suggests that the production of these texts is underpinned by a professional rationale for public intellectualism. But the subject matter of *Into the Red* and Williams's later Mainstream publications in particular suggests that these texts are similar to those which led Ingham and Donnelly to have a 'serious ethical concern'. These texts neither stem from nor feed back into the sociology of sport. Co-authorship with a former Liverpool player (Alan Kennedy) suggests that, for Williams, these texts are more of a commercial sideline than a structured attempt to develop and disseminate the sociology of sport.

Similar conclusions about the sociological worth of these publications can be drawn when they are viewed in the context of the authors' broader careers as sociologists of sport. There is something rather organic about the way Sugden and Tomlinson's approach relates to their broader theoretical orientation to sociology. Indeed, fifteen years before *Great Balls of Fire*, Tomlinson (1984) wrote about the relationship between sociological and journalistic research and writing (see next section). In 2002, Sugden and Tomlinson presented a more detailed outline of their research methodology, listing six overlapping elements: historiography, comparative methods, critical sociology, ethnography and, most importantly for present purposes, investigative research and gonzo (2002). Sugden and Tomlinson have also published articles addressing the methodological and practical issues entailed in this style of research (e.g., 1999b). There is therefore a coherence to Sugden and Tomlinson's broader body of work. By comparison, Williams's work has no apparent roots in, or intellectual connection with, work in the subdiscipline. Where Sugden and Tomlinson's work essentially fulfils the 'critical' remit of sociology, Williams's work is largely celebratory. While Sugden and Tomlinson's FIFA book was shortlisted for the 1998 NASSS Book Award (and indeed was beaten by Sugden's own, *Boxing and Society* [1998]), reviews of Williams *et al.* (2001) cite conceptual incoherence and a lack of primary research and originality (Nash 2001). Furthermore, as recent editors of the *IRSS*, Sugden and Tomlinson have made significant contributions to the subdiscipline as a whole.

The impact on the subdiscipline of these two bodies of work is therefore rather different. While Sugden and Tomlinson have both contributed *to* the subdiscipline and *taken* the subdiscipline to the public, Williams has produced little scholarly writing and has taken little of a sociological nature to a broader public. Sociologists of sport should conduct work that reaches outside the subdiscipline, but such work becomes problematic if it eclipses their academic contribution and becomes an individual's primary or sole orientation. Thus the consequences of disseminating sociological ideas about sport through popular writing may therefore be mixed.[3]

Combining academic and popular writing on sport

A second means by which we might evaluate the public consumption of the work of sociologists of sport is to examine those texts in which academic and popular writing are combined. Probably the first texts of this type (in the UK at least) were edited by Garry Whannel and the aforementioned Alan Tomlinson. Published by Pluto Press on the eve of the Los Angeles Olympics, *Five Ring Circus* (Tomlinson and Whannel 1984) combined chapters from British (James Riordan and Jennifer Hargreaves as well as

Tomlinson and Whannel) and Canadian (Bruce Kidd and Rick Gruneau) sociologists of sport with chapters from David Triesman (academic, trade unionist and latterly Chair of the Football Association) and Sam Ramsamy, Chair of the South African Non-Racial Olympic Committee. The text's central message, that despite recurrent myths about the Olympics the modern games 'have always been bound up with money, power and politics' (Tomlinson and Whannel 1984: x), is a good example of Berger's 'de-bunking' motif of sociology (1966).

Off the Ball (Tomlinson and Whannel 1986) was a similar venture, published immediately prior to the Football World Cup in Mexico. Contributing academics were all British, and more evenly divided between 'sport-specialists' (John Williams, Tony Mason, Alan Bairner and John Sugden) and those for whom sport is one of a number of research interests (Steve Redhead, John Clarke, Chas Critcher and John Humphrey). The collection also included educators working outside the university system at that time (Christine Geraghty, Philip Simpson and Stephen Wagg), journalists (Stuart Cosgrove and Riccardo Grozio) and a freelance researcher (Mario Flamigni). There is thus a distinct shift towards popular writers in this second volume. Its concluding chapter, moreover, is an interview transcript that effectively affords the 'insiders' view of football manager Steve Coppell considerable status relative to the work of academics. Though one may speculate that the dilution of sociological content was in part based on commercial considerations, like its predecessor, the book interrogates sociological concepts such as 'tradition, cultures and national identity' (Tomlinson and Whannel 1986: 2).

Conversely, popular writers have also sought to harness the commercial potential of academic research by making it available to a broader readership. One of the most successful authors/fan-entrepreneurs has been Mark Perryman who co-founded Philosophy Football in October 1994 and subsequently made a number of contributions to *WSC*.[4] Perryman also became prominent in the England Members Club and, like some sociologists of sport already cited (notably John Williams), has been a consultant to government working groups on football. At a point between the publication of his 1999 and 2001 texts, Perryman became employed by the University of Brighton and now works alongside Sugden and Tomlinson. Perryman has also principally published with Mainstream. Three texts are of particular relevance: *The Ingerland Factor: Home Truths from Football* (1999), *Hooligan Wars: Causes and Effects of Football Violence* (2001) and *Going Oriental: Football After World Cup 2002* (2002). Each combined the work of sociologists of sport with other cultural commentators and provided sociologists of sport with an opportunity to engage with a lay audience. What have been the consequences of these engagements?

Perryman's primary concern in *The Ingerland Factor* is to promote the interests and visibility of fans like himself in order to counterbalance negative publicity stemming from more aggressively nationalistic fans (including hooligans) and to ensure freedom for this type of fan in the face of increasingly punitive state restriction (1999: 7). Either Perryman engaged academics for the contribution they could make to this cause or for commercial gain, because there is little evidence to suggest that he holds academic work in high regard. Referring to the growing sports literature post-*Fever*

Pitch, he notes the existence of 'almost every imaginable academic discipline – anthropology, psycho-analysis, business studies, sociology and more – all claiming that they've also got something useful to say on sport, and they insist on saying it too, footnotes and all' (Perryman 1999: 20). From the outset, therefore, Perryman both contests academics' knowledge claims and mocks their presentational style.

The changing content of Perryman's three volumes suggests that he either became increasingly unconvinced of the value of the work of sociologists of sport or that these chapters were thought to have relatively little commercial value. Seven academics contributed to the 1999 collection (Gary Armstrong, Andrew Blake, Ben Carrington, Liz Crolley, Emma Poulton, Steve Redhead and John Williams). In the 2001 edition this was reduced to five (Richard Giulianotti, Poulton, Sugden, Tomlinson and Williams) and just four in 2002 (Blake, Poulton, Wendy Wheeler and Williams). Increasingly it seems, and despite his (part-time) employment within academia, Perryman has been drawn towards journalists and other popular writers.

However, in disseminating the work of eight sociologists of sport to a broader public, these texts did provide a potentially significant forum for public intellectual work on sport. Carrington's (1999) analysis of nationalism and masculinity, Crolley's (1999) use of the sociological literature on gender to illuminate the apparent 'feminization' of football and Giulianotti's (2001) cross-cultural analysis of fan cultures are demonstrably sociological pieces of work in which the authors attempt to convey sociological ideas in non-academic language. Moreover, amongst those who continued to contribute to these volumes, there is little diminution of academic content over time. Poulton's three contributions (1999, 2001, 2002) are all underpinned by the systematic collection of data that distinguishes sociology from the kind of media commentary provided by journalists (illustrated in Philip Cornwall's [2002] contribution). Where Williams cites Baudrillard, Hobsbawm and Stuart Hall in 1999, his 2002 chapter mentions Giddens, Castells and Roland Robertson (Williams 1999, 2002b). Andrew Blake's work actually becomes *more* explicitly sociological, exchanging a discussion of music and football in *The Ingerland Factor* for references to Edward Said's (1978) *Orientalism* (Blake 2002). Many of the chapters authored by sociologists of sport drew upon, or would subsequently appear as, papers published in academic texts.

The impact of such public work is, however, diminished by the context in which these chapters appear. In attempting to adapt their work for a broader readership, sociologists of sport made only occasional reference to academic authors and theoretical ideas. But, revised in this way, academic work begins to take on a very similar appearance to that of popular writers. For instance, Perryman, like Williams, cites Baudrillard and Hobsbawm and uses sociological concepts such as 'risk society' (1999). The distinction between Vivek Chaudhary's (2001) and Poulton's (2001) use of Stanley Cohen's concept of 'folk devils' is hardly apparent. These similarities do not stop some popular writers being critical of sociologists' esoteric language. Simon Inglis, for example, points to obscurantism in academic analyses of stadium redevelopment, or '"socio-spatial transformation" as sociologists would have it' (2001: 88). Within these texts, therefore (c.f. Barnes 1981), we see both the successful dissemination of sociological ideas such that they penetrate the vocabulary of a broader public and the denigration of sociologists for their use of technical language. The cost of dissemination, however, appears to be that the distinctiveness of the sociological approach is diminished.

The impact of this form of public intellectual work is further limited by the criticisms popular writers make of academic contributors. Dougie Brimson, Beatrix Campbell and Dorothy Rowe all explicitly criticize sociological explanations of football hooliganism. Rowe disparagingly suggests that sociological theories invoke 'a model of a human being as a puppet moved by strings controlled by certain features of society' (2001: 56), while Campbell and Dawson cite, 'Classic texts on football hooliganism [which] tend to appeal to the "commonsense" that correlates crime and violence with class' (2001: 69). Brimson is more dismissive of the 'successful careers … [of] "Doctor" this and "Professor" that', based on 'stating the blindingly obvious or formulating ideas based on a combination of guesswork and hearsay … [While] the consequences of such "research" have little or no impact on the real world, occasionally they do. And the results can be catastrophic' (2001: 198).

A rebuttal is not necessary here; suffice to say, the portrayals of these works contain misunderstandings and simplifications.[5] More importantly, for present purposes, these critical engagements suggest that while a broader public has become increasingly aware of sociological concepts, there are no guarantees that the public will become convinced of the greater adequacy of knowledge generated by their use in relation to sport. Indeed, an apparently more significant outcome is to have opened up sociological ideas for a certain amount of ill-informed ridicule.

Two other characteristics of these engagements further limit the impact of this type of public intellectual work. First, the academic writers do not respond in kind to their critics. It may be that academics, conscious of their relatively privileged position, feel that it would be unprofessional for them to directly challenge the explanations of popular writers in this context. There is good reason for this; potentially it would be counter-productive to include critiques of popular ideas in public intellectual work as the very rationale for these engagements is to build bridges between academics and the public. Yet by declining to engage in a debate, the reader is left with nothing but popular writers' questioning of the value of academic knowledge. The format of this conflict of ideas favours sub-confessed former hooligans such as Brimson (2000) as opposed to public intellectuals.

Second, interpretative differences *within* the subdiscipline further constrain the impact of this form of public work. None of the academics attempt to either defend or illustrate sociology's contribution to knowledge. Conversely, we see Armstrong (1999), Williams (2001b) and Giulianotti (2001) critiquing the explanations of hooliganism proposed by the Leicester School and Williams questioning some of the psychological and anthropological work on hooliganism (and, by implication, that of Armstrong). Williams (1999: 185), moreover, refers to 'dull "academic" texts', and Armstrong (1999: 52), ironically, given the context of the publication, refers to 'predictable, media-loving academics'. Perryman is aware of these disagreements (1999: 7), but, unlike an academic editor who might attempt to evaluate between or draw commonalties from the different positions, allows them to pass without comment. Read in isolation, this collection suggests that there are some ideas which are broadly questionable (those emanating from the sociology of sport) and some which have authenticity (those of other cultural commentators).

Texts that combine academic and popular writing on sport have therefore had largely negative consequences for the standing of the subdiscipline. The work of sociologists of sport rarely has a commercial value equal to that of popular writers and such financial imperatives mean that academic contributions are likely to be marginalized or at least compromised over time. Where the editor of a collection is more popularly than academically inclined (compare Perryman's collections with those of Tomlinson and Whannel) there is unlikely to be significant resistance to such pressures. Moreover, not only does the format of such texts mean that the distinctiveness and hence value of the sociological approach is likely to be obscured, but academic contributors may be unwilling to defend themselves from popular writers' critiques. Preoccupied with their own internal differences and disputes, sociologists of sport have turned on each other rather than project the achievements of the subdiscipline. Thus the sociology of sport appears to have gained relatively little from these populist works.

Popular writers' assessments of the sociology of sport

As illustrated in the previous section, popular writers on sport in the UK have had rather more negative than positive comments to make about the work of sociologists. This final section provides an American comparison, examining perhaps the most notorious exchange between sociologists of sport and popular writers in recent years. The exchange involves journalist Jon Entine and his controversial text, *Taboo* (2000). Entine argues that while social and cultural factors interplay with the biological, black athletes dominate certain sports because genetically transmitted traits provide inherent physical advantages.[6] The significance of Entine's text lies in his belief that, 'The decisive variable is our genes – the inherent differences between populations shaped over many thousands of years of evolution' (2000: 113).

Such a view runs directly counter to the social-constructionist orientation of sociology (see Chapter 4). Entine however suggests that his position is a self-evident truth and cites numerous black athletes and coaches in support. Typical of them is Arthur Ashe who stated that, 'Sociology can't explain it [black biological advantage]. I want to hear from the scientists. Until I see some numbers, I have to believe that we blacks have something that gives us an edge ... My heart says "no," but my head says "yes"' (Entine 2000: 80). Entine further portrays his thesis as based on scientific certainty, arguing that 'the issue of whether there are meaningful differences between populations *has all but been resolved*' (2000: 337, emphasis in original). Correlatively he suggests that political correctness explains why many in the genetic science community dispute this (Entine 2000: 271). While Entine sees both sociologists of sport and anthropologists as responsible for and complicit in this political correctness, only the former, he argues, remain intransigently opposed to bio-cultural explanations of race and sports performance (2000: 340).

Taboo's challenge to the ideas generated in the sociology of sport has four aspects. First, Entine portrays the natural science–social science relationship as a paradigm war. This is evident at the outset of the book with the counter-posing of quotes from Gideon Ariel (a biomechanist) and Harry Edwards (a sociologist of sport), and through Entine's argument that a value-laden and politically driven sociological perspective has suppressed the objectivity of scientific investigation. Second, Entine largely disregards the expertise of sociologists who specialize in sport. While Entine cites fifteen sociologists of sport he is, with two exceptions, critical of their work. Although he further acknowledges the help of a number of others (e.g., David Andrews, Jay Coakley, Steve Jackson and Wib Leonard and sports geographer John Bale), his ten-member 'board of advisers' contains six 'natural' scientists, two sociologists of sport (Gary Sailes and Earl Smith), a medical sociologist/anthropologist (Michael Speirs) and one 'mainstream' sociologist (Richard Majors). Third, Entine cites his experiences of attending a NASSS conference as illustrative of how 'ideology can sometimes overwhelm common sense' (2000: 339). Fourth, Entine has repeatedly intervened in debates on the NASSServ discussion list, his dismissive postings clearly irritating many sociologists of sport. What are the characteristics of Entine's assessment of sociological work, and what have been the consequences of this engagement for the sociology of sport?

Somewhat ironically, natural scientists have been more critical of Entine's work than have social scientists.[7] Reviewers in the *Quarterly Review of Biology*, *Nature*, the *American Scientist* and the *American Journal of Physical Anthropology* criticized Entine for falsely assuming 'that "race," as defined by skin color is a meaningful biological and genetic construct' (Dougherty 2001). Entine was also accused of selective use of evidence (Dougherty 2001), providing a 'caricature' of genetics (Achter and Condit 2000) and presenting an argument that was incoherent and internally contradictory (Bogin 2001). The result is a 'thesis … that does not convince' (Malik 2000).

Like their natural-science counterparts, social scientists also referred to Entine's 'selective, partial, and deceptive use of "scientific evidence"' (Wilson 2000: 116) and the illogicality and inconsistency underpinning his conceptualization of 'race' (Valentine 2001; Spickard 2000; Crepeau 2001; Lieberman 2001). Unlike natural-scientist reviewers, they further argue that Entine falsely asserts the neutrality of scientific enquiry (Crepeau 2001: 253) and that his work illustrates that discussions of race and biology are not taboo (Keita 2000). Despite these reservations, social-scientific reviews largely recommend the text to readers. A reviewer in the *International Journal of the History of Sport* describes *Taboo* as a 'well researched book … [which] does an excellent job of combining history and science' (Besseler 2002: 243), while Crepeau (2001: 252), writing in the *Sociology of Sport Journal,* describes *Taboo* as 'an interesting and compelling narrative, which at a number of levels is persuasive'. In *Olympika* Brian Wilson lauds Entine's 'painstaking detail', 'interesting depictions' and historical analysis (2000: 116). These academics, like those discussed in the previous section, conform to certain conventions which mean that they are more measured in their critiques of popular theories than popular writers are in their assessments of sociological work.

The style in which Entine engages with the sociology of sport illustrates two familiar themes: objections to the use of specialist terminology and the absorption of sociological ideas into popular thought. Entine critiques authors of the pioneering studies of stacking in the 1960s and 1970s, for 'invent[ing] phrases soaked in pre-judgement such as "position discrimination" and "positional segregation"' (2000: 275). He also dismisses Laurel Davis's work which 'never got past a jargon-soaked attack to actually address the evidence' (2000: 282). Entine draws upon the empirical evidence collated by various social scientists but somewhat exploitatively, never explicitly acknowledges his debt to the subdiscipline. Despite his acceptance that 'the environment has become the default explanation' (2000: 282), he fails to credit the subdiscipline for the understanding of social and cultural factors that contribute to sporting success. Entine views the significance of cultural factors as commonsensical and historically constant rather than the product of sociological challenges to an intellectual orthodoxy that started in the 1960s with (again ironically) studies of stacking.

Reminiscent of other sociology of sport–lay engagements, Entine seems unable or unwilling to understand the diversity and complexity of academic arguments. Entine does not undertake a systematic examination of the sociology of sport literature, and, in failing to note that some sociologists accept that sports performance has a genetic basis (as cited by many of the reviewers of *Taboo*), falsely portrays the subdiscipline as homogeneous. He criticizes sociological literature on stacking yet fails to mention that such literature has also been widely critiqued within the subdiscipline. (See Chapter 4 and Birrell's [1989: 214] assessment ten years prior to Entine that 'there is no theoretical news in this tradition'.) Entine's problems stem from his highly selective use of literature. This can be seen in his treatment of Laurel Davis's critique of the objectivity of science. Her suggestion that the search for genetic differences between 'races' is based on an a priori belief in their existence (Entine 2000: 282) is never addressed by Entine, even though he inadvertently substantiates Davis's point when quoting Kathy Myburg elsewhere in the text.[8]

Similarly, Entine fails to portray sociological knowledge as methodologically distinct from the impressionistic and anecdotal evidence of some other cultural commentators. For example, Entine shifts from citing 'African American sports writer' Ralph Wiley to academics such as Carole Oglesby and Richard Lapchick, without drawing any distinction between their professional training or the empirical bases of their arguments (2000: 332–3). He further contrasts Martin Kane's (1971) *Sports Illustrated* article, 'An Assessment of Black Is Best', with Harry Edwards's (1971) response published in *Black Scholar*. According to Entine, Kane 'assembled a broad range of informed scientists, coaches and athletes', while Edwards provides 'a polemic in the guise of an academic article' (Entine 2000: 236–7). In fact, in scrutinizing Kane's evidence, Edwards (1971) sought to expose how ill informed Kane's sources were.

However, in contrast to the academic–lay engagements previously discussed, Entine doubly condemns sociologists of sport by juxtaposing their work with that of natural scientists. Entine argues that one can reject sociologists' claims to expertise because of the subjectivity which he argues defines the subdiscipline. Critiquing the work of Margolis and Piliavin, Entine describes their 'hope to combat' racial discrimination as 'an admirable statement but one without any link to the evidence that they proffer' (2000: 279). Entine contrasts a sociology of sport in which, 'The "censor it don't test it" attitude, rooted in the never-never land of post-modernism … is distressingly rampant' (2000: 338) with science defined as 'a method of interrogating reality, not of imposing answers' (2000: 340). Even though Entine describes the work of Harvard geneticists Richard Lewontin as scientifically and politically flawed, he damningly asserts that 'Coming from a geneticist, rather than a sociologist or anthropologist, Lewontin's article had enormous influence' (Entine 2000: 104).

While Entine does correctly identify a subdisciplinary shift away from its positivist origins, he both exaggerates this trend and disingenuously uses it for his own ends. First, Entine fails to convey the level of internal disagreement within the sociology of sport over the appropriate role of values. This appears to be a wilful misinterpretation rather than a lack of understanding, for Entine exploits subdisciplinary divisions to substantiate his portrayal of the sociology of sport as characterized by 'sweeping denunciations couched as moral virtue' (2000: 339). While Entine (2000: 338) cites John Phillips's critique of those 'sports sociologists [who] have voluntarily assumed the burden of telling others what they ought to think and what subjects they should or should not investigate', he neglects to see this as evidence of subdisciplinary heterogeneity. Moreover, he fails to tally his criticisms of the more positivist sociology of sport research on race (i.e. the stacking tradition) with his advocacy of the epistemological approach.

Second, while Entine cites the treatment of Hoberman following the publication of *Darwin's Athletes* (1997) as an illustration of the politically charged character of the subdiscipline, he says nothing of the fact that Hoberman's thesis (discussed in Chapter 4) is diametrically opposed to his own. While prepared to use Hoberman as a data source, Entine never uses knowledge of Hoberman's work to challenge or scrutinize his own belief that political correctness has led to a *lack* of celebration of black sporting success.

Perhaps above all, Entine's text illustrates the vulnerability of sociologists of sport who engage with the public. With regard to race and sport in American society, there has probably been no more prominent sociologist of sport than Harry Edwards. As Professor of Sociology at University of California at Berkeley, Edwards combined advocacy and scholarship, leading the Black Athlete movement to boycott the 1968 Olympic Games and publishing *The Revolt of the Black Athlete* (1969). Tellingly, Entine reserves his most sustained attack for Edwards. The index to *Taboo* contains twelve citations to Edwards, though most of this relates to his activism and media work rather than his academic writing. Entine tries to discredit Edwards by noting that he was once sixth on the FBI's list of 'most subversive Americans' (2000: 226) and, in citing Jesse Owens, who called Edwards a 'self-promoting opportunist' (2000: 230), questions his right to represent black athletes' views. Entine's treatment of Edwards's response to Kane is just one example in a concerted attack on Edwards's credibility. Thus, the most publicly prominent scholar of race and sport comes in for the greatest criticism when the subdiscipline is assessed by a popular writer.

Conclusion

What conclusions can be drawn from this survey of sociologists of sport's populist interventions? First, it should be reiterated that this review is somewhat selective. Indeed, due to the extent of academic–lay engagements (for instance, Lincoln Allison claims to have made in excess of 300 media appearances alone), and due to their ad-hoc nature, it would be impossible to provide a comprehensive overview of the public work of sociologists of sport. Within this broader body of work there may be many examples of the effective dissemination of sociological understanding of sporting phenomena. For instance, a distance-learning student of mine, living in Tanzania when my research on stacking was featured in the *Sunday Times* in 1997, told me that 'everyone' was talking about my claims. This review has, however, indicated that the positive impact of public intellectual work cannot be assumed, and perhaps cannot even be expected. Often, and across a number of different formats and in different cultural contexts, the lay-oriented work of sociologists of sport has largely had a negative impact on the subdiscipline.

While the costs of such engagement may be more apparent than the benefits, certain lessons can be learned. First and foremost, sociologists of sport should retain editorial control over their public work and, preferably, seek to author publications rather than appear in edited collections. In the latter format, at best academics risk their ideas appearing indistinct and, at worst, their ideas risk denigration. In their populist work sociologists of sport also need to exhibit a greater collective consciousness and be prepared to illustrate the subdiscipline's collective knowledge gains, rather than be concerned to forward the work of individuals. It may be that the peculiar opportunity for ego enhancement that sport-related research offers to sociologists contributes towards the visibility of their conflicts in this environment. Sociologists of sport must also be wary that commercial pressures and attractions do not distract from their mission of knowledge dissemination. Finally, sociologists of sport should also be more prepared to extol the merits of the explanations provided by their occupational group relative to those of other cultural commentators for their greater adequacy will not necessarily be apparent to the lay reader.

To what extent does this review illustrate Barnes's (1981) argument that public intellectual work by sociologists inevitably leads to the subject's diminished status? It is clear that many sociological ideas have been absorbed into popular thought although, tellingly for the subdiscipline, perhaps more of these come from the parent discipline than from the sociology of sport itself. A prominent theme, however, is the failure of popular writers to fully grasp the complexities of the academic arguments or their tendency to simplify ideas for presentational ease. Whether this stems from poor dissemination and thus the relative failings of the public intellectual work conducted, or from a more systemic problem, is unclear. While it might perhaps be rash to conclude that the denigration of the sociology of sport is an inevitable consequence of public work, it would certainly seem reasonable to suggest that such engagements are highly problematic and have, to date, done little to raise the status of the sociology of sport in public eyes.

Part IV
Conclusion

10

THE SOCIOLOGY OF SPORT

A 'profession' in process

While writing the concluding chapter to this book I participated on a sub-plenary panel at the British Sociological Association's (BSA) sixtieth annual conference. Sport has had a marginal presence at past BSA conferences, but London's hosting of the 2012 Olympics raised both academic and public consciousness of the social significance of sport. Commenting on the proceedings, a questioner from the floor felt the need to preface his remarks by saying, 'I don't really like sport, but … ' I wondered if anybody attending a round table on race and ethnicity had said, 'I don't really like race, but … ' Had anyone responding to the 'gender and sociology' keynote said, 'I don't really like hegemonic masculinity, but … '? That experience reinforced my reflections from researching this book; despite the myriad ways in which the sociology of sport has engaged with the disciplinary 'mainstream', and the tangible impact in places, the subdiscipline remains semi-detached. For those outside the sociology of sport (and this includes 'mainstream' sociologists as much as the layperson), sport remains something that you like (or dislike) rather than something that you scrutinize from a sociological point of view. As a former head of (a sociology) department said of a colleague of mine, 'He's not a sociologist. He just writes about his hobbies.'

This degree of separation indicates elements of continuity, but a half-century of the sociology of sport has also borne witness to fundamental change. From the preceding chapters a number of particularly significant trends can be identified. While the subdiscipline was initially shaped by its roots in physical education, unequivocally the sociology of sport now bears the hallmarks of a *sociological* discipline. Sociology more broadly may have changed (discussed below), and the sociology of sport may continue to be (in North America), or have increasingly become (in the UK), located in physical education, kinesiology or sports science departments, but the *identity* of people working in the field is essentially that of (a particular type of) sociologists and is distinct from those who identify themselves as, e.g., physical educationalists. This is particularly evident in the degree to which research in a number of empirical areas is located within broader sociological frameworks and responds to similar trends and stimuli.

It is also apparent that the analysis of sport more significantly influences sociological research than has been the case in the past. Some leading social theorists have actively engaged with, and owe a debt to, the sociological study of sport. Long-standing areas of empirical research such as the sociology of race and gender studies contain statements by specialists in those fields which are a far cry from the 'acknowledgements' (Lüschen 1980) or the 'proto-sociological' analyses (Coakley and Dunning 2000a) which sociologists of sport originally identified in the 'mainstream' (see Chapter 2). The shift within sociology towards the analysis of 'culture' has also had a positive impact on the sociology of sport. The interpenetration of 'body' and 'sport' studies has been one of the most marked cases, even if sociologists of the body predominantly seem interested in activities we might more accurately label *sport-related*. Sport is also recognized as a distinctive empirical focus within developing areas such as celebrity studies, and to some it is seen as a *significant* and uniquely valuable area of study. This engagement might not be as comprehensive as sociologists of sport would wish, but the quantitative and qualitative change is readily apparent. This was explicitly acknowledged in the *British Journal of Sociology*'s sixtieth anniversary issue. Reviewing that journal's contents in the first decade of the twenty-first century, Tonkiss (2010) was moved to note the 'significant presence' of sport in the journal, and 'quite a lot' of football in particular. This is not to say that traditional anti-sport prejudice has been entirely overcome, but the days when sociologists of sport would remark on the unsophisticated nature or the fleeting analysis of sport by those in the 'mainstream' have changed forever.

Changes within the subdiscipline are also evident in its 'external' relations. Sports history has been amongst the fields most significantly influenced by an engagement with the sociology of sport. Sports historians may not have had the same initial insecurities that were expressed in the emergent sociology of sport (there was, for instance, no discussion of the relative merits of being sports historians as opposed to historians of sport), but with sports history becoming increasingly sociological, and with fewer sociologists of sport now conducting historical research, it would appear that a significant shift in the balance of power has taken place. What acrimonious relations remain are perhaps more a sign of historians' concerns about the development of their own field, and sociology's influence upon it, than a critique of the sociology of sport per se.

And even though engagement with lay audiences has not generally been beneficial to sociologists of sport, the relationship has not been entirely unproductive either. It may be that the analyses of sport provided by cultural commentators who do not define themselves as sociologists of sport have considerably improved (according to sociological assessments of 'worth'). Whereas the pioneers of the sociology of sport typically argued that such texts were 'the outcome of generally accepted opinion and prejudices about sports' (Wohl 1966: 5), their contemporary counterparts show evidence of the embrace and incorporation of sociological concepts and ideas. Similarly, Coakley argued that in America the subdiscipline emerged 'partly as a response to the awareness of problems generated by muckrakers, and to the call for changes by reformers' (1987: 67), but sociologists of sport now exhibit a relatively collaborative relationship with investigative journalists (see, for instance, the discussion of Sugden and Tomlinson's work in Chapter 9). This may be because sociologists of sport have increasingly accepted the relative adequacy of journalistic work or agreed with its key premises as sociology has become methodologically heterodox and have shown less inclination to attempt to 'solve' the problems of sport and therefore work in its service. But it is also the case that sociologists of sport have become increasingly critical of media production processes and thus have broken the subdiscipline's deference to journalism as an alternative form of cultural analysis. Where sociologists of sport have declined to engage in 'public intellectual' work, their alternative foci have had the unintended consequence of bolstering the subdiscipline. A movement away from applied sociology of sport, and the related movement towards more esoteric and theory-generative approaches to research (particularly apparent in relation to gender) may have equally (or more greatly) benefited the subdiscipline's standing within sociology.

More broadly we can detect three significant developments in the sociology of sport in terms of (1) its empirical scope; (2) its mode of analysis; and (3) its organizational formation. With regard to the first two, the field continues to produce a combined sociology *of* sport and a sociology *through* sport (Gruneau 1976). A sociology through sport is evident in the more widespread theoretical orientation of the subdiscipline today, and also the increasing interest in sport in the other sociological subdisciplines discussed in this book. Particularly amongst sociologists of the body and in relation to Elias's theory (and some would also claim Bourdieu), we can see how sociological understanding has developed *through* an engagement with sport. Concurrently, the shift towards postmodernism and the emphasis on individual experience and fragmented (post-)identities has fostered the acceptance of a diversified research agenda and a more differentiated sociology *of* sport. Sociologists (of sport) are increasingly receptive to research on minority (sporting) groups. Where 1980s British sociology of sport was dominated by researchers addressing broad social concerns such as football hooliganism, contemporary studies are just as likely if not more likely to look at martial-arts subcultures, or the gender politics of 'alternative' sports such as rock climbing or surfing. Where 1980s North American sociologists of sport seemed obsessed with stacking, contemporary studies include the more discrete worlds of women's roller derby and ultra-running.

The orientation of the field towards a sociology *through* sport has also led to a fundamental shift in the definition of 'sport' employed in the subdiscipline. Whereas the initial empirical focus of the subdiscipline was structured by a relatively narrow conception of sport (something that was useful in delineating the sociology of sport from related subject areas), much contemporary research looks at activities that eschew explicit competition or are not institutionally formalized. The aspects of the original definition of sport which are most strongly retained in the field are (1) that activities should have a significant degree of physical exertion and (2) that they should be ludic or playful. Some (e.g., Bairner 2009; Coakley and Dunning 2000a; Ingham and Donnelly 1997) detect an underlying 'anti-sport' agenda, and there is clearly evidence of this. But it should be recognized that the pro- vs. anti-sport debate is not a new characteristic of the field, for it was a source of division between the 'sociologists' and 'physical educationalists' who shaped the subdiscipline's emergence. Those who became ascendant through that debate were the anti-sport advocates (or at least those who defined themselves as more 'critical' sociologists). The situation in contemporary sociology of sport is different only by degree. In the broader scheme of things, the real 'anti-sport' people are those whose beliefs are expressed through disinterest and neglect.

It is, moreover, hard to deny the logic of the definitional shift. In conforming to the 'de-bunking' motif of sociology (Berger 1966), the subdiscipline has exposed contradictions between the perceptions and promises of contemporary (elite) sport and the lived reality of participation. A related 'achievement' of sociologists of sport (an achievement, that is, in terms of being aligned with the principles of sociology more generally), has been to demonstrate the socially constructed character of sport. Sport is gendered, leading to the exclusion and disadvantage of women. Sport is the product of a particular time and place (nineteenth-century Western Europe) and is thus inherently implicated in the relations of different 'races' and ethnic groups. Sport is, at most, only 'relatively autonomous' from the broader system of economic relations and is constituted by, and constitutive of, similar inequalities. If sport is an exclusionary practice, then a sociology *through* sport is logically restricted by these exclusions. For sociologists of sport to pursue the kind of sociological agenda explicit in its origins and contemporary missions, then they must also pursue a broader empirical field than traditional definitions of sport allow. After all, the sociology of religion embraces all aspects of spirituality; the sociology of education embraces pedagogical experiences that take place outside of schools and universities.

Although this should be viewed as an opportunity rather than a threat, it is important also that sport is not entirely 'de-centred', or that the sociology of sport becomes, as Holt (1998) warned of sports history, 'Hamlet without the Prince'. If sociologists of sport cease to emphasize those aspects of sport that illustrate its cultural significance, then it is unlikely that anyone else will. The role of sport within the broader academy will necessarily be weakened and the *raison d'être* of the sociology of sport failed. There is no reason why sociologists of sport should be strictly bound by a particular definition of sport, but neither should their flexibility be a reason to abandon sport altogether.

The primary mode of analysis in the sociology of sport has also changed, for standing in direct contrast to the methodological 'purity' which initially defined the subdiscipline is the multidisciplinarity it exhibits today. In the sense that this represents a fairly radical departure from the field that was originally envisaged, one could deem this to be something of a 'failure'. But this multidisciplinarity is a continuation of the pursuit of aligning the sociology of sport with the sociological 'mainstream' rather than an indication that the subdiscipline's physical education roots have prevailed. For instance, a strong element of this movement has been the embrace of cultural studies, an approach which itself is explicitly multidisciplinary. The embrace of post-structuralism and the incorporation of analytic techniques to 'queer' all kinds of boundaries and definitions (including disciplinary ones) continues this trend through the incorporation of more philosophical modes of analysis. John Urry has argued (1981) that sociology is an inherently parasitic discipline, appropriating what it can from elsewhere and incorporating it into its own canon. In the sociology of sport we initially saw this in relation to the subdiscipline's interdependence with sports history. The incorporation of the anthropology of sport is further evidence that multidisciplinarity is more a consequence of strength than weakness. The degree to which multidisciplinarity has caused a crisis in sports history stands in marked contrast to the degree to which it has been embraced within the sociology of sport. The broadly social-scientific remit of the sociology of sport's most recently established organizing body, the EASS, is further evidence that these changes are organic rather than disruptive for the subdiscipline. The increasing multidisciplinarity of the sociology of sport is therefore concomitant with broader sociological trends.

A third trend in the sociology of sport relates to the geographical distribution of power in the subdiscipline. Again, developments are complex and contradictory. However, compared to the initial composition of the ICSS board, the executive of today's ISSA is much more Anglocentric. Given its initial reliance on UNESCO sponsorship it was inumbent on the ICSS to constitute an internationally representative body and, to this end, the ten members of the 1968 committee (Albonico, Dumazedier, Erbach, Heinila, Lüschen, McIntosh, Novikov, Stone, Takenoshita and Wohl) represented a diverse range of cultures. The seven-member Executive Board of ISSA (2008–11) includes a president from New Zealand, a general secretary from the UK plus an American, Australian, Dane, Swiss and the *IRSS* Editor (also from the UK). (The ten-member 'extended board' and two 'regional representatives' do, however, expand this geographical representation.) The editorship of the *IRSS* has also become increasingly Anglocentric. Initially edited by Andrej Wohl (Polish), Kurt Weiss (Austrian) and Klaus Heinemann (German), subsequent editors have been Jim McKay (Australia), Alan Tomlinson (UK), Janet Harris (USA), Peter Donnelly (Canada) and John Sugden (UK). This 'Anglicization' was significant in prompting the establishment of the EASS in 2001 for, 'up to that time there had been no organization representing experts in the area of sport and social sciences on the European scene.'[1] Tellingly, there are few sociologists of sport from the UK involved in this organization. The NASSS, conversely, has become *less* parochial in recent years. In 2010 it started to develop links with sociologists of sport from Central and South America. The two most recent appointments as editors of the *SSJ* have been Pirkko Markula (Finnish) and Annelies Knoppers (Dutch).

These developments reflect the politics of language. There are, no doubt, outstanding scholars whose influence is largely confined to their own language, but they bear what Donnelly (2004: 6) has called the ethnic cost for non-Anglophones. It is undoubtedly the case that the analysis of the subdiscipline presented here is linked to my own linguistic limitations. Yet it is also the case that all those individuals who transcend the subdiscipline's geographical boundaries communicate in English. As much as journals continue to offer multiple translations of article abstracts, English has increasingly become an axis in the operation of power in academic (sub)disciplines.

Perhaps the main losers in this regard are Europeans, for their relative advantage over researchers from South Korea, Taiwan, etc., appears to be waning as 'English has become the language of cross-linguistic and cross-cultural communication' (Metcalfe 1998: 2).

In addition to simply charting these developments, an assessment of the sociology of sport can be made in relation to the sociological ideas about professions discussed in the introductory chapter. To what extent have sociologists of sport demonstrated that they possess an authoritative and definitive voice over a specific and complex area of study? Has the 'professional project' of sociologists of sport led to market control and social mobility? Is their work both distinctive and distinguished? Does the confidence that sociologists of sport express in their own contributions indicate a high degree of status security? Do they have legitimacy in the eyes of others?

Ironically, perhaps the clearest evidence to suggest that the sociology of sport is seen as a *distinctive* area of study is also the evidence that suggests that it is *not* distinguished. As noted in Chapter 1, for instance, Bourdieu has pointed to the marginality of the sociology of sport. Shilling has made similar comments (2005: 101). Perhaps the clearest and most damning assessment was delivered by Wacquant, who argued that only his association with Bourdieu saved him from 'disappearing into the oblivion of the sociology of sport' (Early *et al.* 1996, cited in Miller 1997: 116). As negative as such statements are, they indicate a taken-for-granted assumption that a clearly identifiable area described as 'the sociology of sport' exists. None of these authors question whether the sociology of sport is a legitimate area of sociological study, only the degree of influence it wields. This is a quite different position to the one in which pioneers of the field operated.

To what extent are sociologists of sport also deemed to be *authoritative* in their own field? The reluctance of authors such as Stuart Hall, Bryan Turner (initially), P. David Marshall, etc., to embark on detailed studies of sport, despite their obvious awareness of its significance to their respective fields, may also be taken as an implicit acceptance that the analysis of sport requires a degree of expertise, acquired through training, commitment, sustained analysis, etc. Against this, we might point to the work of various authors (e.g., Back *et al.* 2001b; Connell 1990; Monaghan 2001; Scambler 2005; Smart 2005; Woodward 2002) who have felt unconstrained to venture into sporting territory and who have generally received approval from sociologists of sport. There is, moreover, little by way of contested interpretation. 'Mainstream' sociologists' sport-related work and studies produced by sociologists of sport tend to be relatively compatible. Indeed, the strongest explicit critiques of the analyses of sociologists of sport came from sports historians in the 1980s and have significantly subsided since. On balance, therefore, it looks as though others recognize that sociologists of sport do something that sets them apart from other sociologists, that their concentrated focus on these social phenomena provides an element of expertise but that there is nothing esoteric or complex about what sociologists of sport do such that it precludes the entry of others into the field. The degree of market domination which sociologists of sport operate is not entirely under their own control; the social mobility it has brought them is limited.

The crux of this argument is that while semi-detachment may entail elements of 'mainstream' neglect, it also enables relative autonomy. This in turn leads to a sense of status security. It is in this light that groups such as the BSASSG can be formed and explicitly state the desire to forward the interests of their members. It is in this light that Maguire could claim that the sociology of sport was in a 'unique position to emphasize to the parent discipline the importance of the body' (1993: 33). Consequently, sociologists of sport have made some rather more confident statements about the field that illustrate a heightened degree of status security. Dunning, for instance, argues that 'the sociology of sport has been one of the liveliest and most fruitful of the parent subject's subdisciplines over the past 20 or so years, if not *the* liveliest and most fruitful' (2004: 17). Carrington similarly counters Wacquant's disparaging remarks by noting that, 'if the sociology of sport is indeed a space of intellectual oblivion … it appears to be in a relatively happy state of effervescent oblivion' (2010: 9–10). It might even be argued that the relative disunity in the contemporary field is an expression of confidence and strength. From the outset there was a 'strong affinity among social scientists in this speciality' (Snyder and Spreitzer 1974/1980: 30) which Dunning (2004) suggests was probably the outcome of a common sense of identity forged through the shared experience of fighting for recognition (see also Ingham and Donnelly 1997). If this is true, the increasing disunity in the field is probably an expression of a greater sense of establishment.

Preoccupied with their own relative marginality, sociologists of sport may fail to see the problems which those in other subdisciplines experience. One might, for instance, look enviously at the significance of the sociology of medicine to the sociological 'mainstream', but less so when one considers the kinds of soul-searching that some sociologists of medicine have undergone, predicting that the lack of theoretical rigour might lead to future decline (Nettleton 2007). Similarly, according to a recent *International Benchmarking Review of UK Sociology* (Trueman 2010), sociology as a whole has become increasingly fragmented with, for instance, an increasing number of sociologists working in business schools. The sociology of sport has its problems and weaknesses, but if sociology teaches us anything it is that we should view such developments within the broader context.

What might become of the sociology of sport in the future? As noted in Chapter 1, there have been calls for the reformation of the field. For instance, Klein has argued that multidisciplinarity has reached such a stage that it seems logical to reform into something he calls 'transnational sports studies' which would see sports scholars relinquish their 'disciplinary passports' (Klein 2007: 885). This call effectively replicates that of Daniels (1966/1969) forty years previously, with the exception that Klein is explicitly against, where Daniels was explicitly in favour of, sociology taking the titular and therefore symbolic lead. But the notion of transnational sports studies is unlikely to meet the requirements of many sociologists of sport because this shift would be likely to impair their sense of legitimacy within the discipline many regard as their home. Rather, the orientation of the EASS illustrates that a strength of sociology lies in the ability to absorb related areas of study and to integrate these additional 'tools' and techniques without undermining the core approach.

A more telling proposal is that of the formation of an area called physical cultural studies (PCS). This movement is most closely associated with David Andrews (2008) who has instituted the term in place of 'sociology of sport' to define the work of the group of scholars that he leads at Maryland University. While Andrews says that he sees 'little point in reprising discussions focused on the name of the field' (2008: 51) in citing 'a debilitating blend of introspective and ineffectual parochialism that has plagued the sociology of sport' (Silk and Andrews 2011: 5), this development promises to have more substantial and enduring ramifications. An *SSJ* special issue on PCS signals how this approach may become increasingly central within the field (Andrews and Silk 2011). Though Silk and Andrews (2011: 8) suggest that PCS 'develops as a complementary field', Atkinson predicts the 'impending demise of the sociology of sport' (2011: 136) with PCS as a 'successor' (2011: 137) or 'potential rival' (2011: 138).

One reason why the development of PCS is so interesting is because the 'problems' identified as stimuli are trends clearly outlined in this book. In a similar vein to the above discussion, Andrews states that contemporary sociology of sport is 'neither exclusively sociological nor … exclusively focussed on sport' (2008: 51). Identifying the development of an embodied sociology as particularly influential on the subdiscipline, he argues that PCS provides a more adequate description of the research now conducted by sociologists of sport. It also circumvents the 'intellectual boundaries and exclusivities' which Andrews (2008: 54) believes both hinders the subdiscipline and are reproduced in the term 'sociology of sport'. Moreover, Andrews argues, PCS could meet the challenges posed by the 'crisis' faced by social scientists of sport by the fragmentation, specialization and scientization which has led sociologists of sport to the 'bottom of the epistemological hierarchy' within kinesiology.

Though Silk and Andrews float the notion that PCS could be better defined as the study of physical culture rather than a cultural studies of the physical, PCS is repeatedly positioned as 'significantly informed by the "Hallian" version of cultural studies' (Andrews 2008: 56; Silk and Andrews 2011: 9). Sharing cultural studies' general orientation to critical theory and literary criticism, PCS similarly seeks to dismantle the boundaries that exist between academic disciplines and fuse concepts and theories from economics, history, media studies, philosophy, sociology, urban studies, cultural studies, etc. (Andrews 2008). PCS can 'be characterized as a critical sensibility and approach toward interpreting culture's role in the construction and experience of the "lived milieu of power"' (Grossberg 1997: 8; cited in Andrews 2008). Empirically, PCS is defined as those 'cultural practices in which the physical body – the way it moves, is represented, has meanings assigned to it, and is imbued with power – is central' (Vertinsky, cited in Andrews 2008: 52). In the call for papers for the *SSJ* special issue, Silk and Andrews (2010), though recognizing that the parameters of PCS are subject to ongoing refinement, highlight as especially relevant 'critical and theoretically informed engagement with various expressions of the physical (including, but by no means restricted to, sport, exercise, fitness, leisure, health, dance and movement-related active embodied practices)'. Silk and Andrews subsequently refer to 'active physicality' (2011: 4) and 'the whole gamut of physical culture' including 'daily living and work-related activities' (2011: 8).

Not only, then, does PCS reflect the multidisciplinarity and supra-sport focus of the field, but also the impact of the sociology of the body (Chapter 6) and the influence of cultural studies (Chapter 3). There are, however, a number of implications to PCS which, I would argue, could impact upon the 'professional project' of sociologists of sport in certain (unintended?) ways. First, the way in which PCS reframes the scope of the field threatens to reduce the distinctiveness of the sociology of sport. While PCS stems from a critique that sport is a 'vague and imprecise noun' (Andrews 2008: 50), this was recognized by the founders of the sociology of sport and to some extent rectified in the early definitional work (Chapter 2). Though liberally applied in contemporary sociology of sport, a precise definition of sport exists and serves as an epicentre for the subdiscipline. In contrast, PCS is *deliberately* vague and imprecise, to the point that, if adopted, PCS (and potentially the sociology of sport) would become undifferentiated from the sociology of the body. Second, in positioning the sociology of sport alongside the sociology of the body and cultural studies, PCS threatens to reduce the relative autonomy of the sociology of sport. Both areas wield greater influence within sociology as a whole, and engagement with these two areas has not been unequivocally beneficial for the sociology of sport, with cultural studies in particular largely failing to 'engage [with] the complex and diverse practices and representation of active embodiment' (Silk and Andrews 2010; see Chapter 3). Third, PCS threatens to be internally divisive to the sociology of sport through the prioritization of one theoretical approach (and the concomitant marginalization of others), and the reducing of the theoretical tensions within the subdiscipline which have previously been seen as a sign of its vitality. Silk and Andrews's (2011) argument that a field in tension has greater progressive potential is rather contradicted by their advocacy of certain methodological, epistemological and ontological boundaries for PCS. Finally, and most problematic of all perhaps, PCS more centrally positions the sociology of sport relative to sports science (and cultural studies). Both, though in different ways, have been relatively resistant to or dismissive of the sociology of sport. Conversely, so much of what the sociology of sport has 'achieved' up until now has come about through the orientation of the subdiscipline towards the sociological 'mainstream'. The historical perspective that has underpinned this review leads to a rather different assessment of the trends and developments in the sociology of sport and suggests that the most beneficial alignment of the subdiscipline has been and will be alongside the sociological 'mainstream'.

Conclusion

The sociology of sport is undoubtedly a product of the time and place of its inception. During the 1960s, subjects such as sociology and physical education were fragmenting into their component parts. These conditions dictated that the sociology of sport would be framed in a particular way, delineated by a specific empirical focus and a particular methodological approach. The precise orientation of the field was the outcome of the combined intended and unintended consequences of the relations of the various actors. Given different dynamics, the field we now know as the sociology of sport could have been subsumed in the sociology of leisure, fused with sports psychology within a broader social science of sport, or it could have become more oriented to the 'service' of sport, becoming more sport sociology than sociology of sport. To paraphrase Marx, sociologists of sport have made their own history but not in circumstances chosen by themselves.

If the sociology of sport was emerging today it would be likely that a different set of dynamics would influence its structure. More recent formations such as media studies or gender studies are explicitly interdisciplinary from the outset. Newer developments in sociology, such as the sociology of the body (Synott 1993: 6) and cultural sociology are claimed not as new areas of study but as 'a special sort of conceptual and methodological enterprise' (Inglis *et al.* 2007: 10). But today's sociologists of sport are just as bounded by the social conditions and historical legacies they find themselves in as were the pioneers of the sociology of sport half a century ago.

In a similar vein, I am conscious that the overview and analysis presented here is structured by my own social context. The contents of this book cannot be disentangled from my European (English), male and middle-class perspective. The conclusions that I have drawn are fundamentally premised on a developmental and relational approach. Central to my perspective has been a desire to illustrate how the sociology of sport has changed over time and how the sociology of sport compares with, and interrelates with, other (occupational) groups with which it cooperates and is in conflict. This is not to say that all analyses are equally adequate or valid. Rather, following Elias, I would suggest that the true value of this analysis lies not in abstract, essentialist and philosophically oriented concepts such 'truth' but in the degree to which the analysis presented here consistently works when subjected to 'reality testing … in the crucible of experience' (Elias 1987: 56).

If at the outset the main aim of the sociology of sport was to raise awareness of the social and sociological significance of sport, then there is evidence to suggest that this has been partially achieved. Sociologists of sport will continue to argue that this influence is not as great as it could or should be. However, it is worth reflecting on the degree to which the achievement of this aim is entirely desirable, for this reveals a central paradox for all subdisciplines. The logical conclusion to this mission is that all sociologists, all those in the various subdisciplines of sport, and other cultural commentators such as journalists, etc., recognize the importance and value of studying sport and integrate the concepts and ideas generated by sociologists of sport into their world view. But ultimately, if this were the case, the sociology of sport as a vocation ceases to exist. There becomes nothing distinct about what sociologists of sport do and therefore no commonalities through which to forge an identity. There can be no 'we' group without a 'they' group against which the 'we' can be defined. *Pace* Andrews, 'intellectual boundaries and exclusivities' are wholly productive for professional groups such as sociologists of sport. While those in the subdiscipline should work to make 'sociologist of sport' a broadly recognized and understandable term, it is equally important that it is seen to be something distinctive.

NOTES

1 Towards a sociology of the sociology of sport

1 See http://www.issa.otago.ac.nz/about.html; http://www.nasss.org; http://www.eass-sportsociology.eu/statutes.html; and http://www.britsoc.co.uk/specialisms/Sport.htm. (Accessed 15 July 2010.)

2 There are, of course, many similar national bodies around the world. A South Korean sociology of sport association was founded in 1990 and has approximately 1,000 members; a Japanese equivalent was founded in 1991 and has approximately 440 members. In France, La Société de Sociologie du Sport de Langue Française was established in 2001, and in Spain the Asociación Española de Investigación Social Aplicada al Deporte was established in 1989 and now has approximately 150 members. My thanks to Ji Hyun Cho, Nobuko Tanaka, Koichi Kiku, Christine Mennesson and David Moscoso-Sánchez for providing this information.

3 The Association for the Anthropological Study of Play (TASP), formed at the 1974 meeting of the North American Society of Sport History, is perhaps the closest to a professional body for anthropologists of sport. However, this body clearly has a more central focus on play and has a North American rather than an international membership. The association produces an annual publication based on the proceedings of its conferences but closed its journal in the mid-1990s indicating that TASP's influence and ambition is considerably less than some of its counterparts in sociology (Blanchard 1995: 20–1). See also the association's website, http://www.tasplay.org.

2 The emergence of the sociology of sport: the invention of tradition?

1 The ICSS was reconstituted as ISSA in 1994.

2 The ICSPE was founded in France in 1958. In 1982 it changed its name to the International Council of Sport Science and Physical Education. See http://www.icsspe.org.

3 Lüschen cites eighty-two active scholars but provides disciplinary backgrounds for eighty-three.

3 Sociology of sport and social theory

1 Others might argue that James's *Beyond a Boundary* (1963) deserves this claim, but see Chapter 4.

2 Paul Hoch's *Rip off the Big Game* (1972) is often also cited in this regard. I have chosen to omit his work here because, despite being a key Marxist work on sport, I do not consider Hoch to have been either a sociologist of sport or indeed a sociologist more generally.
3 I do not pretend that this is anything other than a convenience sample but, given that the absence of reference to sport is such a striking trend, I presume it to be a reliable indicator.
4 Elias also started to write a paper on the relationship between boxing and duelling in England and France. While multiple versions of this paper remain, he never finished the piece and so it remains unpublished.
5 Though some have highlighted the empirical weaknesses of this work. See Franklin 1996.

4 Sport, 'race' and ethnicity

1 The titling of this chapter is complicated by the shifting parameters of the field. Over the period discussed in this chapter there has been a growing sociological critique of the meaningfulness of the concept of biological 'race' (and hence the word's appearance in inverted commas). Allied to the increasing emphasis on issues of (self-)identity this has resulted in a shift towards studies of ethnicity rather than 'race'.
2 The book does not give biographical details for Thompson, but other searches show that there was, at this time, a Richard Thompson writing on race-related issues and working in Canterbury.
3 Most texts refer to the second author of this study as McElvogue rather than Elvogue, but Elvogue is the name that appears on the original article.
4 In the same year, Gajendra Verma and Douglas Darby published *Winners and Losers* (1994). Verma and Darby's detailed empirical research into the patterns of sports participation within British minority ethnic communities helped challenge many myths about the supposed lack of Asian involvement in sport. However, I have not included it in my discussion here as the text lacks a sociological theoretical framework and because Verma and Darby's main disciplinary orientation is education.
5 While some might debate my definition of John Hoberman as a sociologist of sport, his significance to, and participation in, the subdiscipline merits his inclusion here.

5 Sport and gender

1 See http://www.newstatesman.com/2010/09/global-influence-world-2.
2 It should be noted, of course, that feminists are not the only sociologists to question the idea of social science objectivity. In Chapter 9 we see some of the implications of this for the public standing of social science.
3 Feminism is generally categorized into three 'waves'. First-wave feminism, which spanned the end of the nineteenth and beginning of the twentieth centuries, focused mainly on legal inequalities, such as women's right to vote. Second-wave feminism, from around the 1960s to the 1980s, focused on the de-facto, unofficial inequalities which remained, such as in the family, the workplace and, in particular, regarding sexuality and reproductive rights. Finally, third-wave feminism, which arose as a response to the perceived failures of previous forms of feminism, stresses diversity (e.g., women of different ethnicities) and change.

6 Sport and the body

1 Interestingly, one person Frank acknowledges in an endnote is sociologist of sport Kevin Young.
2 The disengagement between the sociology of sport and the sociology of medicine is perhaps surprising given the latter's long-standing and established position within sociology and the potential benefits for sociologists of sport of collaborative links.

Waddington *et al.* suggest that the recent correction of the prior neglect of pain and injury in sport can be attributed to 'the increased incidence of injuries associated with the increased competitiveness of modern sport, and the growing recognition of the increased social and economic significance of injuries' (2006: 8). Young (2004: 1), however, considers it likely that such developments are 'in step' with the development of the sociology of the body as charted in this chapter.

8 Sociology of sport and sports history

1 Aspects of this analysis were developed in a previous book chapter co-authored with Louise Mansfield (Mansfield and Malcolm 2010). I am grateful to Louise for allowing me to draw on that work here.
2 I am grateful to Ronald A. Smith for supplying me with this and other information about NASSH (4 May 2011).
3 The ASSH has no equivalent prize.
4 Dominic Malcolm, Daniel Bloyce and Paul Darby are perhaps exceptions here, though none have yet produced work with the impact of the sociological texts reviewed earlier. Mention should also be made of Paul Dimeo who, whilst trained as a sociologist, has increasingly published historically oriented work and now considers himself more of a sports studies generalist than fixed within either discipline.
5 Johnes cites the *European Sports History Review*, *Football Studies*, *International Journal of the History of Sport*, *Journal of Olympic History*, *Journal of Sport History*, *Nine*, *Olympika*, *Soccer and Society*, *Sports History Review*, *Sport in History*, *Sport in Society* and *Sporting Traditions*. The eight sociology of sport journals are *IRSS*, *SSJ*, *JSSI* and *Sport, Education and Society*, plus *Sport in Society*, *Sporting Traditions*, *Soccer and Society* and *Football Studies*.

9 Sociology of sport and public engagement

1 See http://www.wsc.co.uk/content/category/9/49/72/ (accessed 19 April 2011). Note this list does not backdate to the earliest editions of *WSC* and thus is presented as indicative rather than comprehensive.
2 The Research Assessment Exercise (reformed as the Research Excellence Framework for 2014) is a periodical review of academics' research output which serves as the basis for distributing a considerable proportion of research funding to UK universities.
3 It might be noted that Tomlinson was also one of the founders of the BSASSG and it is perhaps no coincidence, therefore, that the mission statement of that organization makes specific reference to influencing public debate (see Chapter 1).
4 Philosophy Football was primarily known for selling clothing branded with football-related quotes from philosophers and cultural icons.
5 While Brimson argues that academics have failed to see what is 'at the core of the entire [hooligan] issue' – namely the enjoyment hooligans gain from violent engagement – such ideas are central to the Leicester School approach, and, indeed, Williams explicitly refers to the centrality of 'risk and excitement' in his chapter in this book (2001: 49). Similarly, Campbell and Dawson argue that sociologists of sport have overlooked the importance of masculinity in explaining football hooliganism when, again, the notion of masculinity is central to the Leicester School approach, and Williams cites the ideas of Bob Connell and provides the very type of analysis Campbell and Dawson claim is absent. There is also evidence that these readers fail to appreciate the importance of methodology in legitimating sociological knowledge. Campbell and Dawson (2001: 70) for instance argue that Dunning *et al.*'s identification of the importance of class stems solely from their analysis of arrest figures (and not their ethnographic work) and in dismissing academic work as based on 'guesswork and hearsay' Brimson explicitly prioritizes the value of experiential knowledge.

6 Though, he claims, there are no equivalent differences in intelligence: 'It's time to decouple intelligence and physicality' (Entine 2000: 337).
7 See Entine's website (http://www.jonentine.com) for a list of reviews of his work. (Accessed 12 January 2010.)
8 Entine cites Myburgh as arguing that, 'I've been asked many times how an academic can waste time studying the differences between black and white people … I said, "Well if you're a scientist and you're studying obesity, who do you compare obese people with? You compare them with thin people"' (Entine 2000: 79). In so doing, Myburgh, an exercise physiologist, clearly illustrates how research is driven by a priori perceptions of 'race' as a valid category.

10 The sociology of sport: a 'profession' in process

1 See http://www.eass-sportsociology.eu/information.html.

REFERENCES

Abbott, A. (1988) *The System of Professions: An Essay in the Division of Expert Labour*. Chicago, Ill.: University of Chicago Press.

Abrams, P. (1982) *Historical Sociology*. Wells: Open Books.

Achter, P. and Condit, C. M. (2000) 'Not so black and white', *American Scientist*. Available at http://www.jonentine.com. (Accessed 12 January 2010.)

Acosta, V. and Carpenter, L. (1994) 'The status of women in intercollegiate athletics', in S. Birrell and C. Cole (eds), *Women, Sport and Culture*. Champaign, Ill.: Human Kinetics, 111–18.

Allison, L. (1998) 'Biology, ideology and sport', in L. Allison (ed.), *Taking Sport Seriously*. Aachen: Meyer & Meyer, 135–54.

Anderson, E. (2002) 'Openly gay athletes: Contesting hegemonic masculinity in a homophobic environment', *Gender and Society*, 16(6): 860–77.

——(2005) *In the Game: Gay Athletes and the Cult of Masculinity*. New York: State University of New York Press.

——(2009) *Inclusive Masculinity: The Changing Nature of Masculinity*. New York: Routledge.

Andrews, D. (1993) 'Desperately seeking Michel: Foucault's genealogy, the body, and critical sport sociology', *Sociology of Sport Journal*, 10(2): 148–68.

——(1996a) 'The fact(s) of Michael Jordan's blackness: Excavating a floating racial signifier', *Sociology of Sport Journal*, 13(4): 125–58.

——(ed.) (1996b) 'Special issue: Deconstructing Michael Jordan: Reconstructing postindustrial America', *Sociology of Sport Journal*, 13(4).

——(2000) 'Posting up: French post-structuralism and the critical analysis of contemporary sporting culture', in J. Coakley and E. Dunning (eds), *Handbook of Sports Studies*. London: Sage, 106–37.

——(2002) 'Coming to terms with cultural studies', *Journal of Sport and Social Issues*, 26(1): 110–16.

——(2008) 'Kinesiology's *inconvenient truth* and the physical cultural studies imperative', *Quest*, 60(1): 45–62.

Andrews, D. and Jackson, S. (2001a) 'Introduction: Sport stars, public culture and private experience', in D. Andrews and S. Jackson (eds), *Sport Stars: The Cultural Politics of Sporting Celebrity*. London: Routledge, 1–19.

——(eds) (2001b) *Sport Stars: The Cultural Politics of Sporting Celebrity*. London: Routledge.

Andrews, D. and Silk, M. (eds) (2011) 'Special Issue: Physical Cultural Studies', *Sociology of Sport Journal*, 28(1).

Anon. (1976) 'International seminar for sociology of sport, October 2–5, 1975 in Heidelberg', *International Review for the Sociology of Sport*, 11(2): 153–60.
Archer, R. and Bouillon, A. (1982) *The South African Game: Sport and Racism*. London: Zed Books.
Armstrong, G. (1999) 'Kicking off with the wannabe warriors', in M. Perryman (ed.), *The Ingerland Factor: Home Truths from Football*. Edinburgh: Mainstream, 45–58.
Atkinson, M. (2003) *Tattooed: The Sociogenesis of Body Art*. Toronto: University of Toronto Press.
——(2011) 'Physical cultural studies [redux]', *Sociology of Sport Journal*, 28(1): 135–44.
Atkinson, T. (ed.) (2005) *The Body (Readers in Cultural Criticism)*. London: Palgrave Macmillan.
Back, L., Crabbe, T. and Solomos, J. (2001a) '"Lions in black skins": Race, nation and local patriotism in football', in B. Carrington and I. McDonald (eds), *'Race', Sport and British Society*. London: Routledge, 83–102.
——(2001b) *The Changing Face of Football: Racism, Identity and Multiculture in the English Game*. Oxford: Berg.
Bairner, A. (2004) 'Where did it all go right? George Best, Manchester United and Northern Ireland', in D. L. Andrews (ed.), *Manchester United: A Thematic Study*. London: Routledge, 133–46.
——(2007) 'Back to basics: Class, social theory, and sport', *Sociology of Sport Journal*, 24(1): 20–36.
——(2009) 'Sport, intellectuals and public sociology: Obstacles and opportunities', *International Review for the Sociology of Sport*, 44(2–3): 115–30.
Baker, W. J. (1983) 'The state of British sport history', *Journal of Sport History*, 10(1): 53–66.
Bale, J. (1998) 'Review symposium', *International Review for the Sociology of Sport*, 33(1): 83–6.
Bale, J. and Philo, C. (1998) 'Introduction: Henning Eichberg, space, identity and body culture', in H. Eichberg, *Body Cultures: Essays on Sport, Space and Identity*. London: Routledge, 3–21.
Balsamo, A. (1994) 'Feminist bodybuilding', in S. Birrell and C. Cole (eds), *Women, Sport and Culture*. Champaign, Ill.: Human Kinetics, 341–52.
Barnes, J. A. (1981) 'Professionalism in British sociology', in P. Abrams (ed.), *Practice and Progress: British Sociology, 1950–1980*. London: Allen & Unwin, 13–24.
Bateman, A. (2009) *Cricket, Literature and Culture: Symbolising the Nation, Destabilising the Empire*. Farnham: Ashgate.
Beckford, P. (1796) *Thoughts on Hare and Foxhunting*. London.
Berger, P. (1966) *Invitation to Sociology: A Humanistic Perspective*. Harmondsworth: Penguin.
Berghorn, F. J., Yetman, N. R. and Hanna, W. E. (1988) 'Racial participation and integration in men's and women's intercollegiate basketball: Continuity and change, 1958–85', *Sociology of Sport Journal*, 5(2): 107–24.
Berthelot, J. (1991) 'Sociological discourse and the body', in M. Featherstone, M. Hepworth and B. S. Turner (eds), *The Body: Social Process and Cultural Theory*. London: Sage, 390–405.
Besseler, W. (2002) 'Book review: J. Entine, *Taboo: Why black athletes dominate sports and why we're afraid to talk about it*', *International Journal of the History of Sport*, 19(4): 242–3.
Birrell, S. (1988) 'Discourses on the gender/sport relationship: From women in sport to gender relations', *Exercise and Sport Science Reviews*, 16: 459–502.
——(1989) 'Racial relations theories and sport: Suggestions for a more critical analysis', *Sociology of Sport Journal*, 6(3): 212–27.
——(1990) 'Women of colour, critical autobiography, and sport', in M. Messner and D. Sabo (eds), *Sport, Men, and the Gender Order*. Champaign, Ill.: Human Kinetics, 185–99.
——(2000) 'Feminist theories for sport', in J. Coakley and E. Dunning (eds), *Handbook of Sports Studies*. London: Sage, 61–76.
Birrell, S. and Cole, C. (eds) (1994) *Women, Sport and Culture*. Champaign, Ill.: Human Kinetics.
Birrell, S. and Richter, D. (1987) 'Is a diamond forever? Feminist transformations of sport', *Women's Studies International Forum*, 10(4): 395–409.
Blake, A. (1996) *Body Language: The Meaning of Modern Sport*. London: Lawrence & Wishart.

——(2002) 'An other and another World Cup', in M. Perryman (ed.), *Going Oriental: Football After World Cup 2002*. Edinburgh: Mainstream, 90–101.

Blanchard, K. (1995) *The Anthropology of Sport: An Introduction*. Westport, Conn.: Bergin & Garvey.

Bloyce, D. (2004) 'Baseball: Myths and modernization', in E. Dunning, D. Malcolm and I. Waddington (eds), *Sport Histories: Figurational Studies of the Development of Modern Sports*. London: Routledge, 88–103.

Bogin, B. (2001) 'Book review: J. Entine, *Taboo: Why black athletes dominate sports and why we're afraid to talk about it*', *American Journal of Physical Anthropology*. Available at http://www.jonentine.com. (Accessed 12 January 2010.)

Bolin, A. (1992) 'Flex appeal, food, and fat: Competitive bodybuilding, gender, and diet', *Play and Culture*, 5(4): 378–400.

Boorstin, D. J. (1961) *The Image: The Guide to Pseudo Events in America*. New York: Simon & Schuster.

Booth, D. (1997) 'Sport history: What can be done', *Sport, Education and Society*, 2(2): 191–204.

——(1998) *The Race Game: Sport and Politics in South Africa*. London: Frank Cass.

——(2005) *The Field: Truth and Fiction in Sport History*. London: Routledge.

Bourdieu, P. (1978) 'Sport and social class', *Social Science Information*, 17(6): 819–40.

——(1983) 'How can one be a sportsman?', in P. Bourdieu, *Sociology in Question*. London: Sage, 117–31.

——(1984) *Distinction: A Social Critique of the Judgement of Taste*. London: Routledge & Kegan Paul.

——(1987a) 'Programme for a sociology of sport', in P. Bourdieu, *In Other Words*. Cambridge: Polity Press, 156–67.

——(1987b) *In Other Words*. Cambridge: Polity Press.

——(1998a) *On Television*. London: Pluto Press.

——(1998b) 'L'état, l'économie et le sport', *Sociétés et Représentations*, 7: 13–19.

——(1998c) *Practical Reason: On the Theory of Action*. Cambridge: Polity Press.

Bourdieu, P. and Wacquant, L. (1992) *An Invitation to Reflexive Sociology*. Cambridge: Polity Press.

Boutilier, M. and San Giovanni, L. (1980) *The Sporting Woman*. Champaign, Ill.: Human Kinetics.

Boyle, R. (1963) *Sport: Mirror of American Life*. Boston, Mass.: Little, Brown & Company.

Brimson, D. (2000) *Barmy Army: The Changing Face of Football Violence*. London: Headline.

——(2001) 'Fans for a change', in M. Perryman (ed.), *Hooligan Wars: Causes and Effects of Football Violence*. Edinburgh: Mainstream, 198–204.

Brod, H. (ed.) (1987) *The Making of Masculinities: The New Men's Studies*. Boston: Allen & Unwin.

Brohm, J. M. (1978) *Sport: A Prison of Measured Time*. London: Ink Links.

Brooks, S. (2009) *Black Men Can't Shoot*. Chicago, Ill.: Chicago University Press.

Bryson, L. (1987/1994) 'Sport and the maintenance of masculine hegemony', *Women's Studies International Forum*, 10(4): 349–60. Reprinted in S. Birrell and C. Cole (eds), *Women, Sport and Culture*. Champaign, Ill.: Human Kinetics, 47–64.

Burawoy, M. (2005) 'For public sociology', *American Sociological Review*, 70(1): 4–28.

Burdsey, D. (2007a) *British Asians and Football: Culture, Identity, Exclusion*. London: Routledge.

——(2007b) 'Role with the punches: The construction and representation of Amir Khan as a role model for multiethnic Britain', *The Sociological Review*, 55(3): 611–31.

Burke, P. (1980) *Sociology and History*. London: George Allen & Unwin.

Butler, J. (1990) *Gender Trouble: Feminism and the Subversion of Identity*. New York: Routledge.

Caillois, R. (1961) *Man, Play and Games*. Glencoe, Ill.: Free Press.

Campbell, B. and Dawson, A. L. (2001) 'Indecent exposures, men, masculinity and violence', in M. Perryman (ed.), *Hooligan Wars: Causes and Effects of Football Violence*. Edinburgh: Mainstream, 62–76.

Cantelon, H. and Gruneau, R. (eds) (1982) *Sport, Culture and the Modern State*. Toronto: University of Toronto Press.

Carrington, B. (1999) 'Too many St. George Crosses to bear', in M. Perryman (ed.), *The Ingerland Factor: Home Truths from Football*. Edinburgh: Mainstream, 71–86.
——(2000) 'Double consciousness and the black British athlete', in K. Owusu (ed.), *Black British Culture and Society: A Text-Reader*. London: Routledge, 133–56.
——(2010) *Race, Sport and Politics: The Sporting Black Diaspora*. London: Sage.
Carrington, B. and McDonald, I. (eds) (2001a) *'Race', Sport and British Society*. London: Routledge.
——(2001b) 'Whose game is it anyway? Racism in local league cricket', in B. Carrington and I. McDonald (eds), *'Race', Sport and British Society*. London: Routledge, 49–69.
——(2009) *Marxism, Cultural Studies and Sport*. London: Routledge.
Cashmore, E. (1982) *Black Sportsmen*. London: Routledge & Kegan Paul.
——(2002) *Beckham*. Cambridge: Polity Press.
——(2005a) *Tyson: Nurture the Beast*. Cambridge: Polity Press.
——(2005b) *Making Sense of Sports*, 4th edn. London: Routledge.
——(2006) *Celebrity/Culture*. London: Routledge.
Cashmore, E. and Jennings, J. (2001) *Racism: Essential Readings*. London: Sage.
Cashmore, E. and Parker, A. (2003) 'One David Beckham? Celebrity, masculinity and the soccerati', *Sociology of Sport Journal*, 20(3): 214–31.
Caudwell, J. (ed.) (2006) *Sport, Sexualities and Queer/Theory*. London: Routledge.
Cavanaugh, S. and Sykes, H. (2006) 'Transsexual bodies at the Olympics: The International Olympic Committee's policy on transsexual athletes at the 2004 Athens summer games', *Body and Society*, 12(3): 75–102.
Chaudhary, V. (2001) 'Black, brown, blue and white army', in M. Perryman (ed.), *Hooligan Wars: Causes and Effects of Football Violence*. Edinburgh: Mainstream, 77–83.
Christensen, K., Guttmann, A. and Pfister, G. (2000) *International Encyclopedia of Women and Sports*. New York: Macmillan.
Chung, H. (2003) 'Sport star vs. rock star in globalizing popular culture: Similarities, differences and paradox in discussion of celebrities', *International Review for the Sociology of Sport*, 38(1): 99–108.
Clarke, G. and Humberstone, B. (eds) (1997) *Researching Women and Sport*. Basingstoke: Macmillan.
Clement, J. P. (1995) 'Contributions of the sociology of Pierre Bourdieu to the sociology of sport', *Sociology of Sport Journal*, 12(2): 147–57.
Coad, D. (2008) *The Meterosexual: Gender, Sexuality, and Sport*. New York: SUNY Press.
Coakley, J. (1987) 'Sociology of sport in the United States', *International Review for the Sociology of Sport*, 22(1): 63–79.
——(2007) *Sports in Society: Issues and Controversies*, 9th edn. New York: McGraw-Hill.
Coakley, J. and Dunning, E. (2000a) 'General introduction', in J. Coakley and E. Dunning (eds), *Handbook of Sports Studies*. London: Sage, xxi–xxxviii.
——(eds) (2000b) *Handbook of Sports Studies*. London: Sage.
Cohen, G. (ed.) (1993) *Women in Sport: Issues and Controversies*. Thousand Oaks, Calif.: Sage.
Cole, C. (1993) 'Resisting the canon: Feminist cultural studies, sport and technologies of the body', *Journal of Sport and Social Issues*, 17(2): 77–97.
——(2000) 'Body studies in the sociology of sport: A review of the field', in J. Coakley and E. Dunning (eds), *Handbook of Sports Studies*. London: Sage, 439–60.
Cole, C. and Andrews, D. (2001) 'America's new son: Tiger Woods and America's multiculturalism', in D. Andrews and S. Jackson (eds), *Sport Stars: The Cultural Politics of Sporting Celebrity*. London: Routledge, 70–86.
Coleman, J. (1961) *The Adolescent Society*. New York: Free Press.
Collins, T. (2005) 'History, theory and the "Civilizing Process"', *Sport in History*, 25(2): 289–306.
Connell, R. (1987) *Gender and Power: Society, the Person and Sexual Politics*. Cambridge: Polity Press.
——(1990) 'An iron man: The body and some contradictions of hegemonic masculinity', in M. Messner and D. Sabo (eds), *Sport, Men and the Gender Order: Critical Feminist Perspectives*. Champaign, Ill.: Human Kinetics, 83–96.

——(2002) 'Debates about men, new research on masculinities', in S. Scraton and A. Flintoff (eds), *Gender and Sport: A Reader*. London: Routledge, 161–8.

Cornwall, P. (2002) 'Sven, long to reign over us', in M. Perryman (ed.), *Going Oriental: Football After World Cup 2002*. Edinburgh: Mainstream, 183–96.

Costa, D. M. and Guthrie, S. R. (eds) (1994) *Women and Sport: Interdisciplinary Perspectives*. Champaign, Ill.: Human Kinetics.

Cox, R. (2000) 'British Society of Sports History', in R. Cox, G. Jarvie and W. Vamplew (eds), *Encyclopedia of British Sport*. Oxford: ABC-Clio, 48–9.

Cozens, F. W. and Stumpf, F. S. (1953) *Sports in American Life*. Chicago, Ill.: University of Chicago Press.

Crabbe, T. and Blackshaw, T. (2004) *New Perspectives on Sport and Deviance: Consumption, Performativity and Social Control*. London: Routledge.

Craig, P. and Jones, A. (2008) 'Sport and the body', in P. Craig and P. Beedie (eds), *Sport Sociology*. Exeter: Learning Matters, 183–201.

Creedon, P. (ed.) (1994) *Women, Media and Sport: Challenging Gender Values*. London: Sage.

Cregan, K. (2006) *The Sociology of the Body: Mapping the Abstraction of Embodiment*. London: Sage.

Crepeau, R. (2001) 'Book Review: J. Entine, *Taboo: Why black athletes dominate sports and why we're afraid to talk about it*', *Sociology of Sport Journal*, 18(2): 251–3.

Critcher, C. (1979) 'Football since the war', in J. Clarke, C. Critcher and R. Johnson (eds), *Working Class Culture*. London: Hutchison, 161–84.

Crolley, L. (1999) 'Lads will be lads', in M. Perryman (ed.), *The Ingerland Factor: Home Truths from Football*. Edinburgh: Mainstream, 59–70.

Crosset, T. (1995) *Outsiders in the Clubhouse: The World of Women's Professional Golf*. New York: SUNY Press.

——(2000) 'Athletic affiliation and violence against women: Toward a structural prevention project', in J. McKay, M. Messner and D. Sabo (eds), *Masculinities, Gender Relations, and Sport*. Thousand Oaks, CA: Sage, 147–61.

Cunningham, H. (1980) *Leisure in the Industrial Revolution c.1780–c.1880*. London: Croom Helm.

Curry, G., Dunning, E. and Sheard, K. (2006) 'Sociological versus empiricist history: Some comments on Tony Collins's "History, theory and the 'Civilizing Process'"', *Sport in History*, 26(1): 110–23.

Curry, T. (1993) 'A little pain never hurt anyone: Athletic career socialization and the normalization of sports injury', *Symbolic Interaction*, 16(3): 273–90.

——(1994/2002) 'Fraternal bonding in the locker room: A profeminist analysis of talk about competition and women', *Sociology of Sport Journal*, 8(2): 119–35. Reprinted in S. Scraton and A. Flintoff (eds), *Sport and Gender: A Reader*. London: Routledge, 169–87.

Daniels, A. S. (1966/1969) 'The study of sport as an element of the culture', *International Review of Sport Sociology*, 1(1): 153–65. Reprinted in J. Loy and G. Kenyon (eds), *Sport, Culture and Society: A Reader on the Sociology of Sport*. New York: Macmillan, 13–22.

Darnell, S. and Sparks, R. (2005) 'Inside the promotional vortex: Canadian media construction of Sydney Olympic triathlete Simon Whitfield', *International Review for the Sociology of Sport*, 40(3): 357–76.

deCordova, R. (1990) *Picture Personalities: The Emergence of the Star System in America*. Chicago, Ill.: University of Illinois Press.

Deem, R. (1986) *All Work and No Play? A Study of Women and Leisure*. Milton Keynes: Open University Press.

——(1989) 'New ways forward in sport and leisure studies: a reply to Robert Sparkes', *Sociology of Sport Journal*, 6(1): 66–9.

Defrance, J. (1976) 'Esquisse d'une histoire sociale de la gymnastique (1760–1870)', *Actes de la Recherche en Sciences Sociales*, 6: 22–46.

——(1995) 'The anthropological sociology of Pierre Bourdieu: Genesis, concepts, relevance', *Sociology of Sport Journal*, 12(2): 121–31.

Dimeo, P. and Finn, G. (2001) 'Racism, national identity and Scottish football', in B. Carrington and I. McDonald (eds), *'Race', Sport and British Society*. London: Routledge, 29–48.

Dingwall, R. (1983) 'Introduction', in R. Dingwall and P. Lewis (eds), *The Sociology of the Professions: Lawyers, Doctors and Others*. London: Macmillan, 1–13.

Donnell, A. (ed.) (2001) *Companion to Contemporary Black British Culture*. London: Routledge.

Donnelly, P. (1992) 'Special theme issue: British cultural studies', *Sociology of Sport Journal*, 9(2): 103.

——(2003) 'Sport and social theory', in B. Houlihan (ed.), *Sport and Society: A Student Introduction*. London: Sage, 11–28.

——(2004) 'Editorial', *International Review for the Sociology of Sport*, 39(1): 5–6.

Donnelly, P. and Young, K. (1988) 'The construction and confirmation of identity in sport subcultures', *Sociology of Sport Journal*, 5(3): 223–40.

Dougherty, M. (2001) 'Book Review: J. Entine, *Taboo: Why black athletes dominate sports and why we're afraid to talk about it*', *The Quarterly Review of Biology*. Available at http://www.jonentine.com. (Accessed 12 January 2010.)

Dufur, M. (1999) 'Gender and Sport', in J. Saltzman Chafetz (ed.), *Handbook of the Sociology of Gender*. New York: Kluwer Academic, 583–600.

Dumazedier, J. (1964) 'The point of view of the social scientist', in E. Jokl and E. Simon (eds), *International Research in Sport and Physical Education*. Springfield, Ill.: Thomas, 212–17.

——(1966) *Toward a Society of Leisure*. New York: Free Press.

——(1974) *Sociology of Leisure*. Oxford: Elsevier.

Duncan, M. C. (ed.) (2008) 'Special issue: The social construction of fat', *Sociology of Sport Journal*, 25(1).

Dunning, E. (1963) 'Football in its early stages', *History Today* (December).

——(1967) 'Notes on some conceptual and theoretical problems in the sociology of sport', *International Review of Sport Sociology*, 2(1): 143–53.

——(1986a) 'The sociology of sport in Europe and the United States: Critical observations from an "Eliasian" perspective', in C. R. Rees and A. W. Miracle (eds), *Sport and Social Theory*. Champaign, Ill.: Human Kinetics, 29–56.

——(1986b) 'Sport as a male preserve: Notes on the social sources of masculine identity and its transformation', *Theory, Culture and Society*, 3(1): 79–90.

——(1986c) 'The dynamics of modern sport: Notes on achievement-striving and the social significance of sport', in N. Elias and E. Dunning, *Quest for Excitement: Sport and Leisure in the Civilizing Process*. Oxford: Blackwell, 205–23.

——(1992) 'A remembrance of Norbert Elias', *Sociology of Sport Journal*, 9(1): 95–9.

——(1999) *Sport Matters: Sociological Studies of Sport, Violence and Civilization*. London: Routledge.

——(2001) 'Something of a curate's egg: Comments on Adrian Harvey's "An epoch in the annals of national sport"', *International Journal of the History of Sport*, 18(4): 88–94.

——(2002) 'Figurational contributions to the sociological study of sport', in J. Maguire and K. Young (eds), *Theory, Sport and Society*. Oxford: Elsevier Science, 211–38.

——(2004) 'Sociology of sport in the balance: Critical reflections on some recent and more enduring trends', *Sport in Society*, 7(1): 1–24.

Dunning, E. and Curry, G. (2002) 'The curate's egg scrambled again: comments on "The curate's egg put back together"', *International Journal of the History of Sport*, 19(4): 200–4.

Dunning, S. E. and Mennell, S. (eds) (2003) *Norbert Elias*. London: Sage.

Dunning, E. and Rojek, C. (1992) *Sport and Leisure in the Civilizing Process: Critique and Counter-critique*. London: Routledge.

Dunning, E. and Sheard, K. (1979/2005) *Barbarians, Gentlemen and Players: A Sociological Study of the Development of Rugby Football*. London and Oxford: Martin Robertson and Routledge.

Dunning, E., Maguire, J. and Pearton, R. (eds) (1993) *The Sports Process: A Comparative and Developmental Approach*. Champaign, Ill.: Human Kinetics.

Dunning, E., Malcolm, D. and Waddington, I. (eds) (2004a) *Sport Histories: Figurational Studies of the Development of Modern Sports*. London: Routledge.

——(2004b) 'Conclusion: Figurational sociology and the development of modern sport', in E. Dunning, D. Malcolm and I. Waddington (eds), *Sport Histories: Figurational Studies of the Development of Modern Sports*. London: Routledge, 191–206.

Dunning, E., Murphy, P. and Williams, J. (1988) *The Roots of Football Hooliganism: An Historical and Sociological Study*. London: Routledge & Kegan Paul.

Dworkin, S. and Messner, M. (1999) 'Just do … what? Sport, bodies, gender', in M. Ferree, J. Lorber and B. Hess (eds), *Revisioning Gender*. Thousand Oaks, Calif.: Sage, 341–61.

Dyer, K. F. (1982) *Catching up the Men: Women in Sport*. London: Junction Books.

Dyer, R. (1987) *Heavenly Bodies: Film Stars and Society*. London: Macmillan.

Early, G., Solomon, E. and Wacquant, L. (1996) *The Charisma of Sport and Race*. Berkeley, Calif.: Doreen B. Townsend Center for the Humanities.

Edwards, H. (1969/1970) *The Revolt of the Black Athlete*. New York: The Free Press.

——(1971) 'The Sources of the black athlete's superiority', *Black Scholar*, 3(3): 32–41.

——(1973) *Sociology of Sport*. Chicago, Ill.: Dorsey Press.

Edwards, T. (2006) *Cultures of Masculinities*. London: Routledge.

Egan, P. (1812) *Boxiana*. London: Sherwood.

Eichberg, H. (1998) *Body Cultures: Essays on Sport, Space and Identity*. London: Routledge.

Elias, N. (1971) 'The genesis of sport as a sociological problem', in E. Dunning (ed.), *The Sociology of Sport: A Selection of Readings*. London: Frank Cass, 88–115.

——(1978) *What is Sociology?* London: Hutchison.

——(1986a) 'Introduction', in N. Elias and E. Dunning, *Quest for Excitement: Sport and Leisure in the Civilising Process*. Oxford: Blackwell, 19–62.

——(1986b) 'An essay on sport and violence', in N. Elias and E. Dunning, *Quest for Excitement: Sport and Leisure in the Civilising Process*. Oxford: Blackwell, 150–74.

——(1986c) 'The genesis of sport as a sociological problem', in N. Elias and E. Dunning, *Quest for Excitement: Sport and Leisure in the Civilising Process*. Oxford: Blackwell, 126–49.

——(1987) *Involvement and Detachment*. Oxford: Blackwell.

——(2000) *The Civilizing Process: Sociogenetic and Psychogenetic Investigations*. Oxford: Blackwell.

Elias, N. and Dunning, E. (1966) 'Dynamics of sports groups with special reference to football', *British Journal of Sociology*, 17(4): 388–402.

——(1971) 'Folk football in medieval and early modern Britain', in E. Dunning (ed.), *The Sociology of Sport: A Selection of Readings*. London: Frank Cass, 116–32.

——(1986a) *Quest for Excitement: Sport and Leisure in the Civilising Process*. Oxford: Blackwell.

——(1986b) 'Quest for excitement in leisure', in N. Elias and E. Dunning, *Quest for Excitement: Sport and Leisure in the Civilizing Process*. Oxford: Blackwell, 63–90.

Entine, J. (2000) *Taboo: Why Black Athletes Dominate Sports and Why We're Afraid to Talk About it*. New York: Public Affairs.

Erbach, G. (1966/1969) 'The science of sport and sports sociology: Questions related to development – problems of structure', *International Review of Sport Sociology*, 1(1): 59–73. Reprinted in J. Loy and G. Kenyon (eds), *Sport, Culture and Society: A Reader on the Sociology of Sport*. New York: Macmillan, 23–36.

Evans, J. and Hesmondhalgh, D. (2005) *Understanding Media: Inside Celebrity*. Maidenhead: Open University Press.

Falcous, M. and Silk, M. (2006) 'Global regimes, local agendas: Sport, resistance and the mediation of dissent', *International Review for the Sociology of Sport*, 41(3–4): 317–38.

Featherstone, M. (1987) 'Leisure, symbolic power and life course', in J. Horne, D. Jary and A. Tomlinson (eds), *Sport, Leisure and Social Relations*. London: Routledge & Kegan Paul, 139–59.

——(1991) 'The Body in consumer culture', in M. Featherstone, M. Hepworth, and B. S. Turner (eds), *The Body: Social Process and Cultural Theory*. London: Sage, 170–96.

——(ed.) (2000) *Body Modifications*. London: Sage.

Featherstone, M., Hepworth, M. and Turner, B. S. (eds) (1991) *The Body: Social Process and Cultural Theory*. London: Sage.

Featherstone, M. and Turner, B. S. (1995) 'Body and society: An introduction', *Body & Society* 1(1): 1–12.

Ferree, M., Lorber, J. and Hess, B. (eds) (1999) *Revisioning Gender.* Thousand Oaks, Calif.: Sage.

Fine, G. A. (1987) 'One of the boys: Women in male-dominated settings', in M. Kimmel (ed.), *Changing Men: New Directions in Research on Men and Masculinity.* London: Sage, 131–47.

Fleming, S. (1994) *Home and Away: Sport and South Asian Male Youth.* Aldershot: Avebury.

——(2001) 'Racial science and South Asian and black physicality', in B. Carrington and I. McDonald (eds), *'Race', Sport and British Society.* London: Routledge, 105–20.

Fletcher, J. (1997) *Violence and Civilization: An Introduction to the Work of Norbert Elias.* Oxford: Blackwell.

Foucault, M. (1992) *The History of Sexuality.* Harmondsworth: Penguin.

Fowler, B. (ed.) (2000) *Reading Bourdieu on Society and Culture.* Oxford: Blackwell.

Frank, A. (1990) 'Bringing bodies back in: A decade review', *Theory, Culture and Society,* 7(1): 131–62.

——(1991) 'For a sociology of the body: An analytical review', in M. Featherstone, M. Hepworth and B. S. Turner (eds), *The Body: Social Process and Cultural Theory.* London: Sage, 36–102.

Franklin, A. (1996) 'On fox-hunting and angling: Norbert Elias and the "sportisation" process', *Journal of Historical Sociology,* 9(4): 432–56.

Fraser, M. and Greco, M. (eds) (2004) *The Body: A Reader.* London: Routledge.

Freidson, E. (1970) *Profession of Medicine: A Study of the Sociology of Applied Knowledge.* New York: Dodd, Mead & Co.

Gamson, J. (1994) *Claims to Fame: Celebrity in Contemporary America.* Berkeley, Calif.: University of California Press.

Gardiner, S. and Welch, R. (2001) 'Sport, racism and the limits of "colour blind" law', in B. Carrington and I. McDonald (eds), *'Race', Sport and British Society.* London: Routledge, 133–50.

Geraghty, C. (2000) 'Re-examining stardom: Questions of texts, bodies and performance', in C. Gledhill and L. Williams (eds), *Reinventing Film Studies.* London: Arnold, 183–201.

Gerber, E. (1974) *The American Woman in Sport.* Reading, Mass.: Addison-Wesley.

Giardina, M. (2001) 'Global Hingis: Flexible citizenship and the transnational celebrity', in D. Andrews and S. Jackson (eds), *Sport Stars: The Cultural Politics of Sporting Celebrity.* London, Routledge, 201–17.

Gilroy, P. (1987) *There Ain't No Black in the Union Jack: The Cultural Politics of Race and Nation.* London: Routledge.

——(1993) *Small Acts: Thoughts on the Politics of Black Cultures.* London: Serpent's Tail.

——(2000) *Between Camps: Race, Identity and Nationalism at the End of the Color Line.* London: Allen Lane.

——(2001) 'Foreword', in B. Carrington and I. McDonald (eds), *'Race', Sport and British Society.* London: Routledge, xi–xvii.

——(2008) 'The great escape: From Enoch Powell to Hope Powell and beyond', in M. Perryman (ed.), *Imagined Nation: England After Britain.* London: Lawrence & Wishart, 190–6.

Giulianotti, R. (1999) *Football: A Sociology of the Global Game.* Cambridge: Polity Press.

——(2001) 'A different kind of carnival', in M. Perryman (ed.), *Hooligan Wars: Causes and Effects of Football Violence.* Edinburgh: Mainstream, 141–54.

——(2004a) *Sport and Modern Social Theorists.* Basingstoke: Palgrave Macmillan.

——(2004b) 'Introduction: Sport and social theorists – a plurality of perspectives', in R. Giulianotti, *Sport and Modern Social Theorists.* Basingstoke: Palgrave Macmillan, 1–11.

——(2004c) 'The fate of hyperreality: Jean Baudrillard and the sociology of sport', in R. Giulianotti, *Sport and Modern Social Theorists.* Basingstoke: Palgrave Macmillan, 225–40.

——(2004d) 'Civilizing games: Norbert Elias and the sociology of sport', in R. Giulianotti, *Sport and Modern Social Theorists.* Basingstoke: Palgrave Macmillan, 145–60.

Giulianotti, R. and Gerrard, M. (2001) 'Evil genie or pure genius? The (im)moral football and public career of Paul "Gazza" Gascoigne', in D. Andrews and S. Jackson (eds), *Sport Stars: The Cultural Politics of Sporting Celebrity.* London, Routledge, 124–37.

Goffman, E. (1961) *Encounters*. Indianapolis, Ind.: Bobbs-Merrill.

Goudsblom, J. (1977) *Sociology in the Balance: A Critical Essay*. Oxford: Blackwell.

Goudsblom, J. and Mennell, S. (eds) (1998) *The Norbert Elias Reader*. Oxford: Blackwell.

Goulstone, J. (2000) 'The working class origins of modern football', *International Journal of the History of Sport*, 17(1): 135–43.

Green, D., Hebron, S. and Woodward, D. (1987) *Women's Leisure, What Leisure?* London: Macmillan.

Greenberg, D., Hall, R., Hill, R., Johnston, F., Oglesby, C. and Ridley, S. (1998) *Encyclopedia of Women and Sport in America*. Phoenix, Ariz.: Oryx Press.

Greendorfer (1978) 'Socialization into sport', in C. Oglesby (ed.), *Women in Sport: From Myth to Reality*. California: Lea & Febiger, 115–42.

Grossberg, L. (1997) *Bringing It All Back Home: Essays in Cultural Studies*. Durham, NC: Duke University Press.

Grosz, E. (1994) *Volatile Bodies: Toward a Corporeal Feminism*. Bloomington, Ind.: Indiana University Press.

Gruneau, R. (1976) 'Sport as an area of sociological study: An introduction to major themes and perspectives', in R. Gruneau and J. G. Albinson (eds), *Canadian Sports: Sociological Perspectives*. Reading, Mass.: Addison-Wesley, 8–43.

——(1983/1999) *Class, Sports and Social Development*. Amherst, Mass. and Champaign, Ill.: University of Massachusetts Press and Human Kinetics.

Grusky, O. (1963) 'Managerial succession and organizational effectiveness', *American Journal of Sociology*, 69(1): 21–31.

Guttmann, A. (1984) 'The sociological imagination and the imaginative sociologist', in N. Theberge and P. Donnelly (eds), *Sport and the Sociological Imagination: Refereed Proceedings of the 3rd Annual Conference of the North American Society for the Sociology of Sport, Toronto, Canada November 1982*. Fort Worth, Tex.: Texas Christian University Press, 4–20.

——(2008) '*From Ritual to Record* (and the paradigm of modern sports)', in D. Malcolm, *The Sage Dictionary of Sports Studies*. London: Sage, 107–9.

Hall, M. A. (1978) *Sport and Gender: A Feminist Perspective on the Sociology of Sport*. Ottawa: Canadian Association for Health, Physical Education and Sport.

——(1985) 'How should we theorize sport in a capitalist patriarchy?', *International Review for the Sociology of Sport*, 20(1–2): 109–15.

——(1988) 'The discourse on gender and sport: From femininity to feminism', *Sociology of Sport Journal*, 5(4): 330–40.

——(1993) 'Gender and sport in the 1990s: Feminism, culture and politics', *Sport Science Review*, 2(1): 48–68.

——(1996) *Feminism and Sporting Bodies: Essays on Theory and Practice*. Champaign, Ill.: Human Kinetics.

Hall, S. (1998) 'Aspiration and attitude: Reflections on black Britain in the nineties', *new formations*, 33 (spring): 38–46.

Hallinan, C. J. (1991) 'Aborigines and positional segregation in Australian rugby league', *International Review for the Sociology of Sport*, 26(2): 69–78.

Hancock, P., Hughes, B., Jagger, E., Paterson, K., Russell, R., Tulle-Winton, E. and Tyler, M. (2000) *The Body, Culture and Society: An Introduction*. Buckingham: Open University Press.

Haney, D. P. (2008) *The Americanization of Social Science: Intellectuals and Public Responsibility in the Postwar United States*. Philadelphia, Pa.: Temple University Press.

Hargreaves, J. A. (ed.) (1982) *Sport, Culture and Ideology*. London: Routledge & Kegan Paul.

——(1990) 'Gender on the sports agenda', *International Review for the Sociology of Sport*, 25(4): 287–305.

——(1992) 'Sex, gender and the body in sport and leisure: Has there been a civilizing process?', in E. Dunning and C. Rojek (eds), *Sport and Leisure in the Civilizing Process: Critique and Counter-critique*. Basingstoke: Macmillan, 161–82.

——(1994) *Sporting Females: Critical Issues in the History and Sociology of Women's Sports*. London: Routledge.

——(2000) *Heroines of Sport: The Politics of Difference and Identity*. London: Routledge.

Hargreaves, J. A. and Vertinsky, P. (2007a) 'Introduction', in J. A. Hargreaves and P. Vertinsky (eds), *Physical Culture, Power, and the Body*. London: Routledge, 1–23.

——(eds) (2007b) *Physical Culture, Power, and the Body*. London: Routledge.

Hargreaves, J. E. (1986) *Sport, Power and Culture: A Social and Historical Analysis of Popular Sports in Britain*. Cambridge: Polity Press.

——(1987) 'The body, sport and power relations', in J. Horne, D. Jary and A. Tomlinson (eds), *Sport, Leisure and Social Relations*. London: Routledge & Kegan Paul, 139–59.

Harker, R. (1990) *An Introduction to the Work of Pierre Bourdieu: The Practice of Theory*. London: Macmillan.

Harris, J. and Clayton, B. (2002) 'Femininity, masculinity, physicality and the English tabloid press: The case of Anna Kournikova', *International Review for the Sociology of Sport*, 37(3–4): 397–413.

——(2007a) 'The first metrosexual rugby player: Rugby union, masculinity, and celebrity in contemporary Wales', *Sociology of Sport Journal*, 24(2): 145–64.

——(2007b) 'David Beckham and the changing (re)presentations of English identity', *International Journal of Sport Management and Marketing*, 2(3): 208–21.

Hartmann, D. (2003) *Race, Culture and the Revolt of the Black Athlete: The Olympic Protests and their Aftermath*. Chicago, Ill.: Chicago University Press.

Harvey, A. (2001) '"An epoch in the annals of national sport": Football in Sheffield and the creation of modern soccer and rugby', *International Journal of the History of Sport*, 18(4): 53–87.

——(2002) 'The curate's egg put back together: Comments on Eric Dunning's response to "An epoch in the annals of national sport", *International Journal of the History of Sport*, 19(4): 192–9.

——(2004) 'Curate's egg pursued by red herrings: A reply to Eric Dunning and Graham Curry', *International Journal of the History of Sport*, 21(1): 127–31.

Harvey, J. (1986) 'The rationalization of bodily practices', *Arena Review*, 10(1): 55–65.

Harvey, J. and Sparks, R. (1991) 'The politics of the body in the context of modernity', *Quest*, 43(2): 164–89.

Haynes, R. (1995) *The Football Imagination: The Rise of Football Fanzine Culture*. Aldershot: Ashgate Publishing.

Haywood, C. and Mac an Ghaill, M. (2003) *Men and Masculinities: Theory, Research and Social Practice*. Buckingham: Open University Press.

Haywood, L. (2007) 'Producing girls: Empire, sport and the neoliberal body', in J. Hargreaves and P. Vertinsky (eds), *Physical Culture, Power, and the Body*. London: Routledge, 101–20.

Heinemann, K. (1980) 'Sport and the sociology of the body', *International Review of Sport Sociology*, 15(3–4): 41–56.

Helanko, R. (1957) 'Sports and socialization', *Acta Sociologica*, 2(4): 229–40.

Hendry, L. (1973) 'Sports sociology in Britain: Career or commitment?', *International Review of Sport Sociology*, 8(3–4): 117–24.

Henry, F. M. (1964) 'Physical education: An academic discipline', *Journal of Health, Physical Education, and Recreation*, 35: 32–3.

Hill, J. (1996) 'British sports history: A post-modern future', *Journal of Sport History*, 23(1): 1–19.

——(2002) *Sport, Leisure and Culture in Twentieth-Century Britain*. Basingstoke: Palgrave Macmillan.

——(2003) 'Introduction: Sport and politics', *Journal of Contemporary History*, 38(3): 335–61.

——(2006) *Sport and the Literary Imagination: Essays in History, Literature and Sport*. New York: Peter Lang.

Hoberman, J. (1992) *Mortal Engines: The Science of Performance and the Dehumanization of Sport*. New York: Free Press.

——(1997) *Darwin's Athletes: How Sport has Damaged Black America and Preserved the Myth of Race*. New York: Houghton Mifflin.

Hobsbawm, E. (1983) 'Introduction: Inventing tradition' in E. Hobsbawm and T. Ranger, (eds) *The Invention of Tradition*. Cambridge: Cambridge University Press, 1–14.

Hoch, P. (1972) *Rip Off the Big Game: The Exploitation of Sports by the Power Elite*. New York: Anchor Doubleday.

Holland, B. (1995) '"Kicking racism out of football": An assessment of racial harassment in and around football grounds', *New Community*, 21(4): 567–86.

——(1997) 'Surviving leisure time racism: The burden of harassment on Britain's black footballers', *Leisure Studies*, 16(4): 261–77.

Holmes, S. and Redmond, S. (2010) 'Editorial: A journal of *Celebrity Studies*', *Celebrity Studies*, 1(1): 1–10.

Holmlund, C. A. (1989) 'Visible difference and flex appeal: The body, sex, sexuality, and race in *Pumping Iron* films', *Cinema Journal,* 28(4): 38–51.

Holt, R. (1989) *Sport and the British: A Modern History*. Oxford: Clarendon Press.

——(1992/2003) 'Amateurism and its interpretation: The social origins of British sport', *Innovation* 5(4): 19–31; updated and reprinted as, 'The historical meaning of amateurism', in E. Dunning and D. Malcolm (eds), *Sport: Critical Concepts in Sociology Vol. 3*. London: Routledge, 270–85.

——(1998) 'Sport and history: British and European traditions', in L. Allison (ed.), *Taking Sport Seriously*. Aachen: Meyer & Meyer, 7–30.

Holt, R. and Mason, T. (2000) *Sport in Britain, 1945–2000*. Oxford: Blackwell.

Hood-Williams, J. (1995) 'Sexing the athletes', *Sociology of Sport Journal*, 12(3): 290–305.

hooks, b. (1994) 'Feminism inside: Toward a black body politic', in T. Golden (ed.), *Black Male: Representations of Masculinity in Contemporary American Art*. New York: Whitney Museum of American Art, 127–40.

——(2004) *We Real Cool: Black Men and Masculinity*. London: Routledge.

Horkheimer, M. (1964) 'New patterns of social relations', in E. Jokl and E. Simon (eds), *International Research in Sport and Physical Education*. Springfield, Ill.: Thomas, 173–85.

Hornby, N. (1992) *Fever Pitch*. London: Gollancz.

Horne, J., Tomlinson, A. and Whannel, G. (eds) (1999) *Understanding Sport: An Introduction to the Sociological and Cultural Analysis of Sport*. London: Routledge.

Houlihan, B. (ed.) (2003) *Sport and Society: A Student Introduction*. London: Sage.

Howe, P. D. (2004) *Sport, Professionalism and Pain: Ethnographies of Injury and Risk*. London: Routledge.

Hughson, J., Inglis, D. and Free, M. (2005) *The Uses of Sport: A Critical Study*. London: Routledge.

Huizinga, J. (1938/1949) *Homo Ludens: A Study of the Play Element in Culture*. London: Routledge & Kegan Paul.

Hylton, K. (2009) *'Race' and Sport: Critical Race Theory*. London: Routledge.

Ian, M. (1991) 'Abject to object: Women's bodybuilding', *Postmodern Culture*, 3(1): 1–17.

Ingham, A. (1979) 'Methodology in the sociology of sport: From symptoms of malaise to Weber for a cure', *Quest*, 31(2): 187–215.

Ingham, A. and Donnelly, P. (1990) 'Whose knowledge counts? The production of knowledge and issues of application in the sociology of sport', *Sociology of Sport Journal*, 7(1): 58–65.

——(1997) 'A sociology of North American sociology of sport: Disunity in unity, 1965 to 1996', *Sociology of Sport Journal*, 14(4): 362–418.

Ingham, A. and Loy, J. (1973) 'The social system of sport: A humanistic perspective', *Quest*, 19(1): 3–23.

——(eds) (1993) *Sport in Social Development: Traditions, Transitions, and Transformations*. Leeds: Human Kinetics.

Ingham, A., Loy, J. and Swetman, R. D. (1979) 'Sport, heroes and society: Issues of transformation and reproduction', *Working Papers in the Sociological Study of Sports and Leisure*, 2(4). Kingston, Ontario: Sports Studies Research Group.

Inglis, D., Blaikie, A. and Wagner-Pacitici, R. (2007) 'Editorial: Sociology, culture and the 21st century', *Cultural Sociology*, 1(1): 5–22.

Inglis, S. (2001) 'All gone quiet over here', in M. Perryman (ed.), *Hooligan Wars: Causes and Effects of Football Violence*. Edinburgh: Mainstream, 87–94.

International Sociological Association (1998) *Books of the Century*. Available online at http://www.isa-sociology.org/books/vt/bkv_000.htm. (Accessed 22 October 2008.)

Jackson, S. and Scott, S. (eds) (2002) *Gender: A Sociological Reader*. London: Routledge.

James, C. L. R. (1963) *Beyond a Boundary*. London: Hutchison.

Jarvie, G. (1985) *Class, Race and Sport in South Africa's Political Economy*. London: Routledge & Kegan Paul.

——(ed.) (1991a) *Sport, Racism and Ethnicity*. London: Falmer Press.

——(1991b) *Highland Games: The Making of the Myth*. Edinburgh: Edinburgh University Press.

——(2000) 'Sport, racism and ethnicity', in J. Coakley and E. Dunning (eds), *Handbook of Sports Studies*. London: Sage, 334–43.

——(2006) *Sport, Culture and Society*. London, Routledge.

——(2007) 'Sport, social change and the public intellectual', *International Review for the Sociology of Sport*, 42(4): 411–24.

Jarvie, G. and Maguire, J. (1994) *Sport and Leisure in Social Thought*. Routledge: London.

Jarvie, G. and Walker, G. (eds) (1994) *Scottish Sport and the Making of the Nation*. Leicester: Leicester University Press.

Jenkins, R. (1992) *Pierre Bourdieu*. London: Routledge.

Johal, S. (2001) 'Playing their own game: A South Asian football experience', in B. Carrington and I. McDonald (eds), *'Race', Sport and British Society*. London: Routledge, 153–69.

Johnes, M. (2004) 'Putting the history into sport: On sport history and sport studies in the UK', *Journal of Sport History*, 31(2): 145–60.

——(2005) 'British sport history: the present and the future'. Unpublished paper, presented at BSSH Annual Conference, Stirling, September 2005.

Jokl, E. (1964) *Medical Sociology and Cultural Anthropology of Sports and Physical Education*. Springfield, Ill.: Thomas.

Jokl, E. and Simon, E. (eds) (1964) *International Research in Sport and Physical Education*. Springfield, Ill.: Thomas.

Jones, S. G. (1986) *Workers at Play: A Social and Economic History of Leisure, 1918–1939*. London: Routledge.

——(1988) *Sport, Politics and the Working Class*. Manchester: Manchester University Press.

Kane, M. (1971) 'An assessment of black is best', *Sports Illustrated*, 34(3): 76–83.

Kaufman, M. (ed.) (1987) *Beyond Patriarchy: Essays by Men on Pleasure, Power and Change*. Toronto: Oxford University Press.

Kauppi, N. (2000) *The Politics of Embodiment: Habits, Power, and Pierre Bourdieu's Theory*. New York: Peter Lang.

Keita, L. (2000) 'Book review: J. Entine, *Taboo: Why black athletes dominate sports and why we're afraid to talk about it*', *Western Journal of Black Studies*, 24(2). Available at http://www.jonentine.com. (Accessed 12 January 2010.)

Kenyon, G. (1986) 'The significance of social theory in the development of sport sociology', in C. R. Rees and A. W. Miracle (eds), *Sport and Social Theory*. Champaign, Ill.: Human Kinetics, 3–22.

Kenyon, G. S. and Loy, J. (1965/1969) 'Toward a sociology of sport', *Journal of Health, Physical Education, and Recreation*, 36: 24–5, 68–9. Reprinted in J. Loy and G. Kenyon (eds), *Sport, Culture and Society: A Reader on the Sociology of Sport*. New York: Macmillan, 36–43.

Kilminster, R. (2004) 'From distance to detachment: Knowledge and self-knowledge in Elias's theory of involvement and detachment', in S. Loyal and S. Quilley (eds), *The Sociology of Norbert Elias*. Cambridge: Cambridge University Press, 25–41.

Kimmel, M. (ed.) (1987) *Changing Men: New Directions in Research on Men and Masculinity*. London: Sage.

——(1990) 'Baseball and the reconstitution of American masculinity, 1880–1920', in M. Messner and D. Sabo (eds), *Sport, Men, and the Gender Order*. Champaign, Ill.: Human Kinetics, 55–66.

Kimmel, M. and Messner, M. (eds) (2006) *Men's Lives*. Boston, Mass.: Allyn & Bacon.

King, A. (1997) *The End of the Terraces: The Transformation of English Football in the 1990s*. Leicester: Leicester University Press.

King, C. (2004) *Offside Racism: Playing with the White Man*. Oxford: Berg.

King, C. R. (2006) 'Stealing cultural studies: Dialogues with Norman K. Denzin', *Journal of Sport and Social Issues*, 30(4): 383–94.

King, C. R. and Springwood, C. F. (2001) *Beyond the Cheers: Race as Spectacle in College Sport*. New York: SUNY Press.

King, S. (2008) 'What's queer about (queer) sport sociology now? A review essay', *Sociology of Sport Journal*, 25(4): 419–42.

King, S. and MacNeil, M. (2007) '(Post)identity and sporting cultures: An introduction and overview', *Sociology of Sport Journal*, 24(1): 1–19.

Kirsch, G. (1989) *The Creation of American Team Sports: Baseball and Cricket, 1838–1872*. Chicago, Ill.: University of Illinois Press.

Klein, A. (1986) 'Pumping irony: The crisis and contradiction in bodybuilding', *Sociology of Sport Journal*, 3(2): 112–33.

——(1990) 'Little big man: Hustling, gender narcissism, and bodybuilding subculture', in M. Messner and D. Sabo (eds), *Sport, Men, and the Gender Order*. Champaign, Ill.: Human Kinetics, 127–39.

——(1993) *Little Big Men: Bodybuilding Subculture and Gender Construction*. New York: SUNY Press.

——(2007) 'Towards a transnational sports studies', *Sport in Society*, 10(6): 885–95.

Kuhn, A. (1988) 'The body and cinema: Some problems for feminism', in S. Sheridan (ed.), *Grafts: Feminist Cultural Criticism*. London: Verso, 11–23.

Laberge, S. and Kay, J. (2002) 'Pierre Bourdieu's sociocultural theory of sport practice', in J. Maguire and K. Young (eds), *Theory, Sport and Society*. Oxford: Elsevier Science, 239–66.

Lane, J. (2000) *Pierre Bourdieu: A Critical Introduction*. London: Pluto Press.

Lapchick, R. (1975) *The Politics of Race and International Sport: The Case of South Africa*. Westport, Conn.: Greenwood Press.

——(1984) *Broken Promises: Racism in American Sports*. New York: St. Martin's Press.

——(1991) *Five Minutes to Midnight: Race and Sport in the 1990s*. London: Madison Books.

Larson, M. S. (1977) *The Rise of Professionalism: A Sociological Analysis*. Berkeley, Calif.: University of California Press.

Lavoie, M. (1989) 'Stacking, performance differentials, and salary discrimination in professional ice hockey: A survey of evidence', *Sociology of Sport Journal*, 6(1): 17–35.

Lavoie, M. and Leonard, W. (1994) 'In search of an alternative explanation of stacking in baseball: The uncertainty hypothesis', *Sociology of Sport Journal*, 11(2): 17–35.

Leemans, E. J. (1964) 'A sociological approach to sports', in E. Jokl and E. Simon (eds), *International Research in Sport and Physical Education*. Springfield, Ill.: Thomas, 152–9.

Lenskyj, H. (1986) *Out of Bounds: Women, Sport and Sexuality*. Ontario: Women's Press.

Levine, D. (1991) 'Martial arts as a resource for liberal education: The case of aikido', in M. Featherstone, M. Hepworth, and B. S. Turner (eds), *The Body: Social Process and Cultural Theory*. London: Sage, 209–24.

Lewis, R. W. (1996) 'Football hooliganism in England before 1914: A critique of the Dunning thesis', *International Journal of the History of Sport*, 13(3): 310–39.

Lieberman, L. (2001) 'Book review: J. Entine, *Taboo: Why black athletes dominate sports and why we're afraid to talk about it*', *American Anthropologist*, 103(1). Available at http://www.jonentine.com. (Accessed 12 January 2010.)

Lindsey, E. (2001) 'Notes from the sports desk: Reflections on race, class and gender in British sports journalism', in B. Carrington and I. McDonald (eds), *'Race', Sport and British Society*. London: Routledge, 188–98.

Loland, S., Skirstad, B. and Waddington, I. (eds) (2006) *Pain and Injury in Sport: Social and Ethical Analysis*. London: Routledge.

Lorber, J. (1994) *Paradoxes of Gender*. New Haven, Conn.: Yale University Press.

Lowenthal, L. (2006) 'The triumph of mass idols', in P. D. Marshall (ed.), *The Celebrity Culture Reader*. New York: Routledge, 124–52.

Loy, J. (1968) 'The nature of sport: a definitional effort', *Quest*, 10(1): 1–15.

Loy, J. and Booth, D. (2000) 'Functionalism', in J. Coakley and E. Dunning (eds), *Handbook of Sports Studies*. London: Sage, 8–27.

Loy, J. and Elvogue, J. (1970) 'Racial segregation in American sport', *International Review of Sport Sociology*, 5(1): 5–23.

Loy, J. and Kenyon, G. (1969) 'The sociology of sport: An emerging field', in J. Loy and G. Kenyon (eds), *Sport, Culture and Society: A Reader on the Sociology of Sport*. New York: Macmillan, 1–8.

Loy, J. and Sage, G. (1997) 'Sociology of sport: Traditions, transitions, and transformations', *Sociology of Sport Journal*, 14(4): 315–16.

Loy, J., Andrews, D. and Rinehart, R. (1993) 'The body in culture and sport', *Sport Science Review*, 2: 345–70.

Loyal, S. and Quilley, S. (2004) *The Sociology of Norbert Elias*. Cambridge: Cambridge University Press.

Lüschen, G. (1969) 'Sociology of sport in the United States', *International Review of Sport Sociology*, 4(1): 189–90.

——(1970) *The Cross-Cultural Analysis of Sport and Games*. Champaign, Ill.: Stipes.

——(1980) 'Sociology of sport: Development, present state, and prospects', *Annual Review of Sociology*, 6: 315–47.

Lüschen, G. and Sage, G. (1981) 'Sport in sociological perspective', in G. Lüschen and G. Sage (eds), *Handbook of Social Sciences of Sport*. Champaign, Ill.: Stipes Publishing, 3–24.

MacAloon, J. (1998) 'A prefatory note to Pierre Bourdieu's "Program for a Sociology of Sport"', *Sociology of Sport Journal*, 5(2): 150–2.

McCrone, K. (1988) *Playing the Game: Sport and the Physical Emancipation of English Women 1870–1914*. Lexington, Ky.: University of Kentucky Press.

MacDonald, K. M. (1995) *The Sociology of the Professions*. London: Sage.

McDonald, M. (ed.) (2005) 'Special issue: Whiteness in sport', *Sociology of Sport Journal*, 22(3).

McIntosh, P. (1960) *Sport in Society*. London: C. A. Watt.

McKay, J., Messner, M. and Sabo, D. (2000) *Masculinities, Gender Relations, and Sport*. Thousand Oaks, Calif.: Sage.

McKibbin, R. (2002) 'Class, politics, money: British sport since the First World War', *Twentieth Century British History*, 13(2): 191–200.

Mackinnon, C. (1987) *Feminism Unmodified: Discourses on Life and Law*. Cambridge, Mass.: Harvard University Press.

MacNeil, M. (1988) 'Active women, media representations, and ideology', in J. Harvey and H. Cantelon (eds), *Not Just a Game: Essays in Canadian Sport Sociology*. Ottawa: Ottawa University Press, 195–211.

McPherson, B. (1975) 'Past, present and future perspectives for research in sport sociology', *International Review of Sport Sociology*, 10(1): 55–72.

McPherson, B. D., Curtis, J. E. and Loy, J. W. (1989) 'Defining sport', in B. D. McPherson, J. E. Curtis and J. W. Loy (eds), *The Social Significance of Sport*. Champaign, Ill.: Human Kinetics, 15–17.

Magnane, G. (1964) *Sociologie du sport*. Paris: Gallimard.

Maguire, J. (1988) 'Race and position assignment in English soccer: A preliminary analysis of ethnicity and sport in Britain', *Sociology of Sport Journal*, 5(3): 257–69.

——(1993) 'Bodies, sports cultures and societies: A critical review of some theories in the sociology of the body', *International Review for the Sociology of Sport*, 28(1): 33–51.

——(1995) 'Common ground? Links between sports history, sports geography and the sociology of sport', *Sporting Traditions*, 12(1): 3–25.

——(1999) *Global Sport: Identities, Societies, Civilizations*. Cambridge: Polity Press.

——(2005) *Power and Global Sport: Zones of Prestige, Emulation and Resistance*. London: Routledge.

Maguire, J. and Mansfield, L. (1998) 'No-body's perfect: Women, aerobics and the body beautiful', *Sociology of Sport Journal*, 15(2): 109–37.

Maguire, J. and Young, K. (eds) (2002) *Theory, Sport and Society*. Oxford: Elsevier Science.

Maguire, J., Jarvie, G., Mansfield, L. and Bradley, J. (2002) *Sportworlds: A Sociological Perspective*. Champaign, Ill.: Human Kinetics.

Majors, R. (2001) 'Cool pose: Black masculinity and sports', in S. Whitehead and F. Barrett (eds), *The Masculinities Reader*. Cambridge: Polity Press, 209–17.

Malacrida, C. and Low, J. (eds) (2008) *Sociology of the Body: A Reader*. Oxford: Oxford University Press.

Malcolm, D. (1997) 'Stacking in cricket: A figurational sociological re-appraisal of centrality', *Sociology of Sport Journal*, 14(3): 265–84.

——(1999) 'Cricket spectator disorder: Myths and historical evidence', *The Sports Historian*, 19(1): 16–37.

——(2002) 'Cricket and civilizing processes: A response to Stokvis', *International Review for the Sociology of Sport*, 37(1): 37–57.

——(2004) 'Cricket: Civilizing and de-civilizing processes in the imperial game', in E. Dunning, D. Malcolm and I. Waddington (eds), *Sport Histories: Figurational Studies of the Development of Modern Sports*. London: Routledge, 71–87.

——(2008) 'A response to Vamplew and some comments on the relationship between sports historians and sociologists of sport', *Sport in History*, 28(2): 259–79.

Malcolm, D. and Safai, P. (forthcoming) *The Social Organization of Sports Medicine*. New York: Routledge.

Malcolmson, R. W. (1973) *Popular Recreations in English Society, 1700–1800*. Cambridge: Cambridge University Press.

Malik, K. (2000) 'Sporting colours', *Nature: International Weekly Journal of Science*. Available at http://www.jonentine.com. (Accessed 12 January 2010.)

Mangan, A. J. (1981) *Athleticism in the Victorian and Edwardian Public Schools*. Cambridge: Cambridge University Press.

——(1999) 'The end of history perhaps – but the end of the beginning for the history of sport! An Anglo-Saxon autobiographical perspective', *Sporting Traditions*, 16(1): 61–72.

——(2005) 'Series editor's foreword', in E. Dunning and K. Sheard (eds), *Barbarians, Gentlemen and Players: A Sociological Study of the Development of Rugby Football*. London: Routledge, vii–ix.

Mansfield, A. and McGinn, B. (1993) 'Pumping irony: The muscular and the feminine', in S. Scott and D. Morgan (eds), *Body Matters: Essays on the Sociology of the Body*. London: The Falmer Press, 49–68.

Mansfield, L. and Malcolm, D. (2010) 'Sociology', in S. Pope and J. Nauright (eds), *Routledge Companion to Sports History*. London: Routledge, 99–113.

Markovitz, J. (2006) 'Anatomy of a spectacle: Race, gender and memory in the Kobe Bryant rape case', *Sociology of Sport Journal*, 23(4): 396–416.

Markula, P. (1995) 'Firm but shapely, fit but sexy, strong and thin: The postmodern aerobicizing female bodies', *Sociology of Sport Journal*, 12(4): 424–53.

Markula, P. and Pringle, R. (2006) *Foucault, Sport and Exercise: Power, Knowledge and Transforming the Self*. London: Routledge.

Marqusee, M. (2001) 'In search of the unequivocal Englishman: The conundrum of race and nation in English cricket', in B. Carrington and I. McDonald (eds), *'Race', Sport and British Society*. London: Routledge, 121–32.

Marshall, P. D. (1997) *Celebrity and Power: Fame in Contemporary Culture*. Minneapolis, Minn.: University of Minnesota Press.

——(1999/2006) 'The celebrity legacy of the Beatles', in I. Inglis (ed.), *The Beatles, Popular Music and Society*. Basingstoke: Macmillan, 163–75. Reprinted in P. D. Marshall (ed.), *The Celebrity Culture Reader*. New York: Routledge, 501–9.

——(ed.) (2006) *The Celebrity Culture Reader*. New York: Routledge.

Mason, A. (1988) *Sport in Britain*. London: Faber and Faber.

Maynard, M. (2002) '"Race", gender and the concept of "difference" in feminist thought', in S. Scraton and A. Flintoff (eds), *Gender and Sport: A Reader*. London: Routledge, 111–26.
Mead, G. H. (1934) *Mind, Self and Society*. Chicago, Ill.: Chicago University Press.
Medoff, M. (1986) 'Positional segregation and the economic hypothesis', *Sociology of Sport Journal*, 3(2): 297–304.
Melnick, M. and Jackson, S. (2002) 'Globalization American-style and reference idol selection: The importance of athlete celebrity others among New Zealand youth', *International Review for the Sociology of Sport*, 37(3–4): 429–48.
Mennell, S. (1992) *Norbert Elias: An Introduction*. Oxford: Blackwell.
Mennell, S. and Goudsblom, J. (eds) (1998) *On Civilization, Power, and Knowledge: Selected Writings*. Chicago, Ill.: University of Chicago Press.
Mennesson, C. (2000) '"Hard" women and "soft" women: The social construction of identities among female boxers', *International Review for the Sociology of Sport*, 35(1): 21–33.
Mercer, K. (1994) *Welcome to the Jungle: New Positions in Black Cultural Studies*. London: Routledge.
Messner, M. (1987) 'The life of a man's seasons: Male identity in the life course of the jock', in M. Kimmel (ed.), *Changing Men: New Directions in Research on Men and Masculinity*. London: Sage, 53–67.
——(1990) 'When bodies are weapons: Masculinity and violence in sport', *International Review for the Sociology of Sport*, 25(3): 203–18.
——(1992) *Power at Play: Sport and the Problems of Masculinity*, Boston, Mass.: Beacon Press.
——(2000) *Politics of Masculinities: Men in Movements*. New York: Rowan & Littlefield.
Messner, M. and Sabo, D. (1990) *Sport, Men and the Gender Order*. Champaign, Ill.: Human Kinetics.
Metcalfe, A. (1998) 'Sport history in the twenty-first century: A tentative look into the future'. Unpublished paper presented at 5th ISHPES Seminar, Sunny Bay, Bulgaria, 1998.
Miller, L. and Penz, O. (1991) 'Talking bodies: Female body-builders colonize a male preserve', *Quest*, 43(2): 148–63.
Miller, T. (1997) ' ... the oblivion of the sociology of sport ... ', *Journal of Sport and Social Issues*, 21(2): 115–19.
Monaghan, L. (2001) *Bodybuilding, Drugs and Risk*. London: Routledge.
Moore, L. and Kosut, M. (eds) (2010) *The Body Reader: Essential Social and Cultural Readings*. New York: New York University Press.
Moore, P. (ed.) (1997) *Building Bodies*. New Brunswick, NJ: Rutgers University Press.
Morton, H. W. (1963) *Soviet Sport*. New York: Collier Books.
Murphy, P., Dunning, E. and Maguire, J. (1998) 'Football spectator violence and disorder before the First World War: A reply to R. W. Lewis', *International Journal of the History of Sport*, 15(1): 141–62.
Murphy, P., Sheard, K., and Waddington, I. (2000) 'Figurational sociology and its application to sport', in J. Coakley and E. Dunning (eds), *Handbook of Sports Studies*. London: Sage, 92–105.
Murphy, P., Williams, J. and Dunning, E. (1990) *Football on Trial: Spectator Violence and Development in the World of Football*. London: Routledge & Kegan Paul.
Nalapat, A. and Parker, A. (2005) 'Sport, celebrity and popular culture: Sachin Tendulkar, cricket and Indian nationalism', *International Review for the Sociology of Sport*, 40(4): 433–46.
Nash, R. (2001) 'Book review: J. Williams, S. Hopkins and C. Long (eds) (2001) *Passing Rhythms: Liverpool FC and the Transformation of Football*', *Soccer and Society*, 2(3): 123–5.
Natan, A. (1958) *Sport and Society*. London: Bowes & Bowes.
Nauright, J. (1997) *Sport, Cultures and Identities in South Africa*. Leicester: Leicester University Press.
——(1999) '"The end of sports history?" From sports history to sports studies', *Sporting Traditions*, 16(1): 5–13.
Nettleton, S. (2007) 'Retaining the sociology in medical sociology', *Social Science and Medicine*, 65(12): 2409–12.
Nettleton, S. and Watson, J. (eds) (1998) *The Body in Everyday Life*. London: Routledge.
Nixon, H. L. II (1992) 'A social network analysis of influences on athletes to play with pain and injuries', *Journal of Sport and Social Issues*, 16(2): 127–35.

Obel, C. (1996) 'Collapsing gender in competitive bodybuilding: Research contradictions and ambiguity in sport', *International Review for the Sociology of Sport*, 31(2): 185–202.

Oglesby, C. (ed.) (1978) *Women in Sport: From Myth to Reality*. Santa Barbara, Calif.: Lea & Febiger.

——(1998) *Encyclopedia of Women in Sport in America*. Phoenix, Ariz.: Oryx Press.

Owusu, K. (ed.) (2000) *Black British Culture and Society: A Text-Reader*. London: Routledge.

Page, C. H. (1969) 'Symposium summary, with reflections upon the sociology of sport as a research field', in G. Kenyon (ed.), *Aspects of Contemporary Sport Sociology*. Chicago, Ill.: The Athletic Institute, 189–209.

Parratt, C. (1998) 'About turns: Reflecting on sport history in the 1990s', *Sport History Review*, 29: 4–17.

Perryman, M. (1999) *The Ingerland Factor: Home Truths from Football*. Edinburgh: Mainstream.

——(2001) *Hooligan Wars: Causes and Effects of Football Violence*. Edinburgh: Mainstream.

——(2002) *Going Oriental: Football After World Cup 2002*. Edinburgh: Mainstream.

Phillips, J. (1993) *Sociology of Sport*. Boston, Mass.: Allyn & Bacon.

Phillips, M. (2001) 'Deconstructing sport history: The postmodern challenge', *Journal of Sport History*, 28(3): 327–43.

Polley, M. (2003) 'History and sport', in B. Houlihan (ed.), *Sport and Society: A Student Introduction*. London: Sage, 49–64.

——(2007) *Sports History: A Practical Guide*. Basingstoke: Palgrave Macmillan.

Polsky, N. (1967) *Hustlers, Beats and Others*. Chicago, Ill.: Aldine.

Pope, S. (1997) *Patriotic Games: Sporting Traditions in the American Imagination, 1876–1926*. Oxford: Oxford University Press.

——(1998) 'Sport history into the 21st century', *Journal of Sport History*, 25(2): i–x.

Posner, R. A. (2003) *Public Intellectuals: A Study of Decline*. Cambridge, Mass.: Harvard University Press.

Poulton, E. (1999) 'Fighting talk from the press corps', in M. Perryman (ed.), *The Ingerland Factor: Home Truths from Football*. Edinbugh: Mainstream, 119–35.

——(2001) 'Tears, tantrums and tattoos: Framing the hooligan', in M. Perryman (ed.), *Hooligan Wars: Causes and Effects of Football Violence*. Edinburgh: Mainstream, 122–38.

——(2002) 'On the press pack stereotype hunt', in M. Perryman (ed.), *Going Oriental: Football After World Cup 2002*. Edinburgh: Mainstream, 102–15.

Price, J. and Shildrick, M. (eds) (1999) *Feminist Theory and the Body: A Reader*. Edinburgh: Edinburgh University Press.

Price, M. and Parker, A. (2003) 'Sport, sexuality and the gender order: Amateur rugby union, gay men and social exclusion', *Sociology of Sport Journal*, 20(2): 108–26.

Pronger, B. (1991) *The Arena of Masculinity: Sports, Homosexuality and the Meaning of Sex*. London: Gay Men's Press.

Rahman, M. (2004) 'David Beckham as a historical moment in the representation of masculinity', *Labour History Review*, 69(2): 219–33.

Rail, G. (ed.) (1998) *Sport and Postmodern Times*. New York: SUNY Press.

Rail, G. and Harvey, J. (1995) 'Body at work: Michel Foucault and the sociology of sport', *Sociology of Sport Journal*, 12(2): 164–79.

Ramsamy, S. (1982) *Apartheid: The Real Hurdle: Sport in South Africa and the International Boycott*. London: International Defence and Aid Fund for Southern Africa.

Real, M. (1975) 'Superbowl: Mythic spectacle', *Journal of Communication*, 25(1): 31–43.

Redmond, S. and Holmes, S. (eds) (2007) *Stardom and Celebrity*. London: Sage.

Rees, C. R. and Miracle, A. W. (eds) (1986) *Sport and Social Theory*. Champaign, Ill.: Human Kinetics.

Reid, D. (1988) 'Folk football, the aristocracy, and cultural change', *International Journal of the History of Sport*, 5(2): 224–38.

Rein, I., Kotler, P. and Stroller, M. (1997) *High Visibility: The Making and Marketing of Professionals into Celebrities*. Lincolnwood: NTC Business Books.

Richardson, D. and Robinson, V. (eds) (2008) *Introducing Gender and Women's Studies*. Basingstoke: Macmillan.

Riesman, D. and Denney, R. (1951) 'Football in America', *American Quarterly*, 3: 309–19.

Rigauer, B. (1969) *Sport und Arbeit* [*Sport and Work*]. Frankfurt: Suhrkamp Verlag.

——(1981) *Sport and Work*. New York: Columbia University Press.

Risse, H. (1921) *Soziologie des Sports*. Berlin: Reher.

Robbins, D. (2000a) *Bourdieu and Culture*. London: Sage.

——(2000b) *Pierre Bourdieu*. London: Sage.

Roberts, J. M. and Sutton-Smith, B. (1962) 'Child training and game involvement', *Ethnology*, 1: 166–85.

Roberts, J. M., Arth, M. J., and Bush, R. (1959) 'Games in culture', *American Anthropologist*, 61(4): 597–605.

Robinson, V. (2008) 'Men, masculinities and feminism', in D. Richardson and V. Robinson (eds), *Introducing Gender and Women's Studies*. Basingstoke: Macmillan, 55–71.

Roderick, M. (2006) 'The sociology of pain and injury in sport: Main perspective and problems', in S. Loland, B. Skirstad and I. Waddington (eds), *Pain and Injury in Sport: Social and Ethical Analysis*. London: Routledge, 17–33.

Rojek, C. (2001) *Celebrity*. London: Reaktion Books.

——(2006) 'Sports celebrity and the civilizing process', *Sport in Society*, 9(4): 674–90.

——(2009) *Celebrity: Critical Concepts in Sociology*. London: Routledge.

Rowe, D. (2001) 'Keeping with the enemy', in M. Perryman (ed.), *Hooligan Wars: Causes and Effects of Football Violence*. Edinburgh: Mainstream, 54–61.

——(2004) 'Antonio Gramsci: Sport, hegemony and the national-popular', in R. Giulianotti (ed.), *Sport and Modern Social Theorists*. Basingstoke: Palgrave Macmillan, 97–110.

Rowe, D. and Lawrence, G. (1996) 'Beyond national sport: Sociology, history and postmodernity', *Sporting Traditions*, 12(2): 3–16.

Rowe, D., McKay, J. and Lawrence, D. (1997) 'Out of the shadows: The critical sociology of sport in Australia, 1986–96', *Sociology of Sport Journal*, 14(4): 340–61.

Sabo, D. and Panepinto, J. (1990) 'Football ritual and the social reproduction of masculinity', in M. Messner and D. Sabo (eds), *Sport, Men, and the Gender Order*. Champaign, Ill.: Human Kinetics, 115–26.

Sabo, D. and Runfola, R. (1980) *Jock: Sports and Male Identity*. Englewood Cliffs, NJ.: Prentice Hall.

Sage, G. (1980) 'Study of social aspects of sport', in G. Sage (ed.), *Sport in American Society: Selected Readings*. Reading Mass.: Addison Wesley, 1–15.

——(1997) 'Physical education, sociology and sociology of sport: Points of intersection', *Sociology of Sport Journal*, 14(4): 317–39.

Said, E. (1978) *Orientalism*. New York: Pantheon.

——(1994) *Culture and Imperialism*. London: Vintage.

Sailes, G. A. (ed.) (1998) *African-Americans in Sport: Contemporary Themes*. New Brunswick: Transaction.

Scambler, G. (2005) *Sport in Society: History, Power and Culture*. Maidenhead: Open University Press.

Schickel, R. (1997) *Intimate Strangers: The Culture of Celebrity in America*. Chicago, Ill.: Ivan R. Dee.

Scott, S. and Morgan, D. (eds) (1993) *Body Matters: Essays on the Sociology of the Body*. London: The Falmer Press.

Scraton, S. (2001) 'Reconceptualizing race, gender and sport: The contribution of black feminism', in B. Carrington and I. McDonald (eds), *'Race', Sport and British Society*. London: Routledge, 170–87.

Scraton, S. and Flintoff A. (eds) (2002) *Gender and Sport: A Reader*. Routledge: London.

Scraton, S., Caudwell, J. and Holland, S. (2005) '"Bend it like Patel": Centring 'race', ethnicity and gender in feminist analysis of women's football in England', *International Review for the Sociology of Sport*, 40(1): 71–88.

Searle, C. (1990) 'Race before wicket: Cricket, empire and the white rose', *Race and Class*, 31(3): 31–48.

——(1993) 'Cricket as a mirror of racism', *Race and Class*, 34(3): 45–54.

——(1995) 'Lara's innings: A Caribbean moment', *Race and Class*, 36(4): 31–42.

——(1996) 'Towards a cricket of the future', *Race and Class*, 37(4): 45–59.

——(2001) 'Pitch of life: Re-reading C. L. R. James' *Beyond a Boundary*', in B. Carrington and I. McDonald (eds), *'Race', Sport and British Society*. London: Routledge, 199–214.

Sheard, K. (2004) 'Boxing in the Western civilizing process', in E. Dunning, D. Malcolm and I. Waddington (eds), *Sport Histories: Figurational Studies of the Development of Modern Sports*. London: Routledge, 15–30.

Sheard, K. and Dunning, E. (1973) 'The rugby club as a type of "male preserve": Some sociological notes', *International Review of Sport Sociology*, 8(3): 5–24.

Shearman, L. (1992) *Big League, Big Time: The Birth of the Arizona Diamondbacks, the Billion-Dollar Business of Sports, and the Power of the Media in America*. New York: Pocket Books.

Shearman, M. (1887) *Football: Its History for Five Centuries*. London: Longman.

——(1889) *Athletics and Football*. London: Longman.

Shilling, C. (1993) *The Body and Social Theory*. London: Sage.

——(2004) 'Foreword: Educating bodies: Schooling and the constitution of society', in J. Evans, B. Davies and J. Wright (eds), *Body Knowledge and Control: Studies in the Sociology of Physical Education and Health*. London: Routledge, xv–xxii.

——(2005) *The Body in Culture, Technology and Society*. London: Sage.

——(2010) 'Exploring the society-body-school nexus: Theoretical and methodology issues in the study of body pedagogics', *Sport, Education and Society*, 15(2): 151–67.

Shilling, C. and Bunsell, T. (2009) 'The female bodybuilder as a gender outlaw', *Qualitative Research in Sport and Exercise*, 1(1): 141–59.

Shultze, L. (1990) 'On the muscle', in J. Gaines and C. Herzog (eds), *Fabrications: Costume and the Female Body*. New York: Routledge, 59–78.

Shusterman, R. (1999) *Bourdieu: A Critical Reader*. Oxford: Blackwell.

Silk, M. and Andrews, D. (2010) 'CFP: Physical Cultural Studies – Special Issue of Sociology of Sport Journal'. Available online at http://nasssblog.blogspot.com/2009/09/cfp-physical-cultural-studies-special.html. (Accessed 21 February 2011.)

——(2011) 'Toward a physical cultural studies', *Sociology of Sport Journal*, 28(1): 4–35.

Simmel, G. (1917) *Grundfragen der Soziologie* [*Fundamental Questions of Sociology*]. Berlin: Göschen.

Smart, B. (2005) *The Sport Star: Modern Sport and the Cultural Economy of Sporting Celebrity*. London: Sage.

Smith, D. (2000) *Norbert Elias: A Critical Assessment*. London: Sage.

Smith, E. (2007) *Race, Sport and the American Dream*. Durham, NC: Carolina Academic Press.

——(ed.) (2010) *Sociology of Sport and Social Theory*. Champaign, Ill.: Human Kinetics.

Smith, Y. (1992) 'Women of color in society and sport', *Quest*, 44(2): 228–50.

Smith-Maguire, J. (2008) *Fit for Consumption: Sociology and the Business of Fitness*. London: Routledge.

Snyder, E. and Spreitzer, E. (1974/1980) 'Sociology of sport: An overview', *The Sociological Quarterly*, 15(4): 467–87. Reprinted in G. Sage (ed.), *Sport in American Society: Selected Readings*. Reading, Mass.: Addison Wesley, 15–33.

Sparkes, A. and Silvennoinen, M. (eds) (1999) *Talking Bodies: Men's Narratives of the Body and Sport*. Jyvaskyla: SoPhi.

Sparkes, A. and Smith, B. (2007) 'Disabled bodies and narrative time: Men, sport, and spinal cord injury', in J. Hargreaves and P. Vertinsky (eds), *Physical Culture, Power, and the Body*. London: Routledge, 158–75.

Sparkes, R. (1988) 'Ways of seeing differently: Complexity and contradiction in the critical project of sport and leisure studies (response to Rosemary Deem)', *Sociology of Sport Journal*, 5(4): 355–68.

Spears, B. (1978) 'Prologue: The myth', in C. Oglesby (ed.), *Women in Sport: From Myth to Reality*. Santa Barbara, Calif.: Lea & Febiger, 3–15.

Spencer, H. (1861) *Education*. New York: Williams & Northgate.

——(1873) *The Principles of Psychology*. New York: Appleton & Co.

Spickard, P. (2000) 'Book review: J. Entine, *Taboo: Why black athletes dominate sports and why we're afraid to talk about it*', *Journal of Sport History*, 27(2): 338–40.

Spracklen, K. (2001) '"Black pearl, black diamonds": Exploring racial identities in rugby league', in B. Carrington and I. McDonald (eds), *'Race', Sport and British Society*. London: Routledge, 70–82.

St Louis, B. (2003) 'Sport, genetics and the "natural athlete": The resurgence of racial science', *Body and Society*, 9(2): 75–95.

Steinitzer, H. (1910) *Sport und Kultur*. Munich.

Stevenson, C. and Nixon, J. (1972) 'A conceptual scheme of the functions of sport', *Sportwissenschaft*, 2: 119–32.

Stoddart, B. (1995) 'C. L. R. James: A remembrance', in H. Beckles and B. Stoddart (eds), *Liberation Cricket: West Indies Cricket Culture*, Manchester: Manchester University Press, 384–8.

Stoddart, B. and Beckles, H. (eds) (1995) *Liberation Cricket: West Indies Cricket Culture*. Manchester: Manchester University Press.

Stone, G. (1955) 'American sports: Play and dis-play', *Chicago Review*, 9(fall): 83–100.

Struna, N. (2000) 'Social history and sport', in J. Coakley and E. Dunning (eds), *Handbook of Sports Studies*. London: Sage, 187–203.

Stuart, O. (1996) 'Back in the pavillion: Cricket and the image of African Caribbeans in Oxford', in T. Ranger, Y. Samad and O. Stuart (eds), *Culture, Identity and Politics*. Aldershot: Ashgate, 120–8.

Sugden, J. (1998), *Boxing and Society: An International Analysis*. Manchester: Manchester University Press.

—— (eds) (2002) *Scum Airways: Inside Football's Underground Economy*. Edinburgh: Mainstream.

Sugden, J. and Bairner, A. (1993) *Sport, Sectarianism and Society in a Divided Ireland*. Leicester: Leicester University Press.

Sugden, J. and Tomlinson, A. (1998) *FIFA and the Contest for World Football: Who Rules the Peoples' Game?* Cambridge: Polity Press.

——(1999a) *Great Balls of Fire: How Big Money is Hijacking World Football*. Edinburgh: Mainstream.

——(1999b) 'Digging the dirt and staying clean: Retrieving the investigative tradition for a critical sociology of sport', *International Review for the Sociology of Sport*, 34(4): 385–97.

——(eds) (2002) *Power Games: A Critical Sociology of Sport*. London: Routledge.

——(2003) *Badfellas: FIFA Family at War*. Edinburgh: Mainstream.

Sumner, W. G. (1906) *Folkways: A Study of the Sociological Importance of Usages, Manners, Customs, Mores and Morals*. Boston, Mass.: Ginn.

Sutton-Smith, B., Roberts, J. and Kozelka, R. (1963) 'Game involvement in adults', *Journal of Social Psychology*, 60(1): 15–30.

Swartz, D. (1997) *Culture and Power: The Sociology of Pierre Bourdieu*. Chicago, Ill.: University of Chicago Press.

Synott, A. (1993) *The Body Social: Symbolism, Self and Society*. London: Routledge.

Talbot, M. (1988) 'Understanding the relationships between women and sport: The contribution of British feminist approaches in leisure and cultural studies', *International Review of the Sociology of Sport*, 23(1): 31–41.

Theberge, N. (1984) 'A Marxist informed analysis of gender inequality in sport', *Arena Review*, 8(2): 11–19.

——(1985) 'Toward a feminist alternative to sport as a male preserve', *Quest*, 37(2): 193–202.

——(1991) 'Reflections on the body in the sociology of sport', *Quest*, 43(2): 123–34.

——(2000a) 'Gender and sport', in J. Coakley and E. Dunning (eds), *Handbook of Sports Studies*. London: Sage, 322–33.

——(2000b) *Higher Goals: Ice Hockey and the Politics of Gender*. New York: SUNY Press.

Thompson, R. (1964) *Race and Sport*. Oxford: Oxford University Press.

Thorpe, H. (2009) 'Bourdieu, feminism and female physical culture: Gender reflexivity and the habitus-field complex', *Sociology of Sport Journal*, 26(4): 491–516.

Tomlinson, A. (1984) 'The sociological imagination, the new journalism, and sport', in N. Theberge and P. Donnelly (eds), *Sport and the Sociological Imagination: Refereed Proceedings of the 3rd Annual Conference of the North American Society for the Sociology of Sport, Toronto, Canada, November 1982*. Fort Worth, Tex.: Texas Christian University Press, 21–39.

——(2004) 'Pierre Bourdieu and the sociological study of sport: Habitus, capital and field', in R. Giulianotti (ed.), *Sport and Modern Social Theorists*. Basingstoke: Palgrave Macmillan, 161–72.

Tomlinson, A. and Whannel, G. (1984) *Five Ring Circus: Money, Power and Politics at the Olympic Games*. London: Pluto Press.

——(1986) *Off the Ball: The Football World Cup*. London: Pluto Press.

Tonkiss, F. (2010) 'The *British Journal of Sociology* in the 2000s: Sociology in a new century', *British Journal of Sociology*, 61(s1): 343–5.

Trelford, D. (1998) *W. G. Grace*. Stroud: Sutton Publishing.

Trueman, T. (2010) 'UK sociology is at the forefront internationally', *Network*, 105: 14–18.

Turner, B. S. (1984) *The Body and Society: Explorations in Social Theory*. Oxford: Basil Blackwell.

——(1996) *The Body and Society: Explorations in Social Theory*, 2nd edn. London: Sage.

——(2008) *The Body and Society: Explorations in Social Theory*, 3rd edn. London: Sage.

Turner, G. (2004) *Understanding Celebrity*. London: Sage.

——(2010) 'Approaching celebrity studies', *Celebrity Studies*, 1(1): 11–20.

Urry, J. (1981) 'Sociology as a parasite: Some vices and virtues', in P. Abrams (ed.), *Practice and Progress: British Sociology, 1950–1980*. London: Allen & Unwin, 25–38.

Valentine, J. (2001) 'Book review: J. Entine, *Taboo: Why black athletes dominate sports and why we're afraid to talk about it*', *Journal of the Philosophy of Sport*, 28(1): 120–3.

Vamplew, W. (2000) 'History', in R. Cox, G. Jarvie and W. Vamplew (eds), *Encyclopedia of British Sport*. Oxford: ABC-Clio, 178–80.

——(2007) 'Empiricist versus sociological history: Some comments on the "civilizing process"'. *Sport in History*, 27(2): 161–71.

van Krieken, R. (1998) *Norbert Elias*. London: Routledge.

van Sterkenburg, J. and Knoppers, A. (2004) 'Dominant discourses about race/ethnicity and gender in sport practice and performance', *International Review for the Sociology of Sport*, 39 (3): 301–21.

Veblen, T. (1899) *The Theory of the Leisure Class: An Economic Study of Institutions*. London: Macmillan.

Verma, G. and Darby, D. (1994) *Winners and Losers: Ethnic Minorities in Sport and Recreation*. London: Falmer Press.

Vertinsky, P. (1990) *The Eternally Wounded Woman: Women, Doctors and Exercise in the Late Nineteenth Century*. Manchester: Manchester University Press.

——(1994) 'Gender relations, women's history and sport history: A decade of changing enquiry, 1983–93', *Journal of Sport History*, 21(1): 1–24.

Vlot, N. G. (1964) 'Sociological analysis of sport in the Netherlands', in E. Jokl and E. Simon (eds), *International Research in Sport and Physical Education*. Springfield, Ill.: Thomas, 198–211.

Wacquant, L. (1989) 'Corps et âme: Notes ethnographiques d'un apprenti-boxeur', *Actes de la Recherche en Sciences Sociales*, 80: 36–67.

——(1992) 'The social logic of boxing in black Chicago, Ill.: Toward a sociology of pugilism', *Sociology of Sport Journal*, 9(3): 221–54.

——(1995) 'Pugs at work: Bodily capital and bodily labour among professional boxers', *Body and Society*, 1(1): 65–93.

——(2004) *Body and Soul: Notebooks of an Apprentice Boxer*. Oxford: Oxford University Press.

Waddington, I. and Malcolm, D. (2008) 'Eric Dunning: This sporting life', in D. Malcolm and I. Waddington (eds), *Matters of Sport: Essays in Honour of Eric Dunning*. London: Routledge, 1–11.

Waddington, I., Loland, S. and Skirstad, B. (2006) 'Introduction', in S. Loland, B. Skirstad and I. Waddington (eds), *Pain and Injury in Sport: Social and Ethical Analysis*. London: Routledge, 1–13.

Walton, T. (2004) 'Steve Prefontaine: From rebel with a cause to hero with a swoosh', *Sociology of Sport Journal*, 21(1): 61–83.

Watson, N. and Cunningham-Burley, S. (eds) (2001) *Reframing the Body*. Basingstoke: Palgrave Macmillan.

Webb, J., Schirato, T. and Danaher, G. (2001) *Understanding Bourdieu*. London: Sage.

Weber, M. (1904/1930) *The Protestant Ethic and the Spirit of Capitalism*. London: Allen & Unwin.

——(1991) 'Politics as a vocation', in H. H. Gerth and C. Wright Mills (eds), *From Max Weber: Essays in Sociology*. London: Routledge, 77–128.

Weinberg, S. and Arond, H. (1952) 'The occupational culture of the boxer', *American Journal of Sociology*, 57(5): 460–9.

Werbner, P. (1996) '"Our blood is green": Cricket, identity and social empowerment among British Pakistanis', in J. MacClancy (ed.), *Sport, Identity and Ethnicity*. Oxford: Berg, 87–111.

Westwood, S. (1990) 'Racism, black masculinity and the politics of space', in J. Hearn and D. Morgan (eds), *Men, Masculinities and Social Theory*. London: Unwin & Hyman, 55–71.

——(1991) 'Red Star over Leicester: Racism, the politics of identity and black youth in Britain', in P. Werbner, and M. Anwar (eds), *Black and Ethnic Leadership in Britain*. London. Routledge, 146–69.

Whannel, G. (2001) 'Punishment, redemption and celebration in the popular press: The case of David Beckham', in D. Andrews and S. Jackson (eds), *Sport Stars: The Cultural Politics of Sporting Celebrity*. London: Routledge, 138–51.

——(2002) *Media Sport Stars: Masculinities and Moralities*. London: Routledge.

White, P. and Wilson, B. (1999) 'Distinction in the stands: An investigation of Bourdieu's "habitus", socioeconomic status and sport spectatorship in Canada', *International Review for the Sociology of Sport*, 34(3): 245–64.

Whitehead, S. and Barrett, F. (eds) (2001) *The Masculinities Reader*. Cambridge: Polity Press.

Whitson, D. (1989) 'Discourses of critique in sport sociology: A response to Deem', *Sociology of Sport Journal*, 6(1): 66–9.

Williams, J. (1999) 'All abroad! The trans-global football excess', in M. Perryman (ed.), *The Ingerland Factor: Home Truths from Football*. Edinburgh: Mainstream, 185–99.

——(2001a) *Into the Red: Liverpool FC and the Changing Face of English Football*. Edinburgh: Mainstream.

——(2001b) 'Who you calling a hooligan?' in M. Perryman (ed.) *Hooligan Wars: Causes and Effects of Football Violence*. Edinburg: Mainsrtream, 37–52.

——(2002a) *Into the Red*, 2nd edn. Edinburgh: Mainstream.

——(2002b) 'Football's leaving home', in M. Perryman (ed.), *Going Oriental: Football After World Cup 2002*. Edinburgh: Mainstream, 65–80.

——(2003) *The Liverpool Way: Houllier, Anfield and the New Global Game*. Edinburgh: Mainstream.

——(2010) *Red Men: Liverpool Football Club, The Biography*. Edinburgh: Mainstream.

Williams, J. and Hopkins, S. (2005) *The Miracle of Istanbul: Liverpool FC, from Paisley to Benitez*. Edinburgh: Mainstream.

Williams, J. and Kennedy, A. (2004) *Kennedy's Way: Inside Bob Paisley's Liverpool*. Edinburgh: Mainstream.

Williams, J. and Llopis, R. (2006) *Groove Armada: Rafa Benitez, Anfield and the New Spanish Fury*. Edinburgh: Mainstream.

——(2007) *Rafa: Liverpool FC, Benitez and the New Spanish Fury*. Edinburgh: Mainstream.

Williams, J., Dunning, E. and Murphy, P. (1984) *Hooligans Abroad: The Behaviour and Control of England Fans in Continental Europe*. London: Routledge & Kegan Paul.

Williams, J., Hopkins, S. and Long, C. (eds) (2001) *Passing Rhythms: Liverpool FC and the Transformation of Football*. Oxford: Berg.

Willis, P. (1974) 'Performance and meaning: A sociological view of women in sport', unpublished paper, CCCS, Birmingham.

——(1977) *Learning to Labour: How Working Class Kids Get Working Class Jobs*. Farnborough: Saxon House.

——(1982/1994) 'Women in sport in ideology', in J. A. Hargreaves (ed.), *Sport, Culture and Ideology*. London: Routledge, 117–35. Reprinted in S. Birrell and C. Cole (eds), *Women, Sport and Culture*. Champaign, Ill.: Human Kinetics, 31–45.

Wilson, B. (2000) 'Book review: J. Entine, *Taboo: Why black athletes dominate sports and why we're afraid to talk about it*', *Olympika: The International Journal of Olympic Studies*, 9: 115–22.

Wimbush, E. and Talbot, M. (1988) *Relative Freedoms: Women and Leisure*. Milton Keynes: Open University Press.

Wohl, A. (1966) 'Conception and range of sport sociology', *International Review for the Sociology of Sport*, 1(1): 5–18.

——(1969) 'Activity of the International Committee for Sociology of Sport in the years 1964–68', *International Review for the Sociology of Sport*, 4(1): 191–4.

Woodward, K. (2002) *Boxing, Masculinity and Identity: The 'I' of the Tiger*. London: Routledge.

Yetman, N. R. and Berghorn, F. J. (1993) 'Racial participation and integration in intercollegiate basketball: A longitudinal perspective', *Sociology of Sport Journal*, 10(3): 301–14.

Yetman, N. R. and Eitzen, S. (1984) 'Racial dynamics in American sport: Continuity and change', in D. S. Eitzen (ed.), *Sport in Contemporary Society*. New York: St. Martin's Press, 324–44.

Yiannakis, A. (1989) 'Toward an applied sociology of sport: The next generation', *Sociology of Sport Journal*, 6(1): 1–16.

Young, K. (1991) 'Violence in the workplace of professional sport from victimological and cultural studies perspectives', *International Review of the Sociology of Sport*, 26(1): 3–13.

——(1993) 'Violence, risk and liability in male sports culture', *Sociology of Sport Journal*, 10(4): 373–96.

——(ed.) (2004) *Sporting Bodies, Damaged Selves: Sociological Studies of Sports Related Injuries*. Oxford: Elsevier Press.

Young, K. and White, P. (2000) 'Researching sports injury: Reconstructing dangerous masculinities', in J. McKay, M. Messner and D. Sabo (eds), *Masculinities, Gender Relations, and Sport*. Thousand Oaks, Calif.: Sage, 108–26.

Young, K., White, P., and McTeer, W. (1994) 'Body talk: Male athletes reflect on sport, injury and pain', *Sociology of Sport Journal*, 11(2): 175–94.

INDEX